ROUSING THE NATION

ROUSING
THE NATION

*Radical Culture in
Depression America*

LAURA BROWDER

UNIVERSITY OF MASSACHUSETTS PRESS
Amherst

Copyright © 1998 by
The University of Massachusetts Press
All rights reserved
Printed in the United States of America
LC 97-33358
ISBN 1-55849-125-2
Designed by Milenda Nan Ok Lee
Set in Adobe Garamond and Gill Sans Condensed
Printed and bound by Braun-Brumfield, Inc.

Library of Congress Cataloging-in-Publication Data
Browder, Laura, 1963–
Rousing the nation : radical culture in Depression America / Laura Browder.
    p.   cm.
Includes bibliographical references and index.
ISBN 1-55849-125-2 (cloth : alk. paper)
1. American literature—20th century—History and criticism.   2. Radicalism in
    literature.   3.   Literature and society—United States—History—20th
century.   4. United States—Intellectual life—20th century.   5. Motion pictures—
    United States—History.   6. Modernism (Literature)—United
    States.   7. Depressions—1929—United States.   8. Social problems in
    literature.   9. Depressions in literature.   I. Title.
        PS228.R34B76   1998
    810.9'355—dc21   97-33358
                        CIP

British Library Cataloguing in Publication data are available.

This book is published with the support and cooperation of the
University of Massachusetts Boston.

CONTENTS

ACKNOWLEDGMENTS

It is a great pleasure to thank the many people who helped bring this project to fruition.

From the beginning, John Burt, Joyce Antler, and Tom Doherty at Brandeis University, where this book began as a dissertation, helped me to move beyond a purely literary study into a broader work. Their support, insightful readings, and encouragement continue to fuel my work.

John and Joy Kasson provided a wonderfully stimulating five weeks at their 1995 NEH Summer Institute on the Thirties; I'd like to thank them and the other participants in the institute for leading me to think about Depression culture in a new way. Thanks to Leon Fink for his encouraging reading of sections of the manuscript.

At the Federal Theatre Project archives at George Mason University, Lorraine Brown shared a wealth of knowledge with me. I'd also like to thank the staffs at Brandeis and Boston College; at the Library of Congress, Manuscript divisions and Motion Picture division; at the National Archives; at the John Hay Library at Brown University; and at Virginia Commonwealth University interlibrary loan, especially Jeannie Scott.

I could never have completed this project without the cheerleading and criticism of my writing groups, past and present. At Brandeis, Eve Raimon and Ellen Wolff and, at Virginia Commonwealth University, Kathy Fuller and Carol Summers offered me valuable critiques, advice, and humor.

Thanks to Paul Wright, at University of Massachusetts Press, for his long nurturing of this project and for his many helpful suggestions, and to Townsend Ludington, who offered great advice and encouragement at a late stage of the manuscript.

Other friends, family members, and colleagues contributed in a variety of ways to this project. Thanks especially to my father, Andrew Browder, for providing a useful and challenging perspective on the thirties. For their helpful readings and good advice on reshaping the manuscript, thanks to Catherine Ingrassia, Miles McCrimmon, and Charlotte Morse. For everything else, thanks to Merav Gold, Noel Brissenden, Rebecca Kaiser, Sabra Price, Peter Smith, and Lisa Kessler. Finally, thanks to Allan Rosenbaum for all his love and support.

This book is dedicated to the memory of my grandmother, Dorothy Demetracopoulou Lee.

ROUSING THE NATION

INTRODUCTION

FROM UNCLE TOM'S CABIN TO GONE WITH THE WIND

Writing for a Nation in Crisis

The Great Depression was the biggest crisis the United States faced in the twentieth century. With estimates of unemployment rates reaching as high as a third of the American work force, 80 percent of the nation's steel mills shut down, the collapse of the banking system, millions of homeless men and women living in Hoovervilles and riding the rails and millions more living in conditions of almost unbelievable poverty and hardship, Americans had a widespread sense that the center could no longer hold, that the nation was teetering on the brink of failure. Ecological crisis exacerbated economic catastrophe: The dust storms that swept through the Midwest devastated millions of acres of farmland and forced countless farm families on a westward migration. Indeed, to remember a crisis of similar magnitude, Americans had to go back seventy years, to the Civil War.

The Civil War and Depression were, it seemed, America's two great national dramas; it is unsurprising that writers and artists of the thirties, especially those of a radical stripe, often identified strongly with their Civil War counterparts. As Matthew Josephson, former editor of the expatriate modernist magazine *Broom* and a fellow traveler, wrote in his 1930 study *Portrait of the Artist as American,* "It is at the hour of the Civil War that we find an intellectual crisis analogous to our own."[1] Carl Sandburg's magisterial biography of Abraham Lincoln, whose final four volumes appeared in 1939 and which won the Pulitzer Prize the following year, gained enormous popular and critical acclaim. Lincoln Kirstein, in his role as editor of *Hound & Horn,* helped reawaken public interest in Mathew Brady's Civil War photographs, which he called, in 1935, the progenitor of a "classic vision."[2] In his introduction to Walker Evans's *American Photographs* (1938), Kirstein made explicit the comparison between the "moral implication" evident in Evans's Depression photographs and those of Brady. The Civil War, like the thirties, was an age of documentary: Writers and artists had an urgent need to capture, in words or pictures, the emblematic scenes of the crisis, to help audiences understand and interpret the nature of the problems faced by the nation. The last of the Civil War veterans were captured in newsreels as they slowly shuffled along in Memorial Day parades, reminders of a past that was not yet dead. In 1938 Secretary of War Harry H. Woodring stood between the commanders of the United Confederate Veterans and the Grand Army of the Republic during the federally sponsored seventy-fifth anniversary encampment at Gettysburg.[3]

There is no period between the Civil War and the Depression in which the fate of the nation seemed so much in doubt. Like abolitionist writers before them, radical American writers of the thirties were conscious of the import of their historical moment and of the need to persuade a wide readership of the justice of their cause. My use of the term "radical" is deliberately broad; for my purposes, radical writers are those committed to social change and to using literature to try to effect social justice. Although most of the writers I am concerned with joined, or attended meetings of, the Communist Party rather than the Socialist Party, this distinction is not especially important for the purposes of this work. Unlike many recent works on radical literature of the thirties, this one is not concerned with the finer textures of ideological debates within the Communist Party. Rather, its purpose is to explain how American writers in a period of crisis attempted the near-impossible: to present a new vision of America to an audience largely uninterested in its vehicle—the book, the play—and to persuade those audiences to become politically engaged themselves as a result. To attempt this daunting task, these writers looked to their Civil War predecessors.

Civil War writers had been both commercially successful and culturally important. Among the great best-sellers of the nineteenth century, of course, was Harriet Beecher Stowe's *Uncle Tom's Cabin,* which within a year of its publication in 1852 had sold 305,000 copies in America and two and a half million copies all over the world.

Not only did Stowe find it possible to capture a wide and relatively heterogeneous readership with *Uncle Tom's Cabin* (and subsequent dramatic productions of the novel would extend the work's audience even further, in terms both of class and of political sympathies), her work also had a widely acknowledged effect on public policy, as witnessed by Abraham Lincoln's comment upon her visit to the White House: "So this is the little lady who made this big war."[4] Although Stowe may have been exemplary in her effectiveness, she was only one of many writers engaged in the larger national struggle. Frederick Law Olmsted's account of his travels through the South, *The Cotton Kingdom* (1861), was acclaimed by Charles Eliot Norton, James Russell Lowell, and John Stuart Mill, to whom Olmsted dedicated his book. William Dean Howells wrote a campaign biography of Lincoln. Walt Whitman wrote a series of early war poems such as "Beat! Beat! Drums!" and celebrated the rise of "warlike America"; he also visited Civil War hospitals in Washington more than 600 times, an experience he described in "The Wound Dresser." Louisa May Alcott volunteered as a nurse in a Washington hospital and wrote about the experience in *Hospital Sketches* (1863). Charles Eliot Norton turned to the writing of patriotic tracts, including one for soldiers in the field entitled *The Soldier of the Good Cause.* Ralph Waldo Emerson wrote in 1861, the war "has assumed such huge proportions that it threatens to engulf us all—no preoccupation can exclude it, & no hermitage hide us all."[5] Of course, it was not northerners alone who entered the fray; among the many answers in the form of literature to *Uncle Tom's Cabin* was William J. Grayson's poem "The Hireling and the Slave" (1856).

The mid-nineteenth century was a period during which it seems nearly everyone who could read did so. The common school reform movement (1850–59) resulted in high rates of literacy among American workers. As Michael Denning documents in *Mechanic Accents,* the dime novel, primarily intended for working-class readers, was born during the period of the Civil War. Although cheap editions of fiction may have primarily been western tales and adventure stories, they also included other genres; abolitionist publisher James Redpath, whose intended audience for his Books for the Camp Fires was Union soldiers, included an inexpensive version of the novel *Clotelle* by the black abolitionist William Wells Brown.[6]

Moreover, Civil War–era audiences did not observe rigid divisions between "high" and "low" art. As Lawrence Levine has documented in *Highbrow/Lowbrow,* mid-nineteenth-century audiences were heterogeneous: Workers were likely to line up for performances of Shakespeare or to attend the opera, with no consciousness that they were paying obeisance to timeless art. Lowell, Massachusetts, mill girls recalled reading the English poets and essayists as well as literary reviews like *North American Review* and *Blackwood's Magazine.* During their visits to the circulating library, these women might borrow *The Mysteries of Udolpho* and *Charlotte Temple, The Arabian Nights* and *Maria Monk,* or perhaps dip into the latest installment of a Dickens novel featured in a weekly newspaper.[7] Although southern and northern readers may have had very different perspectives on the great crisis consuming America, they were engaged in an ongoing argument with one another, both through reading and viewing the same texts— *Uncle Tom's Cabin* being the obvious example—and in writing rebuttals to one another's work.

Yet by the arrival of the Depression, this had all changed. In accepting the 1930 Nobel Prize for literature, Sinclair Lewis criticized turn-of-the-century critics for "effusively seeking to guide America into being a pale edition of an English cathedral town" and contemporary academics for treating literature as "something dead; it is something magically produced by superhuman beings who must, if they are to be regarded as artists at all, have died at least one hundred years before the diabolical invention of the typewriter." As Levine notes, by the beginning of the twentieth century, the word "culture" was "becoming synonymous with the Eurocentric products of the symphonic hall, the opera house, the museum, all of which, the American people were taught, must be approached with a disciplined, knowledgeable seriousness, and—most important of all—with a feeling of reverence."[8]

Even members of the advertising community were dismayed by what they perceived as plummeting literary standards. A copywriter for the J. Walter Thompson advertising agency wrote an article in the company's internal newsletter, asking if the agency's ads, presented in *True Story* style, were meant to appeal to "the minds of those morons . . . who daily dole out their 2 cents to secure the latest news not only unadulterated but graphically portrayed." In other words, were even advertisements to be dumbed down? The answer from the agency was swift: Yes, a senior copywriter wrote back, the agency must now produce "tabloid copy for tabloid minds."[9] If advertising text was to appear, it was best that it be in the form of a "true confession" or in a style mimicking the tabloid newspapers that by the mid-1920s were easily outselling many "serious" journals. By 1925 the *Daily News,* a New York City paper, approached a million in daily circulation, easily outselling any other paper in the United States. Although, according to contemporary observers, mid-nineteenth-century workers had read the same newspapers, and in the same enormous quantities, as middle-class readers, by the 1930s middle-class and working-class readers were consuming distinctly different kinds of journalism. Moreover, reading rates in general had declined. In 1889, according to John Modell, 89.5 percent of native-born working-class families and 87 percent of Irish-born working-class families in ten northeastern states had significant expenditures for newspapers and books.[10] But by 1925 Robert and Helen Lynd were dismayed to find that Middletown residents had changed their reading habits: "No longer do a Young Ladies' Reading Circle, a Christian

Literary Society (of fifty), a Literary League, a Literary Home Circle, a Literary Fireside Club meet weekly or bi-weekly as in 1890, nor are reading circles formed in various sections of the city, nor does a group of young women meet to study the classics."[11] Most significantly, the Workingmen's Library, founded in 1900, which boasted a librarian hired at $600 a year and which contained, among other things, 210 volumes of fiction, including Thackeray and Dickens, had long since disappeared.[12]

The chasm between working-class and middle-class reading tastes was growing, the gap between "high" and "low" culture becoming ever more vast. Gone were the days when most frontier homes contained well-thumbed editions of Shakespeare, or when working-class youth turned out in droves for an evening of events that might include farce, animal acts, and what twentieth-century audiences would see as "serious" drama. Gone, in fact, was the kind of broad-based audience that would be receptive to the message of the thirties writers, playwrights, and other artists interested in grappling with the issues of the day.

Depression writers were disheartened to find that the readership for "serious" fiction, particularly political fiction, had changed and dwindled. Radical writers at the start of the thirties who wanted to produce proletarian fiction found themselves in the awkward position of wanting to create a new vision of America for a readership that no longer really existed. For the radical Depression novel to succeed, it had to compete with popular culture—with the movies, for instance, which were drawing audiences, in the early thirties, of sixty to seventy-five million a week, a number that corresponds to more than 60 percent of the American population.[13] It would be hard to blame left-wing writers for being wistful about the readership that once was, and for harking back to the Civil War, when a wide readership still existed for fiction and drama of all sorts.

The resonance of the Civil War for Depression writers was of course not confined to radicals; paradoxically, the only Depression novel to come close to the success of *Uncle Tom's Cabin* was the romantically Confederate, by no means abolitionist, *Gone with the Wind* (1936), which won a Pulitzer Prize, sold fifty thousand copies in a day, two million in its first year, and became the source for the 1939 film, which won ten Oscars.[14] Civil War movies included not only *Gone with the Wind* but also, among others, Shirley Temple and Bill ("Bojangles") Robinson in *The Littlest Rebel* (1935) and *The Little Colonel* (1935), the Civil War spy stories *Secret Service* (1931) and *Operator 13* (1934), the nostalgic Confederate film *So Red the Rose* (1934), the Bette Davis vehicle *Jezebel* (1938), for which the actress won an Oscar, John Ford's *Young Mr. Lincoln* (1939) and *Abe Lincoln in Illinois* (1940).[15] While radical writers were struggling to capture a wide audience with their socially conscious novels and plays, Margaret Mitchell seemed to have no problem entrancing the American public with her novel, replete with eye-rolling, childlike, loyal slaves and glorifying marital rape. No wonder so many radical writers felt frustrated by popular culture.

And yet the relationship of many of these radical writers to popular culture was far from uncomplicated. Langston Hughes and Clifford Odets, to take just two examples, were both prominent writers who identified themselves as Marxists. However, they were also Americans who were deeply steeped in the popular culture of their country. It is instructive, perhaps, to consider, by way of contrast, the theories promulgated by members of the Frankfurt School who, fleeing Hitler's Germany, set up shop at Columbia University in 1934. From this base Theodor Adorno and Max Horkheimer would develop and promulgate, from a Marxist perspective, theories of the dehumanizing effects of mass culture on the populace. But even as this was going on, the same writers who decried the numbing effects of mass culture on America were themselves heading out to Hollywood as scriptwriters, directors, and actors. Ten years later, the House Committee on Un-American Activities would have no trouble scaring up the requisite number of present and former leftists for public humiliation. While Theodor Adorno pondered, at Princeton and Columbia, what he termed the "monotonous attraction" of jazz, theorizing that consumers of popular culture, including jazz and the movies, would be reduced to a passive, dependent state, infantilized and incapable of thought or action, in Manhattan, a mere stone's throw away, the Communist Langston Hughes was writing poems celebrating jazz. In 1938 Adorno published his celebrated essay, "On the Fetish-Character in Music and the Regression of Listening," in which he used Marx's definition of the fetish commodity to denounce mass culture. To Adorno, the possibility of real enjoyment of popular music is nonexistent: "the consumer is really worshipping the money that he himself has paid for the ticket to the Toscanini concert." For jazz enthusiasts who take their listening experience seriously, Adorno has even harsher words: "Types rise up from the mass of the retarded who differentiate themselves by pseudoactivity and nevertheless make the regression more strikingly visible."[16] By contrast, in 1938 Hughes wrote and produced *Don't You Want to Be Free?*, a radical play which incorporated blues and spirituals as well as poetry; in the words of his biographer, Arnold Rampersand, the play is "loose-limbed and improvisational in effect, rather than static and rhythmic."[17] In other words, Hughes was using the rhythms of jazz, the blues, and other popular music in his work in order to more effectively promulgate a radical interpretation of African American history. For Hughes, as well as for the writers of the Federal Theatre Project's Living Newspapers from which he drew many of his montage techniques, "high" and "low" categories were not particularly important: the essential thing was to get a message across using any means possible. For Adorno and Horkheimer, "Films, radio and magazines make up a system which is uniform as a whole and in every part." While Adorno was writing that, "Together with sport and film, mass music and the new listening help to make escape from the whole infantile milieu impossible," a few blocks away in Manhattan the most celebrated radical playwright of his generation, Clifford Odets, was packing his bags to go to Hollywood, where he hoped to contribute to making the movies a "genuine art-form for the masses of people."[18]

Some writers might agree with Adorno that popular arts, specifically jazz, operated as a sort of social cement, through displaced wish-fulfillment, distraction, and the intensification of passivity. However, those writers were themselves often active participants in the same popular culture they at times decried. James T. Farrell described in Studs Lonigan a character who shared many of the characteristics of Adorno and Horkheimer's passive consumer of culture, yet Studs had insides as well, an emotional life: He may have illustrated Adorno and Horkheimer's contention that "Real life is becoming indistinguishable from the movies," and yet Studs is not without humanity. Moreover, as I will argue, Studs's cultural complacency is as much linked to his own beliefs about masculinity—the machismo endorsed by Michael Gold, cultural commissar of the Communist Party, and many other radical writers—as to anything. And, most notably, while Farrell created a proletarian culture consumer of whom even Adorno might have approved, he provided his readers with as much sex and violence, as much shock value, as the pulpiest movie or magazine. Farrell wrote a best seller that critiqued other best-selling cultural artifacts.

Ironically enough, the "high art" techniques these writers used in order to write fiction for an audience used to consuming "low art" were uniquely suited to conveying the experience of the dispossessed in a time of trouble. The language experiments of the previous forty years gave writers of the Depression era a set of tools with which to craft the new radical literature. Although modernism may have been—and may still be—associated in the popular imagination with obscure language experiments, it was, in its use of shifting subjectivity and sense of alienation, a perfect vehicle for conveying the experience of the Depression, a time when Yeats's line, "Things fall apart; the centre cannot hold," seemed to sum up the spirit of an age. For a generation of writers appalled by official and commercial cant, for whom public language had lost its ability to convey truth, modernism offered the chance to rebuild language and literature from the ground up. As Malcolm Bradbury and James McFarlane write, modernism is "the one art that responds to the scenario of our chaos. . . . It is the art consequent on the dis-establishing of communal reality and the conventional notions of causality, on the destruction of traditional notions of the wholeness of individual character, on the linguistic chaos that ensues when public notions of language have been discredited and when all realities have become subjective fictions."[19] The credibility gap between optimistic official declarations ("Prosperity is just around the corner" being one of the more egregious examples) and the harsh economic reality experienced by millions, between the snappy language of boosters and the overheard laments of the unemployed, created a space in which a politically committed form of modernism arose.

Modernism offered writers the opportunity to tell a story from a number of different viewpoints, to use perspectives that had not hitherto been used in "serious" literature—those of poor sharecroppers, say, as Walker Evans and James Agee did in *Let Us Now Praise Famous Men*. By offering up the experience of illiterate, impoverished farmers as art, by granting the Gudger, Ricketts, and Woods families subjectivity rather than presenting them as faceless victims of poverty or examples of comic degeneracy (like the subjects of Erskine Caldwell's *Tobacco Road*), Agee and Evans were able to use modernist techniques to powerful advantage. By concentrating their full aesthetic as well as sociological attention on the lives of these families, Agee and Evans insisted on their dignity, their worthiness as subjects. By utilizing dense, writerly language to describe the few daily objects the sharecroppers used, Agee himself treats these things with the importance they had for the families. A range of carefully noted details, like the "nearly fainting munificent odor of muskmelons, in their time, or during picking season the terrible ether odor of hot stored cotton,"[20] forces his readers to honor the sharecroppers with close attention. Evans's photographs, which showed the stark beauty of these objects arranged in a home—a broom leaning in a corner, a frayed cloth hanging on a line—had the same effect. The modern invocation to "make it new" meant, among other things, that it would be possible to see the dispossessed in new ways, to move beyond received ideas and images to new truths. Because the radical writers of the thirties wished to change, if necessary, their readers' historical perspective, to move them from a passive position as spectators at the vast pageant of American history to a position in which they could envision themselves as agents of change, these writers rejected some aspects of modernism: its insular qualities, its emphasis on technical sophistication at the expense of comprehensibility.

The same preconditions that made the task of the radical writer responding to the Depression so much more difficult than that of his or her Civil War counterpart also made the experimental success of the project feasible. As Bradbury and McFarlane write, "The communal universe of reality and culture on which nineteenth-century art had depended was over; and the explosively lyrical, or else the ironic and fictive modes, modes which included large elements not only of creation but of de-creation, were inevitable."[21]

The way that the radicals of the thirties rose to their task accounts for the richness and complexity of the best political fiction and drama of this period. Unlike Stowe and other Civil War writers, they did not have the option of producing what one might call generically encoded literature—sentimental fiction, melodrama—for an audience familiar with the trope. Rather, they used a grab bag of tricks in order to create a new kind of literature that argued for its own importance even as it achieved its artistic and political purpose.

Though the nineteenth-century audiences who moved freely between "culture" and "entertainment" may have vanished, the writers who could produce that particular thirties blend of political messages, experimental techniques, and free movement between high and low culture were more closely akin to their nineteenth-century predecessors than one might suspect. For instance, Dos Passos's *U.S.A.,* which insists on its own modernity on every page, nonetheless features both the driving plot of a nineteenth-century sentimental novel like *Uncle Tom's Cabin,* and the free-wheeling swings between stream-of-consciousness narration, capsule biography, and other seemingly disparate forms that one might expect of a mid-nineteenth-century night at the theater, where audiences might see scenes from Shakespeare interspersed with black-face acts, performing animals, poetic declamations, and dance routines.

Politically engaged Depression writers set themselves a task that few American writers since that time have attempted: creating a literature that would engage the sympathies of a broad-based audience while achieving the linguistic richness and complexity of the literary experiments that had transformed a generation (the "lost generation," in Gertrude Stein's phrase) of American writers. Caught between the populism of the mid-nineteenth-century novelist or playwright and the self-consciousness of the post–World War I artist, burdened with the commitment to social change and public education (about civil rights, about poverty, about the problems of unemployment) that demanded literary expression, a large group of writers, ranging from Nathanael West to his sister-in-law Ruth McKenney, from John Dos Passos to Nathan Asch, from James T. Farrell to Sherwood Anderson, struggled to create a new kind of literature to meet the needs of a nation in crisis. The debate over how to reach a wide audience with a radical message took many forms. The letters columns of Communist Party organs like the *New Masses* were filled with pronouncements about what exactly constituted proletarian literature. At the American Writers Congress of 1935, whose stated purpose was to "reveal, through collective discussion, the most effective ways in which writers, as writers, can function in the rapidly developing crisis,"[22] speakers ranging from Malcolm Cowley to Theodore Dreiser, Kenneth Burke, Earl Browder, general secretary of the Communist Party, Erskine Caldwell, Lincoln Steffens, and Waldo Frank gave talks on how best to create the new, revolutionary literature. Other writers, like James T. Farrell, published scholarly articles on the theoretical basis for radical literature. Still others, like Louis Adamic, wrote popular pieces lamenting the scanty readership for the new work.

Even as these extraliterary debates raged, another form of discussion about how to develop the new literature was taking place within the pages of the radical novels and plays themselves. Just as the argument of *Uncle Tom's Cabin* was rebutted in a number of "anti-Tom" novels, such as *Aunt Phyllis' Cabin; or, Southern Life as It Is* (1852) and *The Planter's Northern Bride* (1854), so radicals of the thirties argued one another's literary and political approaches within the pages of their novels. With the self-consciousness of modernists who knew that their novels were not simply narrated stories but intricate constructions of language, these writers demonstrated within their novels how they themselves would solve the problems of the radical writer without readers.

The discussion between writers, and between the books they wrote, had something of the quality of an ongoing brainstorming session, in which each participant weighs in with an opinion, only to have that notion problematized by the next voice to chime in. In the pages to follow I will show the trajectory of this discussion, which began with John Dos Passos throwing down the gauntlet in his three-volume assault on prevailing forms of American discourse. Once Dos Passos had exhaustively demonstrated the ineffectuality of poetry and of journalism in reaching a mass audience, as well as the unsettling success of advertising, and issued a ringing call for a new kind of radical fiction, it would be up to James T. Farrell to explicate the problem of proletarian readership. Josephine Herbst, in her trilogy, moved on to consider how the experience of writing can itself be politically empowering and to demonstrate the efficacy of incorporating personal history into a larger political narrative. Finally, the Living Newspaper staff of the Federal Theatre Project created a form of radical culture that answered all of the objections and preconditions raised by Dos Passos, Farrell, Herbst, and a host of other radical writers.

This book focuses on the attempts of these authors to represent American history in the light of Depression politics. The radical writers of the 1930s who did not reject modernism totally attempted to rethink modernist fictional techniques in the light of their contemporary political experience. In so doing, they produced a literature that has the subtlety and sophistication of modernism without its hermetic qualities.

The journeys that many writers took in order to discover what America in crisis was all about, and how they could write for this new American audience, were literal as well as metaphorical. In my first chapter I trace the paths taken by many, if not most, radical writers of the Depression. They entered the crisis with a number of important literary and political skills—from the modernist techniques they had acquired in Paris to the advertising and journalism experience they had picked up, out of necessity, while supporting themselves as writers in exile. Although the radical writers of the thirties had seen themselves, in the teens and twenties, as American radicals, many had looked to Europe for a meaningful literary tradition. The Depression was to change this. As writers from Theodore Dreiser to Sherwood Anderson awakened to the depth of the national crisis, many began to acknowledge the need for a literary and political response that would be new and would be specifically American in nature. The question was: What form would this new radical literature take?

Both the inadequacies of the literary responses available at the beginning of the Depression and the model for the new literature were limned most clearly by John Dos Passos. *U.S.A.* is, among other things, Dos Passos's advertisement for his own modernist techniques and a debate on the relative strength of different rhetorical strategies. By showing the political inefficacy of traditional poetic expression, the corruption of journalism, and the terrible strength of the language of public relations, Dos Passos illustrates the need for a new form of radical fictional discourse, one which he pointedly supplies in his ostentatiously inventive trilogy.

Though Dos Passos may have offered at least one highly successful model for a literature that would incorporate the techniques of modernism and of mass culture, he did not address the problem of readership in his trilogy. How would it be possible to write political novels that would be accessible to a wider, working-class audience? James T. Farrell, in his *Studs Lonigan* trilogy, takes up the thorny issue of the vanishing working-class reader and offers a critique of the prevailing tendency within the proletarian literature movement to represent an idealized masculine worker. Studs, although he consumes culture, including novels, voraciously, is impervious to the radical literature of the period. Farrell presents Studs's aggressive masculinity as a construction rather than as an inherent quality and, by pointing up the link between gender and class, demonstrates that Studs, if he is to preserve the exaggerated macho character of the working-class male so celebrated by Michael Gold and other proletarian writers, cannot compromise himself by reading "serious" literature, since to do so would identify him with the genteel strivings of his sisters and other upwardly mobile females. It is only when Studs has become physically weaker and more emotionally open—feminized, in his own term— that he is able to become even vaguely interested in proletarian novels.

Although Farrell may have offered a critique of the idealized masculine worker, his trilogy, since it is told from Studs's point of view, lacks a female perspective. It would be up to Josephine Herbst to bridge Dos Passos's concern with the radical writer and Farrell's focus on the reader, to offer a blueprint for transforming readers into writers and, not incidentally, to ratify women's domestic experience as political. Herbst's trilogy brings the public sphere into the private, and the private sphere into the public, an effect intensified by her inclusion in the trilogy of her own family documents, including newspaper clippings and letters. Herbst's women begin understanding themselves as political subjects through reading family letters and other documentary materials and attain their fullest political development when they leave the domestic sphere to become documentarians in their own right. By presenting her characters as moving from a purely personal interest in their family history to an understanding of that history as part of a larger political context, and by using the documents of her own family's past as raw material, Herbst offers her audience what is in effect a "history from below" which encourages readers to consider their own familial pasts in a more political light.

Herbst may have demonstrated a way in which readers could become radicalized through using their own history to see themselves in a larger historical framework, but she was still faced with the problem that every novelist must wrestle with: No matter how radicalizing a novel may be, it is still designed to be consumed in private, by one person at a time. For a collective radicalizing experience, another medium would be necessary. The theoretical issues that concerned novelists such as Farrell were enacted in concrete form in the productions of the Living Newspapers of the Federal Theatre Project.

Derived from a theatrical form that had developed in the Soviet Union in the 1920s, the Living Newspapers were collaboratively written plays based on news events of the day and drawn from documentary sources such as the *Congressional Record*. These plays were performed for audiences that often had no experience with theater, and they dealt with such topics as the current plight of the American farmer and his betrayal by the federal government; the problems caused by the monopolies held by the big utility companies; and the collusion between racketeers and courts in the Dutch Schulz case. I focus on the productions of the Federal Theatre Project, whose playwrights included

Zora Neale Hurston and Sinclair Lewis, as multicultural, polyphonic attempts to rethink and represent America to itself—to forge a national drama that, rather than being star-based and produced only for the elite, would be written and produced both by luminaries and by unknown writers, directors, and actors and would concern itself with the experience of those who had hitherto escaped noncaricatured representation in drama—workers, tenant farmers, the homeless, African Americans. Living Newspaper audiences were far from passive; they yelled back at the stage and often left the theater arguing loudly about what had taken place.

Given the problems that radical writers had attracting audiences, and given their interest in popular culture, it is only natural that so many of them ended up in Hollywood, making movies about the social issues of the decade. After all, if the Living Newspapers, produced over a four-year period, could attract cumulative audiences of twenty-five million, why not write for a medium that attracted as much as three times as many people each week? Thus the final chapter examines the social films of the period and shows how the ideas radical writers had previously expressed in novels, plays, and manifestos survived (or failed to survive) by the time they reached the big screen. Specifically, I focus on a Living Newspaper, *One-Third of a Nation,* that was produced as a film by Paramount in 1939.

As Popular Front ideology merged into wartime suspiciousness and Cold War paranoia after World War II, what it meant to be a radical writer changed. It is hardly news that the political novel is not thriving in this country. The schism between the radical left and the literary avant-garde that began at the end of the thirties has become a chasm. Postwar authors did not employ the techniques of modernism to effect political change, as did writers ranging from those we have considered to now forgotten novelists like William Rollins, author of *The Shadow Before,* and Clara Weatherwax, author of *Marching! Marching!,* whose novels, if not always fully successful, were extremely experimental. The "radicalism" of postwar writers tended to be concerned not with a political vision but with what one might call lifestyle issues. Kerouac and the other Beats agitate, in their work, for the freedom to do more drugs and have more sex; the work of more conservative experimental writers of the fifties and sixties, like William Gaddis and Donald Barthelme, is not even engaged in this limited form of political rebellion. Although one might argue that Thomas Pynchon offers a more political vision, his are the politics of paranoia; he is a conspiracy theorist more than anything. Young experimental writers today are far more likely to be aware of the modernists of the twenties than of those of the thirties, because the earlier work has a closer kinship to the experimental works of the postwar period. Moreover, postwar writers of all stripes have become more interested in the individual quest and less interested in the fate of the group. Perhaps, after the war, the notion that understanding our history can help us to change anything has come to seem absurd. Thus even a contemporary political novel like Ella Leffland's 1983 *Rumors of Peace,* which concerns a young girl's struggle to understand the events of the Second World War, is focused only on this young girl's intellectual and spiritual development. In a sense, historical understanding is used in this novel more for personal growth than for political change. Although one could argue that E. L. Doctorow, particularly in *Ragtime,* presents us with the kind of documentary modernism that the thirties novelists attempted, there are important differences between his work and that of his forebears. In *Ragtime,* we get history as pageant; Doctorow maintains an ironic distance from his famous characters. The common denominator among almost all of his characters is the fact of their celebrity, no matter in what area it has been achieved. A revolutionary and a famous mistress are given equal weight in the book, and this has the effect of flattening out historical meaning, of focusing reader attention more on the odd coincidences attending these characters' intersections than on the texture of history itself. What we get is a kind of spectacular sleight-of-hand.

In the sixties, when journeys to discover the heart of America took place, as they had with great frequency during the thirties (there was practically a cottage industry in this genre, with writers from Edmund Wilson to Sherwood Anderson, from Dreiser to Dos Passos, contributing their efforts), these journeys tended to be much more about the discovery of the self (as in John Steinbeck's *Travels with Charley*) than the discovery of the other. On film, in movies like *Easy Rider,* America turned out to be a grim place indeed.

The thirties was really the last time in American history that radical writers felt themselves welcomed into a larger conversation about what it meant to be American; it was the last time, too, that radicals grappled with the question of how to create a literature that would be technically and politically sophisticated and yet able to attract a wide audience. *Gone with the Wind* may have outsold the *U.S.A.* trilogy, and audiences today may be more familiar with Kaufman and Hart's *You Can't Take It with You* than with *One-Third of a Nation;* that does not mean that Dos Passos, Herbst, Farrell, the creators of the Living Newspapers, and all the other radical artists who were discussing, arguing, and writing their way into this debate had failed in their purpose. Rather, they left behind a wealth of material that, read today, may still offer fruitful answers to the revitalization of American literary and political culture.

CHAPTER ONE

THE ROAD

In Search of America

"I am in the position of most writers nowadays," Sherwood Anderson explained in the introduction to *Puzzled America,* his 1935 travel memoir. "Formerly, for a good many years, I was a writer of tales. It might be that I should have remained just that, but there is a difficulty. There are, everywhere in America, these people now out of work. There are women and children hungry and others without enough clothes."[1] Sixteen years earlier, Anderson had published *Winesburg, Ohio.* Widely condemned at the time of publication for its sexual frankness, the collection had won Anderson the admiration of American modernists. The stories may have taken place in an American town, but it was, as Anderson said, a mythical town; the stories were examinations not of the life of a people but of the loneliness of individuals. Whereas those stories had titles like "Hands," "Sophistication," and "Drink," Anderson's need, by the midthirties, to understand and report on the condition of the country led him to write a book with chapter headings like "A Union Meeting," "At the Mine Mouth," "Revolt in South Dakota," and "Night in a Corn Town." By the thirties, it would be impossible for him to write, as he had in his 1922 memoir, *A Story Teller's Story,* that to a true artist "All morality then becomes a purely aesthetic matter."[2]

Anderson was by no means alone in either his puzzlement or his attempts to understand and represent the new America. Throughout the thirties, writers like Nathan Asch, Edmund Wilson, James Rorty, Theodore Dreiser, John Dos Passos, and Louis Adamic took to the road in search of America.

The accounts they published of their trips would be the most unmediated expression of the central project of radical writers in the thirties: the attempt to describe a crisis-ridden America in terms that would move a wide readership to political activism. Rather than encourage armchair traveling in their descriptions of unfamiliar corners of the country, these accounts were designed to awaken readers to the responsibilities of citizenship, to help them find kinship with a wide range of Americans, including the homeless, laborers, and African Americans. Working in a tradition of American literary journeys that stretched back to Crèvecoeur's *Letters from an American Farmer* (1782), the politically engaged writers of the Depression era produced narratives that most strongly echoed works like Frederick Law Olmsted's *Cotton Kingdom* (1861), his account of a journey through the South, or *Specimen Days,* Walt Whitman's account of working in a Civil War hospital in Washington, D.C. Like northern chroniclers of the antebellum South and of the Civil War, the writers of the thirties portrayed an uneasy landscape and an uncertain future.[3]

Like previous chroniclers of America in a state of crisis, writers of the thirties were spurred on to take their cross-country journeys by their recognition that something had gone terribly wrong and that they needed to understand what it was. Worse, perhaps, was the feeling that their old intellectual habits had become irrelevant, that a literature that did not address the crisis at hand was a literature not worth writing. What is clear from many of the accounts is the extent to which these writers, even as they struggled to both survive and describe it, felt baffled by America and uncertain about their place in it. Theirs was to be a mission both personal and political, both experiential and literary. Disgusted by the ease with which the public relations industry had used the language of Americanism to effect dubious goals, writers struggled to find new language and new literary tools to describe the country that seemed in many ways foreign to them. In their travelogues, as well as in much of the radical fiction and drama of the decade, writers were coming to grips with the necessity for new forms and techniques. They would use the skills of the muckrakers, offering statistical accuracy in order to stir outrage. They would employ the lessons of the modernists while experimenting with the text that was America. Finally, as those who had labored on tabloids and in the advertising industry understood all too well, radical writers, were they to succeed, would have to compete with the styles and techniques of mass culture. Sometimes moved, often shocked, and occasionally bored by what they saw, these writers were rediscovering America for themselves and for their readers. Whereas in the twenties many of these writers had traveled to Europe for inspiration, cheap living, and the intellectual and emotional support of their peers, now they had come home, and they wanted to know what home was.

Statistics can indicate, but not fully express, the trauma of the Depression. The voices recorded in Studs Terkel's *Hard Times* vividly recapture the anguish of the times. "We were struggling, just desperate to be warm. No blankets, no coats," a blacksmith's daughter recalls. "My father lost his job and we moved into a double-garage," another recollects. "We had a coal stove, and we had to each take turns, the three of us kids, to warm our legs. It was awfully cold when you opened those garage doors." A coal miner's son tells us that "My first real memories come about '31. It was simply a gut issue then: eating or not eating, living or not living." A worker recalls: "I'd get up at five in the morning and head for the waterfront. Outside the Spreckles Sugar Refinery, outside the gates, there would be a thousand men. You know dang well there's only three or four jobs. . . . A thousand men would fight like a pack of Alaskan dogs to get through there. Only four of us would get through." The struggle for warmth, for food, for employment caused enormous emotional strain: "Remember, too, the shock, the confusion, the hurt that many kids felt about their fathers not being able to provide for them," a labor organizer recalls.[4]

The home to which American writers returned had become a place where, following the stock market crash, the gross national product had fallen 29 percent from its high point in 1929 to its nadir in 1933; where during the same period construction dropped by 78 percent, consumption expenditures by 18 percent, and investment by 98 percent, and unemployment rose from 3.2 to 24.9 percent. Home was a place where, in 1932, police under the orders of Henry Ford opened fire on three thousand strikers at his River Rouge plant in Detroit, killing four and seriously wounding fifty others. In June of the same year an event took place which came to seem emblematic of the government's broken promises to the people: the Bonus March on Washington, D.C. The Bonus Marchers, a ragged army of three thousand Great War veterans, began traveling from Portland, Oregon, to Washington, D.C., to demand the immediate payment of the World War I bonus Congress had promised them would be paid in 1945. Eventually, twenty thousand men converged on the nation's capital, and although a House bill calling for immediate payment of the bonus was defeated in the Senate, the Bonus Marchers stayed on in an encampment in Anacostia Flats, a visible and much-reported-on presence. Acting on his own, General Douglas MacArthur ordered troops to disperse the marchers—a dispersal that was effected with the aid of tear gas and bayonets. The spectacle of soldiers setting fire to the encampments of the veterans and their families was shocking to many. These were the heroes of 1918, after all, who had become, as a popular 1933 film, *Heroes for Sale,* would have it, men with no prospects and no hopes.[5]

As bank failures swept the nation, President Hoover's optimistic declarations that "Nobody is actually starving" came to ring hollow to those standing in soup lines and living in the makeshift shacks so sarcastically dubbed "Hoovervilles" or those, perhaps, who benefited from the Princeton eating clubs' innovative scheme to send their table scraps to the poor. The horror of the Dust Bowl, a natural disaster fueled by careless use of farmland, gave rise to the decade's sobriquet, the Dirty Thirties. The drought, which began in 1930 and worsened in the following year until the Dakotas and Montana became nearly as arid as the Sonoran desert, affecting every state but Maine and Vermont in the years from 1930 to 1936, ultimately caused a million migrants to head west for California.[6]

Though a sweeping look at the big picture can provide a sense of the general misery in the country, it is perhaps on the local level, and in the most mundane details, that it is easiest to appreciate the impact of the Depression on every facet of daily life. As Ruth McKenney reported in *Industrial Valley,* her 1939 study of the rubber workers and rubber companies in Akron between 1932 and 1936, dog licenses dropped from 9,000 in 1931 to 2,900 in 1932; people could no longer afford to keep pets. Some 900,000 fewer streetcar fares were reported in the same period. For the first time that year, crippled schoolchildren would not get new state-funded braces and crutches at the beginning of the school year. Property tax valuations went down 30 percent. Milk consumption dropped by 60 percent from 1930 to 1931. Some schools closed altogether for lack of funds, while others went on drastically reduced schedules, including a five-week forced vacation in 1932. Farmers in the surrounding countryside rioted at farm foreclosure sales. Akron banks closed.[7]

Franklin D. Roosevelt took office when every bank in the nation was closed, when thirty million families were without regular incomes, and when private charity had reached its highest level in history. Although public spending on welfare was more than double what it had been in the twenties, it was not nearly sufficient to stem the tide of misery. Roosevelt's first hundred days, in which he began what Robert S. McElvaine has termed "the most significant period of reform legislation in American history,"[8] were marked by a great willingness to try whatever it took to get the country on track. "The country needs and, unless I mistake its temper, the country demands bold, persistent experimentation. It is common sense to take a method and try it: If it fails, admit it frankly and try another. But above all, try something."[9] Experimentation led to the creation of dozens of "alphabet soup" agencies (including the cultural agencies of the Federal Arts Projects, which would be so important in determining the shape of 1930s arts) and the development of a social welfare infrastructure unprecedented in size and scope. Yet, though the New Deal and its programs could alleviate much suffering, there was still plenty of misery left to go around. And writers joined the philosophers, economists, politicians, and ordinary Americans who were engaged in endless debate about what the Depression meant and how to make the country better.

As Malcolm Cowley reported of Edmund Wilson, "He began reading history and economics instead of symbolist poetry, and his second wife, a friendly woman without strong convictions, complained that he used to wake her in the middle of the night to discuss the political situation."[10] Wilson took his cross-country journey after finishing *Axel's Castle,* his critical work on the symbolist movement, published in 1931. The methods he had employed as a literary critic were useful to him as he traversed the country, documenting such events as the dedication of the Empire State Building, an Indian corn dance, a miner's strike in Kentucky. As Cowley pointed out,

> In writing his reports, Wilson utilized the same methods that he had developed in writing criticism. That is he began each of them by describing a scene and a situation, much as if he was expounding the subject matter of a book little known to his readers; then he told about the events he witnessed and the comments he heard, as if he were summarizing a plot and suggesting its moral atmosphere, then finally he made his critical comments, which were brief and sometimes expressed by his choice of concrete details. His report on Dwight Morrow was like a short book review; his section on the Ford plant was a formal essay based on parallels and contrasts.[11]

In other words, America had become Wilson's text, and *The American Jitters* was almost a sampler of styles and techniques as he struggled to find the form most appropriate to describe each region, each condition. In stark contrast to his cool, measured portraits of three suicides in Brooklyn, his descriptions of Hollywood employ stream of consciousness, sly sexual innuendo, and a hint of the grotesquery that Nathanael West would use with effectiveness a few years later in *The Day of the Locust* (1939). Wilson's concern for literary form is echoed in scores of travel narratives of the thirties as writers struggled to come to terms with the difficulties of representing a devastated America.

Similarly, in the introduction to *Where Life Is Better,* his 1936 account of his cross-country trip, James Rorty explained that "In certain chapters I have resorted to the greater concreteness and enlarged perspective of the fictional and poetic forms, chiefly as a practical means of handling difficult material. I have tried to make these experiments reinforce rather than break the narrative and expository sequence, and to fuse the journalistic material into a rough synthesis."[12] To convey properly the realities of a country whose miseries seemed often to beggar conventional descriptions, it would be necessary to use the avant-garde techniques of the twenties: shifting perspectives, stream of consciousness, fragmented language, juxtapositions of seemingly unrelated images—that is, to use "literary" technique rather than the more straightforward journalism of the muckrakers.

Not all the writers who embarked on these voyages had been modernists. Louis Adamic, whose *My America* was "an attempt to draw a partial picture of *my* America between 1928 and 1938 . . . the period during which I became an American writer,"[13] was in some sense a direct literary descendant of the muckraking novelists of the earlier part of the century.

Dynamite, Adamic's fictional account of the McNamara bombing trial in Los Angeles, came out in 1931. As Adamic recalled, Upton Sinclair had given him the impetus to write it. "He was then still a regular Socialist, a member of the party, but not averse to hearing the truth, even if unfavorable, about radicals and their movements and politics. The Cantrell story, as I reeled it off to him, fascinated the novelist in him."[14] The novelist in Upton Sinclair, or in any of the other muckrakers, for that matter, did not produce much that would be recognizable to the modernists as good literature. The muckraking novel, of which Sinclair's *The Jungle* (1906) remains the best-known example, was heavy on investigative research, dense with fact, but light on character development, formal innovation, and the fresh use of language. Though marked by a passion for social justice and effective in exposing corruption, the muckraking novel had no formal pretensions. In *The Jungle,* the main character, Jurgis, has no inner life whatsoever. His only function is to move from one horrifyingly bad job to the next, in order to afford Sinclair ample space to describe, in language that, while evocative, remains perfectly conventional, the stomach-turning conditions under which Jurgis works.

The radical literature of the thirties wedded the solid reportage and moral outrage of the muckrakers and the literary experimentation of the modernists. Modernists became wary of literary experimentation for its own sake: Art for art's sake seemed obscene in a time of crisis. On the other hand, the muckrakers found that the literary experiments of the previous decades could not be ignored. Like the modernists, journalists would now become interested in the way the story got told, who told the story, what shape it had, and what the process of shaping the narrative was. By decade's end, James Agee would exemplify the self-consciousness of this journalism in *Let Us Now Praise Famous Men,* copyrighted in 1939 though not published until 1941. Although ostensibly a report on the daily lives of southern tenant farmers, Agee's text, as he wrote in the preface, "is intended, among other things, as a swindle, an insult, and a corrective."[15] It is as much about the problem of representation as about the sharecroppers who are its subject.

The way that each writer tackled the job of representing American life varied, of course: Nathan Asch, for instance, was "taking the trip to find the flesh, the blood, the living spirit to animate the skeleton of a novel. I had in my mind to write a book about America, and for weeks before, little bits of tissue, things I had seen, had heard, had floated before my inside eye and ear, that of themselves made no sense at all, but which set opposite must make clear, explain, explain, and all together somehow form a whole." Although Asch begins *The Road* with fragments of stories, which he then contrasts with the reality of what actually happened, he soon begins to wrestle with feelings of futility: "It didn't matter whether I wrote a book or not. Nothing mattered except to take a gun and kill someone. It was that feeling that had now possessed me, and I went to the bus station, and waited all night." He worries about the problem of representation: "In a book that one wanted to write maybe it was not possible to be absolutely objective, but if it were possible, I was going to be. There would be no wish fulfillment in my novel, or I might have stayed in New York and argued what I wanted America to be." However, after touring a prison in Bismarck, North Dakota, living in a Sea Islands boardinghouse with decaying aristocratic ladies, spending the night with a sheepherder on the plains of Montana, Asch feels overwhelmed by the voices he has heard and decides the time has come for a new kind of literature: "What was I going to do with these people? Write stories of them? I had not started to write stories, any more than I wanted to write the legend of man's hunger in youth, or of the fascinating terror of pretty, objective, in the hills of Africa, murder in the afternoon."[16]

The modernist novels to which Asch more than obliquely refers include Knut Hamsun's *Hunger* (1890), in which the representation of starvation is as a purely individual experience, removed from wider social events or implications: a form of representation that is clearly unacceptable in the context of the Depression. The safari and bullfighting subjects of Hemingway's *Death in the Afternoon* (1932) and *Green Hills of Africa* (1935) also prove inadequate, not only because they are removed from the life experience of most Americans but because Hemingway can be seen as aestheticizing violent death. Asch proposes a way out of these literary traps, however.

> I wanted to write of the legend of men's hunger for always, of death every day, little and not dramatic death, death from watching your children so hungry they were too weak to play, death from not having a job, death from seeing

someone you love sick and not having the money to call a doctor; death from night after night of sleeplessness and worry;—and not in one elaborate, exceptional case, but in ten, hundred, thousand, million cases; in all of America.[17]

The writers who embarked on these trips were not simply, as cultural historian Richard Pells claims, "cherish[ing] the pure, unadorned 'facts' of daily life. Before the simple human drama of the depression experience there was no need to embroider, to speculate, to theorize, to indulge in the conventions of 'art.' "[18] In fact, like Rorty, they were using a wide range of fictional techniques to create a new form of literature. And in their portrayals they were battling an even more insidious and powerful version of reality: that provided by the world of advertising and mass culture. As Dos Passos would in *U.S.A.,* the writers who took these trips felt the need to strip away the veneer of public relations that they had themselves, in some cases, created. Sherwood Anderson had started as a copywriter, and Rorty took the very title of his book, *Where Life Is Better,* now used with the bitterest irony, from a "boost" pamphlet he himself had written ten years previously for an organization called Californians, Inc. Rorty's book is suffused with contempt for the mass culture that was the steady diet of most Americans. Ninety-five percent of the population, he wrote, "don't think; the press, the radio, the movies do not give them the materials of thought, but instead give them obsolete stereotypes." Radical writers would have to find a way to lift their voices above the hubbub of the competition while restoring to language the meaning that public relations had stripped from it. As a character in Nathan Asch's 1930 novel *Pay Day* complains, after hearing the news of Sacco and Vanzetti's execution,

> Try to think of a way to reach them, the rulers of the country for whose benefit all this was arranged, as a warning, as a lesson. Somehow try and wake them up. Words mean nothing to them. They're old, stale, they've been used too much. A wrong decision in a boxing match is an injustice. A bandit shooting a greasy bootlegger is a crime. A straw hat worn after the fifteenth of September a horror. . . . Headlines. Two men are hounded and framed into death. More headlines. Always the same. The sports page is more interesting, the comics page more amusing. Why read what's under the headlines?[19]

Radical writers were taking the perspective of anthropologists while trying to identify with the subjects of their research. "You, the reader," wrote Anderson, "must imagine the writer as going about, constantly puzzled as you are."[20] Just as these alienated intellectuals were trying to get out there and discover America for themselves, they were replicating this journey in their fiction.

They were trying to make the familiar strange to their readers, to make the strange familiar.

Rorty, like other writers, worried about his own relationship to his community and his nation. Describing the Connecticut town in which he lived, as a neighbor of the former muckraking icon Ida Tarbell, and the failure of the contemporary artist to "enjoy a self-respecting, intelligible relationship to [his] community," Rorty went on to ask:

> What has happened to us in America? Have we lost all instinct for reality, all aptitude for human relationships? Is that one of the consequences—perhaps the major consequence—of our "progress"? Does that explain the intolerable flimsiness of these parasitic swank-artistic communities—why they seem like paste diamonds set in an ugly matrix of economic and social chaos? Are artists really quaint?[21]

Finding a social purpose as an artist, of course, informed much of the discourse of the period, from agonized late-night discussions between friends whose conversations, as Granville Hicks later said, could have filled several volumes to the American Writers Congress of 1935, which included Dos Passos, Josephine Herbst, James T. Farrell, and Waldo Frank. As Henry Hart noted in the introduction to the published record,

> From 1930 on, more and more American writers . . . began to take sides in a world struggle between barbarism (deliberately cultivated by a handful of property owners) and the living interests of the mass of mankind. Within the last five years, those whose function is to describe and interpret human life—in novel, story, poem, essay, play—have been increasingly sure that their interests and the interests of the propertyless and oppressed, are inseparable.[22]

Writers on radical literature of the thirties have attempted to define exactly what they meant by the proletarian writer or the radical writer. Whether or not they belonged to the Communist Party, whether they strayed in and out of radical movements, there was a large group of writers in the thirties engaged in a common purpose: to rediscover and redefine America to itself, in order that readers might themselves adopt a new relationship to their nation and its past—as agents rather than as spectators to some great historical pageant. The new fiction, thus, would be a call to activism. During the thirties, especially during the Popular Front period (1935–39),[23] radicals wrestled to reclaim the term "Americanism" from conservatives.

This effort was, one might say, a culture-wide attempt to ratify an American identity. For instance, the 1932 Literary Guild volume, *America: As Americans See It,* featured pieces by prominent writers: Sherwood Anderson's essay "The Times and the Towns"; James Weldon Johnson's "The Creative Negro"; Upton Sinclair's "Graft in America." As is clear from this list, modernists mingled freely with muckrakers; Communists like W. E. B. Du Bois (writing on "Black America") stood cheek to jowl with liberals like Bruce Bliven, managing editor of the *New Republic.* The experience of Native Americans, women, hoboes, and cowboys was discussed; illustrations stressed the connections between "high" and "low" art (refrigerators and gasoline pumps were presented as art; examples of early-nineteenth-century folk art were included as well as recent photographs by Bruehl and Stieglitz); other illustrations included those by modernists like Charles Sheeler, Ben Shahn, and Edward Hopper as well as documentary photographs and cartoons by such *Masses* stalwarts as Art Young and Robert Minor.[24]

What may be hard to remember is the extent to which fellow traveling took place: Not only did many people drift in and out of the Communist Party but radicals then, unlike now, were hardly ghettoized. On the Federal Arts Projects, for instance, radicals like Richard Wright, Nathan Asch, and Josephine Herbst worked side by side with less radical writers like Eudora Welty. Murals produced under the liberal Constance Rourke's stewardship often contained radical references (the public library depicted in Hoit Towers in San Francisco contains a full complement of texts by radical authors like Martin Andersen Nexo). So while it is important to draw distinctions between camps, it is also necessary to keep in mind the extent to which the conversation about American identity took place all the way along the political spectrum. Between Constance Rourke's celebration of an American tradition that was "various, subtle, sinewy, scant at times but not poor"[25] and Earl Browder's assertion that "Communism is twentieth century Americanism" lay plenty of room for debate.

It may be true that writers were in often anguished disagreement about what path to take to create the new literature. What is equally true is that the writers in contention were often those who, in previous decades, would have had little to say to one another. Although no single life can be representative of a generation, there are clearly those whose paths seem to typify some important trends. Joseph Freeman, one of the founders of *New Masses* and among the chief literary critics of the Communist Party, is interesting not only for his views—among them a defense of modernism as a politically useful literary form—but also as an exemplar of the journey taken by many radical writers of the thirties. Having emigrated from Russia as a child, Freeman grew up in the Williamsburg section of Brooklyn, a Jewish ghetto which would in the teens and twenties be the setting for such early immigrant novels as Anzia Yezierska's *Bread Givers* and Abraham Cahan's *Rise of David Levinsky*. This was also the site chosen by Samuel Ornitz—another founder of *New Masses* who in the fifties would become one of the Hollywood Ten—for his bitter satire on the immigrant novel, *Haunch, Paunch, and Jowl*. Later, the Williamsburg section was described by Michael Gold in *Jews without Money*, by Daniel Fuchs in his Williamsburg trilogy, by Henry Roth in *Call It Sleep*.

Freeman, born in 1897, came of age as an early radical. As he writes in his autobiography, *An American Testament*,

> Loud was the middle-class protest in those days. . . . The discontent expressed by Steffens, Tarbell and Baker in the magazines was echoed in the novels of Booth Tarkington, Frank Norris, David Graham Philips, Winston Churchill and Upton Sinclair. Those of us who began to read and think at this time became accustomed to the idea, first, that American capitalism was corrupt from top to bottom; second, that art and politics were closely related. Both ideas come from purely American sources. The scene involved was the United States alone; the muckrakers were native-born Americans.[26]

For an immigrant, an American identity could be a radical identity—these were real Americans, concerned with specifically American issues. However, for a young writer, the muckrakers provided little literary inspiration. The muckrakers are, in a sense, an easy target. They may have written crudely, political urgency propelling their message forward when literary technique failed to do the job. In language designed to shock, Sinclair would detail the conditions of a meat-packing plant, or Tarbell would expose the machinations of Standard Oil. This was journalism that would get the job done, would arouse a public to demand pure food legislation or child labor laws, and it was literature that went hand in hand with the photographs of Jacob Riis and Lewis Hines.[27]

Yet it was not the kind of literature that most young Americans wanted to write. Growing up, reading Floyd Dell's 1912 critique of Dreiser's "nineteenth century, passive attitudes," Freeman writes that it seemed to him that

> The writer's "artistic" self had nothing to do with his social self. In his novels he might be a nineteenth century pessimist; in his travel books, essays and articles he must be a twentieth century socialist. This was being like employers who went to church on Sundays and shot strikers on weekdays; or like myself, whose ideas were slowly and stubbornly trickling towards socialism, and whose poetry flowed secretly from the vanished village.

Although the muckrakers might be politically inspirational, and indeed might serve as models for American citizenship, they could not serve as models for aspiring literati. As the college student Freeman asked, "Could one create Art in America? Nonsense! America was a wild marketplace, hysterical with the shrieks of hagglers." Echoing this complaint, Malcolm Cowley, an almost exact contemporary of Freeman's, recalled in the thirties that in college "It seemed to us that America was beneath the level of great fiction; it seemed that literature in general, and art and learning, were things existing at an infinite distance from our daily lives. For those of us who read independently, this impression became even stronger: the only authors to admire were foreign authors." Cowley may well have been describing Freeman himself when he wrote:

> A Jewish boy from Brooklyn might win a scholarship by virtue of his literary talent. Behind him there would lie whole generations of rabbis versed in the Torah and the Talmud, representatives of the oldest Western culture now surviving. Behind him, too, lay the memories of an exciting childhood: street gangs in Brownsville, chants in a Chassidic synagogue, the struggle of his parents against poverty, his cousin's struggle, perhaps, to build a labor union and his uncle's fight against it—all the emotions, smells and noises of the ghetto. Before him lay contact with another great culture, and four years of leisure in which to study, write and form a picture of himself. But what he would write about in those four years were Keatsian sonnets about English abbeys, which he had never seen, and nightingales he had never heard.[28]

Though a familiar lament for American writers of previous generations, this longing for an older, more stable world was perhaps exacerbated by the uncertainties produced by World War I. An orientation toward European culture and a European aesthetic was, as Freeman writes, "very pleasant for young men removed from productive labor, anxious to forget a world rendered bitter by the war." This may have been generally true—for youths with political beliefs the schism was even more extreme, as we have seen in Freeman's case. Whether repelled for aesthetic reasons by the growth of mass culture—a culture that many of these writers contributed to in their jobs as copywriters or as newspaper reporters—or horrified by the climate of political intolerance that came with the call to war and lingered after it in the Palmer raids, young artists found America an inhospitable place: As William Carlos Williams would write, "Such men, right thinking but prey to isolation by the forces surrounding them, became themselves foreigners in their own country."[29]

Rather than trying to create art in the wild marketplace, these young writers and artists headed for Paris. In 1921 Harold Stearns completed his editing of *Civilization in the United States,* a well-received collection of essays by thirty intellectuals on the problems talented young men and women faced in finding satisfying uses for their gifts in this country. Having delivered the finished manuscript to his editor, he embarked for Paris, providing an answer by example to those young artists and intellectuals whose dilemma the volume was intended to address.[30]

The life lived there has been documented to death, ossified in perhaps its most concrete form by Hemingway's quite mythological *A Moveable Feast,* his 1960s account of cafe life among the modernists. However, for the purposes of this narrative, it is useful to remember a few things: first of all, the sheer numbers of writers, composers, and artists who spent a year or a decade in Paris in the teens and twenties. Among them were, to name but a few, Virgil Thomson; Sherwood Anderson; Sylvia Beach; Kenneth Burke; Josephine Baker; Gilbert Seldes, the managing editor of *The Dial,* which published T. S. Eliot and Hart Crane; Matthew Josephson, the coeditor of *Secession* and associate editor of *Broom,* later to become a prominent figure in thirties leftist circles; Claude McKay, one of the inner circle on the *Liberator* (which was *The Masses* in its midtwenties incarnation); Ezra Pound; John Dos Passos; Hart Crane; the journalist Dorothy Thompson (who with her husband Sinclair Lewis would host radical salons in the thirties); Waldo Frank; e.e. cummings; Josephine Herbst; Nathan Asch.

And while all these writers, most of them modernists, were in Paris, they were, as Freeman writes, "on a lark, traveling, drinking, loving, and—perhaps most important of all—learning to work steadily every day at the profession of journalism." Those who, unlike Virgil Thomson, did not have academic fellowships or wealthy patrons to support them (and Thomson seems to have been a veritable genius at attracting backers) had to rely on hackwork. John Dos Passos was a roving foreign correspondent; Dorothy Thompson worked for the *Philadelphia Ledger*'s Paris desk; Matthew Josephson worked for the *Paris Telegram,* an English-language racing sheet, to give but a few examples. The journalistic and advertising jobs they took on would reemerge recontextualized in the thirties: Already their high-art ambitions were tempered by the reality of having to work in the world of mass culture. Many of these writers were already aware of the problems of truth in journalism, in that, as William Wiser notes, to "take revenge for the meager salary—a marginally living wage only because of the favorable exchange rate—reporters treated the news as something of a joke, extending the most trivial items into extravagant features or inventing unverifiable dispatches out of whole cloth." And, as Freeman, himself a newspaperman, was to write, the "public avidly followed a press which, concealing the truth about Mooney and Billings, Sacco and Vanzetti, devoted pages to beauty contests and lust murders."[31]

Finally, the artistic movements in Paris—dada and futurism—that were outgrowths of the First World War, and in which many American artists dabbled or to which they were at least exposed, were those that tended toward either anarchy—the in-your-face behavior of dadaists who held art exhibitions in public urinals—or worship of the machine. As F. T. Marinetti, perhaps the foremost proponent of futurism, explained, "We glorify war, the sole hygiene of the world. We glorify militarism, patriotism, the destructive gestures of the anarchists: the beautiful idea which kills: the contempt for women."[32] In its celebration of crowds, industrial machinery, speed, violence, its yearning for what Marinetti would term "the metalization of man," futurism was an aesthetic of destruction, a longing for an order beyond that of the human. Traces of futurist thought could be found in the social realist painting of the twenties and thirties, and more than traces in the Fascist art of the period. Although both dada and futurism may have appealed to young artists who were beginning to think hard about the possibilities of demolishing previous forms of art, they could never be lasting solutions to the problem of how to make art that mattered. Dada may have mocked the institutionalization of art, but the humor was in the form of an in-joke, accessible primarily to a small coterie of artists educated in that tradition. Dada was, as Cowley would say, the final manifestation of the religion of art, and futurism was an ideology that allowed little form for the expression of sentiments less monolithic than those of the machine.

Rebuked by comrades at home for his dedication to art and his lack of dedication to revolution, Freeman came back to America, part of a wave of writers of all ideological stripes who drifted homeward throughout the twenties because they were homesick, or they had run out of money, or it was simply high time. Yet, as Matthew Josephson recalled, "After our *Wanderjahre* we came home, some earlier, some later, with no little fear or trembling, to what we considered the non-culture of our native land."[33]

Even back home, in Greenwich Village where many of them ended up, it would take a while for their European orientation to change. Even while appreciating things American, they did so from the perspective of admiring foreigners. Still in Paris, Cowley wrote "poems about America, poems that spoke of movies and skyscrapers and machines, dwelling upon them with all the nostalgia derived from two long years of exile. I, too, was enthusiastic about America; I had learned from a distance to admire its picturesque qualities." However, the admiration of the tourist was very different from that of the citizen. Cowley writes of the difficulty "of reproducing in New York the conditions that had seemed so congenial to us abroad, and of continuing to praise the picturesque American qualities of the Machine Age and the New Economic Era while living under their shadow."[34] As Matthew Josephson, who had returned from his Paris years to edit the avant-garde magazine *Broom*, ruefully noted, "We had tried to give expression to some elements of the modern myth of America as a machine economy and a society of the Masse Mensch. But there were as yet no helpful social arrangements by which the artist himself might escape the peril of being caught and mangled by the assembly lines."[35]

Conversely, many expatriates realized that they would never be European, despite their best efforts. As Virgil Thomson put it, "A French composer I could never be anyhow; I had always known that. It was all right to be a foreigner working in France, but not a pseudo-Gallic clinger-on." Logically, then, the task remained to carve out an identity separate from that of the Europeans by whom he was surrounded: "I considered the creation of an American music by myself and certain contemporaries to be a far worthier aspiration than any effort to construct a wing, a portico, or even a single brick that might be fitted on to Europe's historical edifice."[36]

Though American artists were beginning, in the twenties, to turn back to native sources for their inspiration, these sources were not necessarily radical ones. Matthew Josephson returned from his *Wanderjahre* in Paris to work on the high-modernist magazine *Broom*. As Freeman writes of his experiences working on the Communist Party–identified *Liberator*, the reborn version of *The Masses*, in 1922,

> At the moment when liberal writers sought wisdom at the shrine of Eliot, Pound, Proust and Joyce, Michael Gold was reporting the coal strike in Pennsylvania and the clothing workers' convention in Cleveland; and Mary Heaton Vorse and John Dos Passos sent us eyewitness accounts of life in the new Russia. Later the two literary tendencies were to meet on more or less common ground under the crushing effects of a great economic crisis; but that meeting was ten years off.[37]

Indeed, there was often a certain degree of tension between the two groups. Poet Claude McKay, who was central to the *Liberator* staff, recalls in his autobiography *A Long Way from Home* that, when he argued for the inclusion in the magazine of a spread of e.e. cummings poems, temporary editor-in-chief Robert Minor told "me that if I liked such poems I was more of a decadent than a social revolutionist."[38]

The *Liberator* offices may have been only a few doors down from the *Dial*, where Van Wyck Brooks, Lewis Mumford, and Kenneth Burke were helping to develop another school of American literature, but they were still worlds apart.

Yet, as early as 1925, Samuel Ornitz, Floyd Dell, author of the quintessential bohemian novel *The Moon Calf,* Upton Sinclair, John Howard Lawson, Waldo Frank, Mary Heaton Vorse, and Van Wyck Brooks were willing to serve on the executive committee of a proletarian writers' league, the newly founded American wing of a similar group in the Soviet Union. It is important to note, though, that the aims of this proletarian writers' group would be somewhat different from those of proletarian literature organizations ten years later. Whereas the American Writers Congress of 1935, which included many of the same writers (as well as a host of others) and at which Earl Browder presided as head of the Communist Party, saw proletarian literature as further-ing the interests of an entire class, the 1925 group saw it as an extension of work on behalf of the labor movement. As Freeman writes, "There was a long period in American history—the first quarter of our century—in which the progressive intelligentsia felt sympathetic towards labor. To assist labor in one way or another, to give your talents and energies, was considered rather noble. The middle classes, pressed hard by the expanding trusts, often allied them-selves with labor."[39] Much of the energy of the muckrakers earlier in the century had been directed toward exposing the shocking conditions endured by workers; events like the 1911 Triangle Shirtwaist factory fire, in which more than 140 women plunged to their deaths from the burning building or were asphyxiated inside it, stirred public outrage.[40]

In the twenties the 1926 Communist-led strike by 16,000 Passaic textile workers, where police clubbed men, women, and children and firemen turned hoses on strikers, sparked national and international outrage and sympathy for the strikers and impelled liberals to join with radicals.

One of the outgrowths of this outrage would be the formation of the *New Masses,* a magazine edited by Joseph Freeman, Mike Gold, Hugo Gellert, James Rorty, and John Sloan, whose editorial board would boast a broad range of American writers and artists, including experimental playwrights like Eu-gene O'Neill, Susan Glaspell, and Elmer Rice; journalists like Mary Heaton Vorse; future NAACP leader Walter White; literary critics like Van Wyck Brooks, Lewis Mumford, Edmund Wilson, and Waldo Frank; poets like Carl Sandburg, Claude McKay, and Louis Untermeyer; bohemian fixtures like Floyd Dell; and a range of other writers including Lola Ridge, Genevieve Taggard, Cornelia Barnes, John Dos Passos, Sherwood Anderson, and Max Eastman. Though the magazine would come to be identified with the Communist Party, only two of its founding members (out of fifty-six) were Party members, and perhaps ten more were sympathetic to the Party's purposes. The founding of this magazine represented an important moment in the development of a self-consciously American radical literature; as Dos Passos wrote, "Ever since Columbus, imported systems have been the curse of this country. Why not develop our own brand?" And Mike Gold seconded this emotion, agreeing that "American writers in general and the *New Masses* writers in particular ought to set sail for a new discovery of America."

Yet, many of the writers who would be identified with radicalism in the thirties were aspiring modernists and bohemians in the twenties. It was a period when it was possible to make a decent living writing books and magazine articles or as copywriters, public relations workers, editors, a time when many writers could enter the middle class. Although the executions of Sacco and Vanzetti in 1927, after seven years of investigation, trials, and failed appeals, may have galvanized, for a while, a broad range of liberal intellectuals to a common cause, it would take the crash to bring together the radical writers, the aesthetes, and the critics—like Van Wyck Brooks who, in his 1918 essay "Letters and Leadership," had bemoaned the lack of a common spiritual heritage or national fabric of spiritual experience—into, if not a unified cause, at least a single conversation.

By the midthirties, the single conversation was taking place in a number of periodicals, which addressed the concerns of writers in search of an American identity—and which used the tools of modernism and documentary to effect this goal. Perhaps one of the best examples is *Direction,* published between 1934 and 1940 (including a special issue called *American Stuff* devoted to the off-hours writing and art of Federal Writers Project and Federal Art Project employees).[41] A typical issue, that of January 1938, included a conversation between John Dos Passos and Theodore Dreiser, paintings by workers on the WPA Art Project, an article on Le Corbusier, and a feature called "Magnifying the News," in which a newspaper story on industrial espionage, and more particularly on companies spying on their employees, was selectively magnified to show the most horrifying portions of the piece—a variation of the reexaminations and deconstructions of news that so many fiction writers were engaged in throughout the thirties. Perhaps even more telling was the "Cultural Front" column for the April 1938 issue:

A new group called DESCENDANTS OF THE AMERICAN REVOLUTION has organized to "maintain the freedom-loving traditions of Americans, and to defend democratic institutions." Its membership will be limited to those who can prove descent from a man or woman of Revolutionary times, and its purpose is also to offset the reactionary influence of groups such as the *Daughters of the American Revolution.* Among the sponsors are Stuart Chase, Malcolm Cowley, John Haynes Holmes, Mary K. Simkhovitch, George Soule, Mary Hillyer, Elizabeth Faragoh.[42]

The stress on the Americanism of radicals was a theme echoed in other articles in *Direction,* such as "Americanism—What Variety?" by William Zeuch in the July/August 1938 issue.[43] The "Cultural Front" column also contained a list of recommended books for readers of *Direction,* among them *People's Front* by Earl Browder; *Under the Open Sky* by Martin Anderson Nexo, a Danish proletarian writer whom Mike Gold claimed as one of his greatest influences;[44] and Archibald MacLeish's *Land of the Free,* which married his poetry to documentary photographs by Dorothea Lange, Russell Lee, Walker Evans, Ben Shahn, and other Farm Security Administration photographers. Modernism, documentary, radical politics, and not incidentally, a stress on the positive value of the WPA-sponsored arts projects, merged in this periodical.

Direction was far from being singular in its concerns. What is most striking about the little magazines of the thirties is their heterogeneity. There were some, indeed, that fit received ideas about radical literature of the thirties, magazines with names like *Blast: Magazine of Proletarian Short Stories* (whose ad copy promised "more force and vitality than a dozen bourgeois magazines put together"), *Dynamo, Anvil, The Left,* and its successor, the *New Quarterly,* whose ads promised that its editorial bias "will be frankly proletarian and revolutionary." Yet there were a host of others, like the *Windsor Quarterly,* published in Hartland Four Corners, Vermont, and *Contempo,* from Chapel Hill, North Carolina, or *Smoke,* from Providence, Rhode Island, whose lists of contributors contained some surprising bedfellows. A glance at the table of contents in 1934 and 1935 for *The Magazine,* out of Beverly Hills, offers Josephine Herbst in the same issue as the agrarian Caroline Gordon, Robert Penn Warren with the radical poet Muriel Rukeyser, C. Day Lewis and William Carlos Williams. In 1933 the list of contributors to *Contempo: A Review of Books and Personalities* included Ezra Pound and Upton Sinclair, Theodore Dreiser and William Faulkner, Josephine Herbst and Paul Green. *Windsor Quarterly* published Elizabeth Bishop and R. P. Blackmur as well as the future Hollywood Ten member Alvah Bessie and Meridel Le Seuer. Communists, Fascists, liberals, and conservatives could and did appear in the same magazines. Radical writers were hardly ghettoized; rather, they were able to address the same audiences as their more conservative colleagues.

It is perhaps unsurprising that Joseph Freeman and Malcolm Cowley have served in this discussion as exemplars of the different paths that American writers took to the activism of the Depression years. After all, Freeman was to become one of the contributing editors of the important 1935 anthology *Proletarian Literature of the United States,* and Cowley's accounts of his own and other writers' journey toward radicalism in the twenties and the thirties, *Exile's Return* (1934) and *The Dream of the Golden Mountain* (1964), remain indispensable sources. It would seem natural to extend this focus as we move into the 1930s, or to look at a figure like Michael Gold, who served as perhaps the Communist Party's foremost literary spokesperson. What may seem a more surprising choice, however, is the person whose position seems to me to be somehow paradigmatic of the leftist writer in the thirties: Ruth McKenney.

McKenney, who, born in 1911, was a little over a decade younger than the writers we have been considering, is best known today as the author of *My Sister Eileen,* the best-selling account of her family life during her childhood. This autobiography, first published in 1938, was a collection of McKenney's *New Yorker* pieces; a second anthology would appear two years later under the title *The McKenneys Carry On.* Both volumes were critically acclaimed, especially the first, of which the *Books* reviewer confidently asserted, "If anyone thinks women are constitutionally devoid of humor—of course, no sensible person could think so, but if anyone did think so, he would only have to read Ruth McKenney to learn the extent of his error."[45] "As richly American as a three-decker sandwich," wrote M. L. Elting in *Commonweal,*[46] *My Sister Eileen* went through more than a dozen printings and became first a Broadway play, then a 1942 Hollywood film directed by Alexander Hall and starring Rosalind Russell and Brian Aherne. In 1955 Richard Quine directed a musical version with Betty Garrett, Janet Leigh, and Jack Lemmon; the Broadway version of this musical was entitled *Wonderful Town.* In the memoir's introduction, McKenney discusses her omissions from the book of "the awful things my sister Eileen and I lived through when we were growing up," including the summer she and Eileen spent "in a deserted monastery in Columbus, Ohio, fighting a brood of oversize and somewhat insane bats."[47] The book's chapter titles may give a fair idea of its general flavor: "Hun-gah" is subheaded "Eileen learns to play the piano and I take elocution lessons," while "A Loud Sneer for Our Feathered Friends" is further explained as "We go to a girls' camp and don't think much of it, also about birds," and "The Gladsome Washing Machine Season" is subheaded "Father feels like King Lear, with good reason." This text would hardly position McKenney as a radical writer of the time. But McKenney wrote other books: In 1939 and 1940 her works included a campaign pamphlet through Workers Library Publishers entitled *Browder and Ford for Peace, Jobs, and Socialism; The McKenneys*

Carry On, an anthology of her *New Yorker, Woman's Day,* and *Publishers Weekly* stories, which appeared not only in a Grosset and Dunlap edition but also in an abbreviated edition for the armed services; and *Industrial Valley,* a documentary account of the 1932–36 successful rubber strike in Akron, Ohio. As if this weren't enough, between 1938 and 1946 the prolific McKenney penned the "Strictly Personal" column for *New Masses,* where she also appeared on the masthead among the editors. McKenney moved easily from popular autobiography to documentary labor history to radical pamphleteering. She moved in high Communist Party circles, spending her vacations with Earl Browder and his family. Moreover, sister Eileen was married to Nathanael West, author of the apocalyptic Los Angeles novels *Miss Lonelyhearts* (1932) and *The Day of the Locust* (1939)—modernist novels that offered a scathing critique of mass culture and the Hollywood dream factory. McKenney, thus, was situated as the radical vortex of the neat triangle of mass culture, documentary, and modernism.

Even in the light work that made McKenney's popular reputation, she offers us a child's-eye view of the cultural transformations that had shaped the radical writers of the thirties. In *My Sister Eileen,* she writes that "The nicely brought up child of today lives on a prissy milk-and-water movie diet of colored cartoons, costume pictures with noble endings, and banal dramas starring his favorite radio comic. The Mickey Mouse vogue among the juniors demonstrates what fearful changes Will Hays, the Legion of Decency, and Aroused Parenthood have wrought in a mere twenty years or so" (3). She writes of her total involvement, as a child, in mass culture and of her and Eileen's movie-judging system that gives the chapter its name: "No Tears, No Good." Writing about her immersion in cinema, and the aversion of intellectuals to this art form—as she says, "back in 1919 and 1920 people who had pretensions to culture, at least in the Middle West, wouldn't be caught dead in a movie house" (9)—she humorously treats her and her sister's desire to be swept away on a tide of unthinking emotion: exactly what the writers of the thirties would fight against.

During the same period, Americans' infatuation with Continental culture is described in her chapter "Hun-gah," in which McKenney, in response to her lace-curtain-Irish aunts' desire to make their nieces "cultured," takes elocution lessons from the Paris-trained Madame DuLak in her Studio of the Voice. Madame DuLak, who has nothing but contempt for Ruth's idol, Joyce Kilmer, is an Europhiliac—and Amerophobic—as they come, and the play in which the young McKenney demonstrates her skills is a perfect parody of modernist pretensions: "I sat on the steps of what was supposed to be a cathedral. From the time the curtain went up until at last it went down, I sat on those steps, chanting the word 'hunger' at more or less one-minute intervals. . . . It was a Greek-chorus idea. The play was exceedingly symbolical" (24).

The girls' aunts, of course, had hoped for "Eileen at the piano bringing tears to the eyes of her relatives with a splendid performance of 'Narcissus,' the selection where you cross your hands on the keyboard" (21). In fact, much of the humor of *My Sister Eileen* revolves around the efforts of these aunts to inculcate the girls with middlebrow culture. Culture, in this definition, is something that both bores and uplifts; the aunts buy them theater tickets because they "thought we should sit at the feet of Shakespeare and quit going to those horrid movies all the time" (70), but the chaperoning aunts themselves are always "somewhat bored" (70). When a scandalized neighbor tells Mr. McKenney about the girls' exposure to Noel Coward and demands a halt to the excursions, the girls beg to be allowed one more show. However, the next week's offering, Maxwell Anderson's *What Price Glory?*, an antiwar drama which was to become a successful production of the radical Group Theatre, is seen by the censorious neighbor as "the last straw. She said that *showed* you what Noel Coward could do" (75). Radicalism, in this equation, is seen as even more threatening than the risqué sexuality and double entendres of a Noel Coward play.

McKenney neatly, albeit lightly, lays out the dilemma that would face writers in the thirties, confronted by audiences who might secretly be enthralled by the mass-market newspaper serials of "virtue triumphant and sin abashed" (81), yet who, if they were genteel, would, like Aunt Molly, "who was considered very high-toned by the rest of the family" (82), claim that Mr. Galsworthy was their favorite author. Caught between "tales of flappers gone bad" (81), on the one hand, and predictable, high-minded offerings on the other, through which one suffered because culture, like medicine, was supposed to taste bad if it was to work, one would be hard pressed to find an artistic model to emulate in the pages of *My Sister Eileen*. It is hard to find a phase of intellectual and cultural development that McKenney misses, though. The bohemian Greenwich Village life is represented (it seems to consist mainly of trimming fungus off the bathroom ceiling of a disgusting basement apartment and picking up dates at New Theatre League dances), and we even see Ruth becoming a journalist (she interviews Sir Randolph Churchill for her school newspaper and ends up becoming drunk with him and searching with him for his lost sock under a hotel bed).

Nor does McKenney neglect the political arena. Just as she satirizes the cultural pretensions and anxieties of middle-class Americans of the teens and twenties, so too does she make fun of the myths of success so central to American life.

> You know, the growing lad dashes out into the blistering wintah breeze to sell a mean newspaper. In about two months the head slugger in the circulation department recognizes true genius in the budding banker; he equips the ambitious boy with a Colt machine gun and from there on in our lion-hearted hero overcomes all obstacles including competitors and winds up complaining about labor unions to the president. (111)

Needless to say, this is not the model she feels able to emulate; McKenney's own work experiences include a job in a print shop, where "I was the center of a big ideological and sociological struggle" (114). McKenney sides not with the Republican boss but with the linotype operators, who are "belligerent Ingersoll atheists, enthusiastic Eugene Debs Socialists, old-time Wobblies, and passionate union men" (116). This first job becomes the site of McKenney's radical conversion—a trope that was a staple of radical thirties fiction. What would appear in straight form in Robert Cantwell's *The Land of Plenty* (1934) as a chapter headed "The Education of a Worker," and would be echoed in dozens of other novels, is comically handled in *My Sister Eileen:* "Unlike the embryo banker who learns thrift and how to get ahead on his first job, all I ever learned was never to bet on an ex-champion's return bout, and what was wrong with the capitalistic system and God" (118).

If this volume was all that McKenney produced, one would be hard pressed to make a case for her as a radical writer, for *My Sister Eileen,* while it echoes many of the themes of other radical writers, hardly challenges the prevailing social order. However, *Industrial Valley,* her nonfiction novel, not only exemplifies radical documentary of the period but serves perhaps as its avatar. Using only two fictitious names in her collective biography of the strikers, McKenney traces the strike's progress using excerpts from newspaper headlines, vital statistics, and editorial comments on national and local affairs. Of this work Malcolm Cowley, writing in the *New Republic,* declared: "For the last eight years, people have been arguing about proletarian literature; it has been praised, reviled and more recently buried in potter's field, but the interesting point is that it has rarely been written. 'Industrial Valley' is perhaps the best American example of that manner and medium. Even though it is based completely on fact, I also offer it as one of our best collective novels."[48]

Industrial Valley was well received by both radical and mainstream critics: The Third Writers Congress voted it the outstanding piece of nonfiction of the year, Albert Maltz (later to become one of the Hollywood Ten) characterized it as "brilliant history" in his *New Masses* review, and Lewis Gannett, writing in the *New York Herald Tribune,* declared that, "for sheer dramatic excitement, for effective organization as a story, there isn't one among all the strike novels to match this essentially true story." Even John L. Lewis wrote a letter to McKenney, expressing his appreciation for the work.[49]

The carefully researched *Industrial Valley* stands not just as exemplar for its genre but as explanation for the genre's importance. Unlike Asch, Rorty, Anderson, and others who documented their journeys through America, McKenney keeps herself entirely out of the story. Thus we do not get the naked methodology of those works—the discussions of how best to represent American culture, to tell the American story. What McKenney does instead is to contrast the official truths of Akron, Ohio, as expressed by newspapers and Chamber of Commerce releases, with the unofficial, yet very real, suffering of the population there, as documented by the numbers of people applying for relief, the numbers freezing to death, the number of suicides. Through these often surreal juxtapositions, McKenney forces readers to consider the distance between these two accounts:

News Item   *February 24, 1932*
A very large gray rat bit Phyllis Smith, aged six months, about fifty times as she lay in her crib early this morning. Doctors at Children's Hospital barely saved the infant's life.

Don't Hoard   *February 25, 1932*
Akron citizens who had three cents for a *Times-Press* or a *Beacon Journal* were considerably startled to read a large advertisement urging them to stop hoarding their money.
The best people in town sponsored the don't-hoard-your-dollar-bills program, Akron's most spectacular anti-Depression campaign.

Again and again, McKenney juxtaposes the booster rhetoric of official sources with the harsh realities experienced by Akron citizens. Henry Ford announcing that "This nation is on the threshold of an inconceivably bright future" and the editorial in the *Beacon Journal* on New Year's Eve, 1932, stating that "The best cause for merrymaking tonight is that this greatest of jinx years is dead and that the community may turn its face at least hopefully to another" both lead readers to question a wide range of official verities.[50]

What my choice of *Direction* as exemplary magazine and McKenney as a paradigmatic figure may indicate is that I cast a fairly wide net in my discussion of radical fiction of the period.[51] While I am interested in the debate among writers on how best to convey a radical message within a novel or play, I examine this discussion not primarily as it was played out in the editorials and letters columns of magazines like *New Masses,* or even during meetings of the radical writers' organizations of the period, but as it was embodied within the texts themselves. Thus each chapter will examine an exemplary approach to the problem of creating an aesthetically sophisticated, politically engaged literature for a mass audience.

The questions that McKenney addressed in her writing would be echoed by a generation of radical writers who, through turning stale official rhetoric upside down, through adapting the techniques they had learned on their European sojourns to American purposes, and through experimenting with the very structure of the novel and the play, would create a literature peculiarly suited to a nation in crisis.

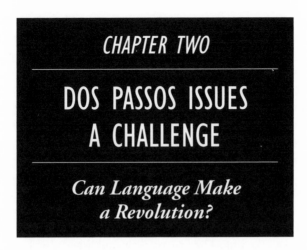

CHAPTER TWO

DOS PASSOS ISSUES A CHALLENGE

Can Language Make a Revolution?

Although many radical writers were involved in the debate over the shape the new literature should take, it was John Dos Passos who, in his *U.S.A.* trilogy, most clearly identified both the literary forms that could no longer be effective in a time of crisis and, in his own trilogy, the form that could work.

Between 1930 and 1933 John Dos Passos published the three volumes— *The 42nd Parallel* (1930), *Nineteen Nineteen* (1932), and *The Big Money* (1933)—that would appear, with the addition of the hitherto unpublished introductory sketch "U.S.A." as an assembled trilogy, *U.S.A.* The trilogy's scope is vastly ambitious, not only in subject matter but in aesthetic terms: Among the techniques Dos Passos uses to describe America during the first three decades of this century are stream-of-consciousness autobiographical passages, capsule biographies of notable inventors, more traditional narratives which are interwoven with one another in nearly Tolstoian terms, and "Newsreels" composed of montages of newspaper headlines, popular songs, and news fragments.

The *U.S.A.* trilogy, with its depiction of characters ranging from Wobblies to public relations magnates, from radical journalists to Harvard-educated aesthetes, has been seen by many critics as the great historical narrative of American life in the first decades of this century. As Donald Pizer notes, "Dos Passos had in the late 1920s already begun to characterize himself as a 'historian' of American life, and he was to use this designation for the remainder of his career."[1] *U.S.A.*, as Melvin Landsberg notes, can certainly be considered "an American epic."[2] It is indeed, as Dos Passos intended, "a historical rather than a personal representation of twentieth-century American life."[3] And yet, though it certainly functions as a work of history, it is perhaps more significantly a work of historiography, a nearly 1,400-page debate on the question of who is entitled to tell the truth about American history and how that truth can be told most effectively—or, to be more precise, who will get to influence public opinion, who will get to define what are received ideas about such crucial issues as the causes of the First World War, on whose side justice lies in labor disputes, and the innocence or guilt of Sacco and Vanzetti.

John Dos Passos was as well situated as any writer to document the changing shape of American history and literature. Indeed, his education as a writer echoed that of many of his radical compatriots in the thirties, from his early suspicion of American art, to his education among the European modernists, to his political awakening. The first article he published after his 1916 graduation from Harvard was entitled "Against American Literature."[4] He was ambivalent about Woodrow Wilson and impressed by the antiwar speeches of Max Eastman. During the war he drove an ambulance in France, a rite of passage for so many American writers.[5] Upon his return to the United States, Dos Passos lived in Greenwich Village where he wrote novels and supported himself primarily through journalism. He became one of the first editors of *New Masses* and protested the execution of Sacco and Vanzetti. His reaction to that event echoed that of the subway rider overheard in Nathan Asch's 1930 novel *Pay Day* who complained, after the execution, that "A straw hat worn after the fifteenth of September [is] a horror. . . . Headlines. Two men are hounded and framed into death. More headlines. Always the same."[6] In fact, it was the case of the two Italian anarchists, convicted of murder and sentenced to the electric chair, which was to prove formative for Dos Passos as a writer and as a political thinker.

In *Facing the Chair: Sacco and Vanzetti: The Story of Two Foreign Born Workmen,* a pamphlet produced by Dos Passos for the Sacco and Vanzetti Defense Committee in 1927, just before the execution of the two anarchists, Dos Passos wrestles with the meaning of Americanism and laments the meaninglessness to which language has been reduced. The national spirit, for Dos Passos, is embodied by one of the lying witnesses for the prosecution, who "learned Americanism all right, he suffered from no encumbering ideas of social progress; the law of dawg eat dawg was morbidly vivid from the first." This successful American, rather than becoming politically engaged, knows how to profit from the national pride of others: "No protests from him about the war. He and his sister and another man dressed up in uniforms and collected money for some vaguely phoney patriotic society, The American Rescue League." In *Facing the Chair,* which is itself filled with affidavits from the trial's participants, as well as an appeal from Eugene Debs and a demand for investigation from the American Federation of Labor, Dos Passos writes of the "Affidavits, affidavits read alternately by counsel in the stillness of the yellowvarnished courtroom. Gradually as the reading goes on the courtroom shrinks." The accretion of language has no effect in securing justice: "Tragic figures of men and women grow huge like shadows cast by a lantern on a wall; the courtroom becomes a tiny pinhole through which to see a world of huge trampling forces in conflict."[7] The futility of the language in the courtroom, as well as, finally, the ineffectuality of his own literary efforts to secure justice for the two anarchists, proved to be a turning point for Dos Passos. The anarchists were executed on August 23, 1927, and by September Dos Passos had begun work on the first volume of the *U.S.A.* trilogy. In *U.S.A.,* which ends with the execution of Sacco and Vanzetti, he would not only, like Asch, express frustration at the poverty of American language to express political truth; he would go further by proposing, and providing the model for, an entirely new kind of fiction, one which would offer a discourse about America that would be both truthful and rhetorically effective.

Although Dos Passos's earlier novels, most successfully *Manhattan Transfer* (1925), had been highly experimental, and though Dos Passos became increasingly radical throughout the twenties, a fact reflected in his coverage for *New Masses* of such events as the 1925–26 Passaic textile workers' strike, it would not be until he wrote *U.S.A.* that he would address the questions posed by Asch's fictional subway rider. As Landsberg writes, "The [Sacco and Vanzetti] affair supplied a new impetus for his studying American society—its leaders, its myths, its ideologies, its sources of information."[8]

Fueled by outrage, in *U.S.A.* Dos Passos fused his journalistic experience and his knowledge of modernist technique to document American life in the first three decades of this century. Perhaps even more significantly, he posed the aesthetic and political questions about the very process of creating this new vision of America that would be hotly debated by radical writers throughout the thirties.

Who would be allowed to write the story of their time was perhaps the focal question for writers and artists of the thirties, and Dos Passos may have best framed the issues of representation with which those writers were struggling. At a time when writers argued, in and out of print, about how most effectively to offer a vision of American history and of the current crisis, and how to impress most strongly upon readers the necessity of political activism, it was in

Dos Passos's trilogy that representatives of these various forms of discourse—newspapermen, public relations men, muckrakers, and artists—battled it out to see who would get to tell the truth (or their truth) so effectively as to change the course of history.

Did the Depression Really Exist?

It is easy for us to forget that, initially, the question of whether the Depression actually existed was central to public discourse. As Gilbert Seldes wrote in his 1932 "Short History of a Depression,"

OCTOBER 1, 1929: It could not occur.

OCTOBER 23, 1929: It wasn't occurring.

NOVEMBER 1, 1929: It hadn't happened.

NOVEMBER 15, 1929: It was purely a technical operation in the market.

NOVEMBER 20, 1929: It had restored brains to thinking and money to productive enterprise. . . .

MARCH 20, 1930: Good news of Good Times. Also Buy Now. Workingmen, unable to understand plain English, riot for jobs. . . .

APRIL 20, 1930: Purely psychological. . . .

MAY 17, 1930: Prosperity fails to keep date with President Hoover. Reported eaten by bears.

MAY 25, 1930: Motor car manufacturers decide to restore prosperity by selling motor cars to each other.

JUNE 3, 1930: Inasmuch as nothing was lost (except paper profits) the condition of America is sound. The sound is hollow. . . .

DECEMBER 31, 1931: In accordance with orders issued at various points, the depression ends.[9]

Dos Passos and other writers of the thirties were writing against a background of government and business denials of the fact that there was a Depression at all. As one of the final newspaper headlines in *The Big Money* reads, "MARKET SURE TO RECOVER FROM SLUMP."[10] "U.S. CHAMBER OF COMMERCE URGES CONFIDENCE" (521), reads another. Still a third trumpets: "PRESIDENT SEES PROSPERITY NEAR" (521).[11]

To be sure, the onslaught of the Depression posed a public relations challenge to both government and business. Both responded with creative solutions: President Hoover himself was responsible for naming the crisis, on the theory that "Depression" sounded, in 1929, less alarming than "panic" or "crisis," the traditional terms for economic collapse. To a generation of writers trained in the language of public relations, official expertise in naming the crisis away and other government attempts to massage public opinion could only seem ominous. In the terrible economic crisis facing the country, the government seemed to operate on the theory that what people didn't see they wouldn't have to know about (and as many observers have pointed out, it was easy to miss the families living in cardboard shacks or picking through garbage heaps—you had to know where to look for them). It was not long before the ironies of the distance between government discourse and economic truths gave rise to a new language, used not only by radical writers but by the population at large: As Gilbert Seldes notes about Hoover, "He became a sad joke for second-rate entertainers: the Hoover Flag was pockets turned inside out, and a comedian, hearing that business was going up would ask 'Is Hoover dead?' "[12] Hoover's assurances that American hoboes were better nourished than ever before, his talk of the confidence and courage of the American people and of the bracing effect of adversity, could finally only further embitter the country and widen the gulf between lived experience and official rhetoric.[13] It was not only Hoover who was to blame: Business, government, and academics all worked to present a rosy, if misleading, picture, for the ostensible good of the country. "The American Economic Association, meeting in Washington in December 1929, deliberately announced outdated forecasts indicating recovery by June 1930, because its members felt that to give out their current estimates would be against the public interest."[14] The boosterism of the twenties could only be seen as a public insult, however, in the thirties.

As Robert McElvaine notes, "Hoover was the first important figure in American politics to use the techniques of modern public relations on a massive scale. Hoover was generally seen in the twenties as a 'human symbol of efficiency,' a super businessman who could solve any problems that might arise."[15] Though the gap between official rhetoric and lived reality may have been increasingly apparent to writers before the thirties (after all, who would be more conscious of the manipulation of language?), the Depression experience finally laid bare the artifice and failure of advertising and of massaging the facts. Not only were facts massaged but the subject, one might say, was changed. As Asch's subway rider complained, newspapers were likely to devote more space to sensational tidbits than to hard, and hard to digest, news.

Indeed, in the same Newsreel from which the headlines on economic conditions cited above were taken, other headlines declare: "MAKER OF LOVE DISBARRED AS LAWYER," "PLAY AGENCIES IN RING OF SLAVE GIRL MARTS," and "POLICE KILLER FLICKS CIGARETTE AS HE GOES TREMBLING TO DOOM" (520).[16] The difference between the "news" the public read and the important facts the public lacked access to (or worse, ignored) was to infuriate socially conscious writers of the thirties. James T. Farrell's oafish working-class protagonist, Studs Lonigan, would briefly skim a headline on Mussolini's rise to power before his attention was diverted by an article on the gang rape of a teenager; the journalists Josephine Herbst depicts in her trilogy of novels are cowards, opportunists, or worse.[17]

The Newsreels: Repackaging the Truth

It is telling that Dos Passos presented his headlines in sections labeled "Newsreels," for if writers were infuriated by the contents of newspapers, it was the actual newsreels shown in the movie theaters that provided the American public with the most insidiously packaged distractions and disinformation. Throughout the thirties, articles appeared in radical publications attacking the newsreels and analyzing their packaging of the news. The *New Masses,* for instance, devoted a series of articles to pointing up the shortcomings of the "March of Time."[18] Another Communist Party–backed magazine, *New Theatre,* called that newsreel "a first class example of biased opinion substituted for factual reporting."[19] Even the decidedly nonradical monthly *Scribner's,* in an irony-tinged article on the newsreels, noted that during the 1934 governor's race in California, when Upton Sinclair ran and nearly won on his End Poverty in California (EPIC) program, "Certain newsreels showed tramps and bums pouring into the state on freight trains, expressing their determination to go to California and live off the government if Sinclair won. The scenes were staged, if not actually faked." However, the article's author, Thomas Sugrue, asserted that "Nothing like it has happened since." In general, he preferred to lay the shortcomings of the newsreels at the feet of their audience, for "The American is apathetic; it is for him that the newsreels have injected comedy, novelties, features, and the expert filming of sports events. History either bores or frightens him."[20] Radical writers, by contrast, laid the blame for the newsreels' impoverishment at the doorstep of their producers. For them, the newsreels were a cause—and the public's willingness to uncritically attend to them, a symptom—of the rhetorical crisis they, as American writers, faced.

Yet it would be Dos Passos who would most effectively limn the crisis in narrative and who would issue a call, in *U.S.A.,* to "rebuild the ruined words."[21] Dos Passos offers us the problem and the solution neatly wrapped in a single package: He not only tells us how words came to be ruined but proposes a model for redemption in the form of his own creation.

In effect, Dos Passos is giving us in his trilogy an overview of how easily digestible lies about America came to be produced, and of the deleterious effects of letting lies become accepted truths. By showing us how public relations men managed to bust unions, manipulate public opinion on the war, and pump money into the coffers of corporations at the expense of poor people, he sets the stage for the debacles of the thirties. Throughout the trilogy we trace a group of characters who use different strategies to try to tell their versions of events in America. There are journalists who attempt to tell the truth but cannot, due to their failure to control the means of production. They usually end up as cynical drunks or are absorbed into the public relations machinery. There are artists—the category into which Dos Passos himself would most naturally fall—who don't last too long as artists, never seem to get their message heard, and are inevitably transmogrified into the most effective, least honest category of historians, the public relations men. Their message may be a lie, but it is inevitably accepted as the truth. That process is graphically illustrated: More than once, a narrative section devoted to the manufacture of some particularly noxious form of propaganda is followed by a Newsreel section in which that propaganda is presented as a newspaper headline, as fact.

These Newsreels are at the heart of the book: montages of high and low sources, newspaper headlines concerning important political events and sensational tidbits, songs both sentimental and overtly political in which important historical events are narrated, the letters of condemned men and the declarations of presidents. By putting them side by side, Dos Passos gives each declaration equal weight. And within the Newsreels we see the obsessions that are to dominate the trilogy—both the technology that makes the newsreels possible and the way that, just as different versions of the truth can be given equal weight, conversely, the same message can be used in many different ways.

Dos Passos's question—Who gets to tell the story?—is, of course, linked to the question of who gains the means of production necessary to tell the truth. Thus newspapers and newspaper technology play a major role in the trilogy. For example, Fenian (Mac) gets his start as a sometime radical working for his uncle's linotype business. "The first print Uncle Tim set up on the new machine was the phrase: Workers of the world unite; you have nothing to lose but your chains."[22] However, even owning the means of production is not enough to disseminate a radical message. The legal apparatus of the state still has the power to shut down Uncle Tim's shop. And so Fenian, out of a job, goes to work for a distributor of erotic literature, who seems to have few problems getting his message across and who, moreover, is able to use "high" literature to sell "low" literature.

The relationship between "high" and "low" forms of literature is a theme that runs throughout the novel. In the first "Camera Eye" section of the trilogy we are treated to Dos Passos's memory of his father "riding backwards through the rain in the rumbly cab . . . reciting *Othello* in his lawyer's voice" (*FP,* 52), an upper-class paterfamilias declaiming great verse for the edification of his son; it is a "noble" scene. And yet, pages later, Dos Passos undercuts this effect by having Doc Bingham, the peddler of racy literature, recite different lines from the same scene of *Othello* to his companions on a train for, having thus gotten attention, he can be sure of an audience for his wares. (Later, when Fenian tries to ask him for his salary, Doc Bingham will again use Shakespeare as a distraction, a change of subject.)

This scene functions in a number of ways. The repeated use of *Othello* in related but widely disparate contexts serves to blur the boundaries between high and low culture and to desanctify treasured items in our canon. The scene echoes the scenes of the Duke and the Dauphin, those great lowbrow Shakespeareans, in *Huckleberry Finn.* And, perhaps most importantly, it illustrates the use of art not to democratize but to drown out democratic debate, not to bring political issues to light but to block their examination. Not only does Doc Bingham quote Shakespeare as a way to entice customers to buy his wares, but he also accomplishes the goal of silencing a political discussion.

"Well, at last Teddy has a chance to carry out his word about fighting the trusts." "I'm telling you the insurgent farmer vote of the great Northwest . . ." "Terrible thing the wreck of those inauguration specials."

But Doc Bingham was off:

> Most potent grave and reverend signiors,
> My very noble and approved good masters,
> That I have ta'en away this old man's daughter
> It is most true; true, I have married her.

"They won't get away with those antitrust laws, believe me they won't. You can't curtail the liberty of the individual in that way." "It's the liberty of the individual business man that the progressive wing of the Republican party is trying to protect." (*FP,* 61)

But Doc Bingham continues his recitation of Shakespeare and silences the debate: " 'The farmer vote,' the other man began shrilly, but nobody was listening. Doc Bingham had the floor" (62).

Even as the Newsreels, the Camera Eye sections, and the biographies are doing important work within the text, it is the most conventional, least experimental portions of the novel that contain the strongest parts of Dos Passos's argument. There's a paradox here: While Dos Passos is working hard to persuade us of the viability of his new form, and while he populates his novel with ineffectual, morally weak artist characters, he uses, in the narrative sections, the structure of a fairly conventional novel, centering around characters with representative aspirations. These characters exist as types rather than individuals. For instance, Mac, the character who starts off working for a pornographer, is soon put on a train by Dos Passos and made to appear at every site in America and Mexico where there is a possibility for radical action. In this he is no more fortunate than the protagonist of Sinclair's *The Jungle*, who seems to exist only so that he can be dragged around to every shockingly bad working environment in the country. However, even as Dos Passos draws his readers into considering his theories of representation through these characters, he distances the reader from them both by insisting on staying at an ironic remove from them and by making them so flat, so typical, that it is nearly impossible for a reader to empathize with any one of them. His distancing humor is often quite effective, as when discussing the childhood of the successful public relations executive, Richard Ellsworth Savage. He notes that, after setting up a fudge-selling business with a friend of his, "Skinny bought the boxes and did most of the work, but Dick convinced him that it wouldn't be fair for him to take more than ten percent of the profits because he and his mother put up the original capital."[23] This parody of capitalist rhetoric may be funny, but it does nothing to draw the reader closer to the character, or indeed to individuate Dick Savage from any other capitalistic paragon. Indeed, if Dos Passos is interested in proving the inefficacy of conventional art as a vehicle for political protest, he cannot make his characters in the narrative sections so unique, so vital, that they overwhelm his rhetorical point about modes of expression.

Character as a Rhetorical Device

Each character, thus, carries a part of his argument. The character of J. W. Moorehouse offers Dos Passos an opportunity to air his view of the commercialization of political discourse in America, focusing specifically on the Creel Committee on Public Information, the World War I coalition of advertisers hired by the government for the purposes of marketing the war. Richard Ellsworth Savage offers an object lesson in the ways in which Dos Passos teaches us to distrust art and the motivations of the storyteller. And, finally, Mary French, the one woman in the entire trilogy who has any political consciousness, shows us the ineffectuality of radical discourse.

J. W. Moorehouse enters the world as an advertisement, an investment, literally incarnating his parents' devotion to his maternal grandfather: "they decided to call the kid John Ward after Mrs. Moorehouse's father who was a farmer in Iowa and pretty well off" (*FP,* 190). And, propitiously for his future in marketing history to the masses, Moorehouse gets his start in life working for a book-distributing firm: "he received a congratulatory note from them saying he was the first agent they had ever had who sold a hundred consecutive sets of Bryant's *History of the United States*" (192).

Moorehouse, in fact, tries out most of the available means of interpreting America. After he gives up his first efforts to be an artist, he becomes a journalist. But writing about "Mrs. Piretti whose husband had been killed in a rumpus in a saloon on Locust Street or Sam Burkovich who'd been elected president of the Ukrainian singing society, or some woman with sudsy hands whose child had been slashed by a degenerate" (*FP,* 260) depresses him. No wonder that Mr. McGill, the steel plant manager who gives him his first big public relations job, tells him, "Oh, drop [newspaper work]; there's no future in that" (263).

It doesn't take long for Moorehouse to do just that, and before long he is writing public relations material for the steel firm, scoring his first real success in the field because

> a strike came on at Homestead and there were strikers killed by the mine guards and certain writers from New York and Chicago who were sentimentalists began to take a good deal of space in the press with articles flaying the steel industry and the feudal conditions in Pittsburgh as they called them, and the Progressives in Congress were making a howl, and it was rumored that people wanting to make politics out of it were calling for a congressional investigation. (*FP,* 269)

Moorehouse is a representative of what the muckrakers, who formed the generation of political writers just before Dos Passos, were up against in exposing terrible conditions in the meat-packing plants, coal mines, and steel mills of America. Moreover, at least in Dos Passos's description, Moorehouse and those like him are testament to the failure of the muckraking novel: For Moorehouse, the efforts of the reformers provide an opportunity for a new profession. As he tells his boss, "It was the business of the industry to educate the public by carefully planned publicity extending over a term of years" (269). Indeed, the brand-new profession of public relations springs from what Moorehouse sees as "this new unexploited angle of the relations between capital and labor" (271).

Dos Passos demonstrates the success of Moorehouse's program against the reformers by highlighting selections from newspapers in the Newsreels: In Newsreel XXIV, for example, there is a chunk of text that sounds as though it could have been written by J. W. Moorehouse himself:

> suppose now that into this delicate medium of economic law there is thrust the controlling factor of an owner of a third of the world's tonnage, who regards with equanimity both profit and loss, who does not count as a factor in the cost of operation the interest on capital investment, who builds vessels whether they may be profitably operated or not and who charges rates commensurate in no certain measure with the laws of supply and demand; how long would it be before the ocean transport of the whole world had broken down completely? (*NN*, 157)

This fragment, which appears along with other news items culled from the *Chicago Tribune*, appears to be an attack on Soviet shipping practices; others refer to labor unrest or draft dodging. Another news fragment reads: "the winning of the war is just as much dependent upon the industrial workers as it is upon the soldiers. Our wonderful record of launching one hundred ships on Independence Day shows what can be done when we put our shoulders to the wheel under the spur of patriotism" (195). This bears a remarkable similarity to the rhetoric Moorehouse uses in his Rotary Club speeches and in his talks with Judge Planet, a lawyer on the side of the mine owners, and G. H. Barrow, a union leader who has sold out. "The great leaders of American capital, as you probably realize, Mr. Barrow," Moorehouse tells them, "are firm believers in fair play and democracy and are only too anxious to give the worker his share of the proceeds of industry if they can only see their way to do so in fairness to the public and the investor" (*FP*, 284). This approach to what the judge euphemistically calls "a new field in the shape of an agency to peaceably and in a friendly fashion settle labor disputes" (284) will result in the many bashed heads and ruined strikes that occur in the course of the trilogy. It will also result in positive newspaper coverage of events that we know, through the narrative sections of the work, to be painful blows to the workers of the country. Nowhere in the Newsreels does Dos Passos represent the muckrakers' version of events: Clearly, the reformers are not proving effective in getting their message distributed, since the rhetoric of Moorehouse and those like him is powerful enough to shape political discourse in America.

We do see the effects of the reform movement represented in various ways, both artistically, through the "little theater" movement in which Eleanor Stoddard and Eveline Hutchins are involved, and more significantly, through the character of Mary French, who is inflamed by reading works like *The Jungle*, Ernest Poole's *The Harbor*, and Veblen's *The Theory of the Leisure Class*. However, by the end of *The Big Money* we will have seen just how futile are Mary's efforts at reform.

Yet, while the reformers are faltering, Moorehouse and his ilk are getting stronger, and nowhere is this more apparent than in the section on the Creel Committee, the propaganda effort of the U.S. government to sell the war, in which Moorehouse makes his reputation. The work of the Creel Committee was a watershed event in the history of American public relations. Advertising leaders formed the National War Advisory Board and offered their services to the government for fund-raising and recruiting purposes.

> As the J. Walter Thompson agency observed, the war gave advertising men "an opportunity not only to render valuable patriotic service . . . but also to reveal to a wide circle of influential men . . . the real character of advertising and the important function which it performs." *Printers' Ink* [the professional journal for advertisers] later concluded that advertising had fully capitalized on its opportunity. Wartime advertising had shown that "it is possible to sway the minds of whole populations, change their habits of life, create belief, practically universal, in any policy or idea."[24]

The slogans of the Creel Committee show up in the Newsreels, only to be exposed as hollow: A headline reading "HELP THE FOOD ADMINISTRATION BY REPORTING WAR PROFITEERS" (*NN,* 189) is preceded by a scene in which Joe, the merchant seaman, runs into an old acquaintance who has become a stool pigeon for the government: "the minute he touched him Joe knew he'd never liked the guy, eyes too close together." In classic informer fashion, Tex explains that he has been hired by a secret service agent to look for "reds, slackers, German spies, guys that can't keep their traps shut . . . an' he turns around and hands me a job if little Willie makes good. . . . Twenty-five a week and servin' my country besides" (186). Naturally, while civil liberties are being destroyed in response to the government propaganda campaign, the true war profiteers not only are not being informed upon and punished but are being rewarded for their service. The system is corrupt. As Rasmussen, the Standard Oil engineer who is benefiting from the war, says, "there isn't any public since the war. The public'll damn well do what it's told . . . what we've got to do is make a few key men understand the situation. Moorehouse is the key to the key men" (307). Indeed, Moorehouse slides easily from writing public relations material for the war to doing the same thing on behalf of Standard Oil. There is little hint in *U.S.A.* that this is a situation that will change—if anything, Moorehouse becomes more successful as the volumes progress—but there are many signs that this is a deplorable state of affairs.

While public relations is flourishing, what of art? Art and those with pretensions to being artists generally get short shrift in the trilogy. Some of the most despicable characters, such as J. W. Moorehouse and Dick Ellsworth Savage, begin with creative aspirations. And Eleanor Stoddard, who starts off with artistic ambitions herself, soon learns that the important thing is not to make art but to look like an artist and thus sell oneself. It's all of one piece: the transformation of artists into advertisers and the discovery that an honest or artistic appearance matters much more than what is actually produced. Thus Moorehouse's secretary, Janey Williams, has as her first bosses the "brains of the firm" and the "firm's bay window" (*FP,* 170), as Jerry Burnham, the first of many cynical journalists, analyzes the situation.

J. W. Moorehouse is a character who is allowed little humanity. From his introduction, when we see him as a struggling songwriter exploiting and then forgetting his "spinster" piano teacher, there seems to be little hope for him, and it is clear, even when he is an adolescent reading *Success* magazine, that not only will he not be a character with whom the reader will want to sympathize but, more importantly, he will not be a character with much dimension. A more interesting character, and the most notable of all the failed artists in the trilogy, is Richard Ellsworth Savage whose life—absent father, Harvard degree, and work as an ambulance driver in the war—most clearly parallels that of Dos Passos.[25] With his carefully crafted verses and his pretensions ("The night he told Ned he was going to France they got very drunk on orvieto wine in their room and talked a great deal about how it was the fate of Youth and Beauty and Love and Friendship to be mashed out by an early death, while the old fat pompous fools would make merry over their carcasses" [*NN,* 112]), Dick Ellsworth Savage seems most emblematic of those characters who use art principally as a means of social ascension and whose art has very little to do with his, or anyone else's, American experience.[26]

Loving Art, Evading Truth

Most of the artists and art lovers in this most American book will have nothing to do with any authentically American art. Love of art is often tied to anglophilia and to snobbery, as witness Eleanor Stoddard's English teacher: "she'd occasionally have her more promising pupils, those who seemed the children of nicer parents, to tea in her flat . . . and talk to them about Goldsmith and Doctor Johnson's pithy sayings and *cor cordium* and how terrible it was he died so young" (*FP,* 227). Not only is art English, it is entirely divorced from the messy business of living: The English teacher "made [Eleanor] feel that Art was something ivory white and pure and noble and sad" (228).

Dos Passos brings up and derides an attachment to things European in other ways. For instance, Eleanor, who is thought by her employer to have "an indefinable air of chic" (*FP,* 228) and is assumed to be French by many of her customers at the lace shop where she works, is transformed by her boss into a Frenchwoman: "Eleanor would have to be French from now on; so she bought her twenty tickets to the Berlitz school and said she could have the hour off in the morning between nine and ten if she would go and take French lessons there. . . . [Eleanor] began to slip a phrase in now and then as unconcernedly as she could when she was talking to the customers, and when there was anybody in the shop Mrs. Lang called her 'Mademoiselle' " (235). This scene is significant in two ways, both for what it says about an attraction for the Continental, about "culture" as a sign of upward mobility, and also, as we have seen with Janey's employer, for what it says about the importance of appearances, no matter what the reality behind them might be. And it is fitting, after all, that Eleanor becomes an interior decorator. Through her apprenticeship with her English teacher and in the lace shop she has received a thorough education in the language of appearances and is thus able to enhance the images of her clients by surrounding them with symbolically loaded items of furniture and bric-a-brac.

Dick Ellsworth Savage, even when he isn't looking over first editions of Beardsley and Huysmans and Austin Dobson, is reading upper-class periodicals such as *Smart Set* and *The Black Cat.* His art is always either completely irrelevant to the experiences of himself and those around him or made for the purpose of social advancement, as when he "delighted [his patron] so by dedicating to him a verse translation of Horace's poem about Maecenas that he worked up with the help of the trot, that Mr. Cooper made him a present of a thousand dollars to take him through college" (*NN,* 104). Even his sexual activities have a literary cast: As "they were sitting side by side on the sand talking about India's Love Lyrics that Hilda had been reading aloud that afternoon, she suddenly jumped on him and mussed up his hair and stuck her knees into his stomach" (101). And when Hilda, his clergyman's wife, spurns him, "he wrote a very obscure poem full of classical references that he labeled,

'To a Common Prostitute,' and sent to Hilda, adding a postscript that he was dedicating his life to Beauty and Sin" (105).

Not only is this silly and pretentious, it reveals a talent, which we shall see further developed in Dick's dealings with Daughter, the Texan he impregnates, for using art as a way of distancing himself from experience and of putting women in their places. In this, too, Savage seems a more extreme version of Dos Passos, who in all of *U.S.A.* can scarcely bring himself to describe a woman in human terms. With the exception of Mary French, the reformer, every woman in the trilogy, from Mac the Wobbly's wife to Janey Williams, Moorehouse's secretary, to Annabelle Strang, his first wife, to Margo Dowling, the movie actress, is an apolitical whiner. Female characters tend to see their husbands' interest in social issues as a threat to their earning power and for this reason make no bones about discouraging their political activity. The wife of Mac's radical uncle, the printer, cries out that she hopes the strike he supports will be broken: "Didn't I tell you, Tim O'Hara, no good'll ever come with your fiddling around with these godless labor unions and social-democrats and knights of labor" (*FP,* 46). And the woman Mac later marries will echo these words as she urges him to work harder and harder in order to buy her more and more things. "Maisie read a lot of magazines and always wanted new things for the house, a pianola, or a new icebox, or a fireless cooker. . . . Whenever she found *The Appeal to Reason* or any other radical paper round the house she'd burn it up" (133). Even in the cultural arena, women lose out: When Moorehouse and his first wife, Annabelle, travel to Paris, she "said that museums gave her a headache, spent her days shopping and having fittings with dressmakers" (214). Interestingly, one of the few female storytellers in the novel seems to be Jeanne, Dos Passos's nurse whom he discusses in a Camera Eye section:

> when everybody had gone to bed she would take you into her bed
> and it was a long scary story and the worst of the wolves howled through the streets gloaming to freeze little children's blood was the Loup Garou howling in the Jura and we were scared and she had breasts under her nightgown and the Loup Garou was terribly scary and black hair and rub against her and outside the wolves howled in the streets and it was wet there and she said it was nothing she had just washed herself. (147)

With none of Savage's highbrow pretensions, the nursemaid tells a story simply for the purpose of getting sexual gratification from her charges. Unfortunately, most of the women in the text are not even granted this degree of resourcefulness. Any stories they tell will be crude, superstitious tales, such as those told by "longfaced Red Cross women workers giving each other goose-flesh with stories of spitted Belgian babies and Canadian officers crucified and elderly nuns raped" (*NN*, 112). Cut off from the high culture of Savage and his ilk, the women of *U.S.A.* seem to dwell in a realm of consumer greed and bloody superstition. If the male characters in the novel demonstrate the poverty of American discourse, the female characters, for the most part, emblematize the culture's resistance to any discourse outside the commercial. Maisie will go so far as to burn her husband's radical papers, and the only magazines she reads tell her what to buy; the only art that interests Annabelle is the art of packaging herself in more attractive dresses. The female focus on things, to the exclusion of ideas, is one more obstacle to creating an informed citizenry, a populace that will be awakened by language rather than lulled into a stupor by words that have lost their original meaning. And thus Savage's treatment of the women in his life seems like a crueler, cruder, more aestheticized version of Dos Passos's treatment of the women in his text.

Yet Savage's cultural contempt for women, and his use of art to dismiss them, is also part and parcel of the way that he uses his aesthetic awareness to distance himself from entire classes of people. For Savage, artistic development is linked not with a movement toward democratization but with a move away from it, into a more rarefied, homogeneous atmosphere. "Perhaps it was the result of living in the Yard that he got to know all the wrong people, a couple of Socialist Jews in firstyear law, a graduate student from the Middle West who was taking his Ph.D. in Gothic, a Y.M.C.A. addict out from Dorchester who went to chapel every morning. . . . He went to all the football rallies and smokers and beernights, but he could never get there without one of his Jewish friends or a graduate student, so he never met anybody there who was anybody" (*NN*, 105). It is only when he is accepted by the WASPy Wigglesworths that Dick starts to grow as an artist: "a scrubbylooking little man was reading aloud a story that turned out to be Kipling's 'The Man Who Would Be King.' Everybody sat on the floor and was very intent. Dick decided he was going to be a writer" (107). He does flirt with some progressive ideas; "Dick found himself getting all worked up about the New Freedom, Too Proud to Fight, Neutrality in Mind and Deed, Industrial Harmony between Capital and Labor" (108). (The latter idea, of course, is one that we have already seen J. W. Moorehouse massage into the public consciousness.) Yet, despite this, Dick's ideological commitment can perhaps be seen most clearly in a scene that takes place on his last night in Cambridge before leaving for France and the ambulance corps. After he and the younger Wigglesworth have the above-mentioned discussion of Beauty and Truth, "They sat on the cold tombstone a long time without saying anything, only drinking, and after each drink threw their heads back and softly bleated in unison Blahblahblahblah" (112).

Savage's aestheticization of his wartime experience begins the instant he steps on board ship: "Sailing for France in early June was like suddenly having to give up a book he'd been reading and hadn't finished" (*NN*, 112). It continues as he journeys on: "All the way to Paris the faintly bluegreen fields were spattered scarlet with poppies like the first lines of a poem; the little train jogged along in dactyls; everything seemed to fall into rhyme" (113). Because he experiences his life as a graceful or graceless work of literature, he is able to remove himself from the horror of war, and to escape the consequences of his own experience. Surrounded by maimed and dying men, Savage can't seem to do much more than get drunk and have long discussions about literature and architecture. Although, after a long night working as an orderly in a military hospital, he will walk home "thinking of the faces and the eyes and the sweatdrenched hair and the clenched fingers clotted with blood and dirt and the fellows kidding and pleading for cigarettes and the bubbling groans of the lung cases" (218), such moments are rare. More typically, he thinks of Swinburne and vows that, "By gum, he must write some verse: what people needed was stirring poems to nerve them for revolt against their cannibal governments." One might see this as engagement with a political and social problem, with a more democratic, less aesthetic response than Savage has thus far exhibited. And yet, even in these revolutionary moments, he sees himself as far removed from the conflict that he hopes to incite: "he was so busy building a daydream of himself living in a sunscorched Spanish town, sending out flaming poems and manifestoes, calling young men to revolt against their butchers, poems that would be published by secret presses all over the world" (219). There never seems to be any question that he himself will be manning the barricades, and indeed, he has soon forgotten his revolutionary impulses in favor of the next meal, the next drink, and the next woman whose suffering he can aestheticize.

This one is a suicidal prostitute called Dirty Gertie who is being abused by her madam. Witnessing this scene, Dick "felt terrible. When he got home he felt like writing some verse. He tried to recapture the sweet and heavy pulsing of feelings he used to have when he sat down to write a poem. But all he could do was just feel miserable so he went to bed" (*NN*, 354). However, his poetic nastiness peaks when he impregnates the Texan Anne Elizabeth, then refuses to marry her. After sending her out into the rain, and ultimately to her suicide, "He thought of Anne Elizabeth going home alone in a taxicab through the wet streets. He wished he had a great many lives so that he might have spent one of them with Anne Elizabeth. Might write a poem about that and send it to her. And the smell of the little cyclamens" (392). His response—to write a poem—is so inadequate to the situation, has so little to do with his responsibility to Anne Elizabeth, that his callousness comes across as shocking. For Savage, the little cyclamens are no more or less important than the ruin of Anne Elizabeth's life: His art enables him to distance himself not only from the experience of the populace as a whole but from the individual pain he has caused. His divorce of language from moral responsibility makes him perfectly suited for a role in shaping the burgeoning consumer culture of postwar America. And indeed, as he tells her, "I've just been offered a very fine position when I get out of the service, but I can't take a wife and child at this stage of the game, you must understand that" (391). The fine position, writing public relations material for Standard Oil, has been offered by none other than J. W. Moorehouse.

There is, in fact, an almost touching scene that occurs between the two men as they are dining at Moorehouse's Long Island mansion. Moorehouse, concerned about his possibly too liberal forays into the stock market and about his wife's confinement to a sanitarium, tells Savage that " 'I've managed to do pretty well in everything except that . . . I'm a lonely man. . . . And to think once upon a time I was planning to be a songwriter.' He smiled. Dick smiled too and held out his hand. 'Shake hands, J.W.,' he said, 'with the ruins of a minor poet' " (*BM,* 493). This scene is telling, not least in the way it permits Dos Passos and his readers to have a little laugh at the expense of Moorehouse. Although, in this scene, the public relations mogul is still powerful, Dos Passos makes clear to the reader that this situation will not be long-lasting. With his money tied up in the stocks, and with the market starting to tremble, it is likely that Moorehouse faces ruin. Even he may not be able to dictate the public vision of America forever. A new spokesman will be more necessary than ever before.

As for Savage, he clearly has no moral authority to bolster his poetic talent. Lacking an ability to empathize with another, even to see, let alone represent, the struggles of another constituency, he is unfit for the task of rewriting America. It makes perfect sense that he joins Moorehouse's public relations empire, and even more sense that the account on which he makes his reputation as an ad man is none other than that of Doc Bingham, the peddler of erotic literature whom we first encountered in the early pages of the trilogy as he was using Shakespeare to cheat his employees and to sell risqué books. Bingham's fortunes have risen—he has now become a patent medicine king. Savage's campaign for the worthless medicine gains Moorehouse's approbation: "Of course," Moorehouse tells him, "selfservice, independence, individualism is the word I gave the boys in the beginning. This is going to be more than a publicity campaign, it's going to be a campaign for Americanism" (*BM*, 494–95).

Advertising America

Indeed, Bingham's rhetoric, which was alternately Shakespearean and progressive during the early years of the century, has taken on a patriotic tone: "in my day the path was harder for a young man entering life with nothing but the excellent tradition of moral fervor and natural religion I absorbed if I may say so with my mother's milk. We had to put our shoulders to the wheel in those days and it was the wheel of an old muddy wagon drawn by mules, not the wheel of a luxurious motorcar" (*BM*, 498). Bingham has skillfully managed to cram an astonishing number of clichés into this short speech, invoking not only the pioneer virtues of self-sufficiency and toughness but also his mother and religion.

In so doing, Bingham firmly positions himself as a man of the 1920s, the first decade in which language was systematically debased for commerce. The Metropolitan Casualty Insurance Company issued a pamphlet called *Moses, Persuader of Men,* which described the prophet as a "Dominant, Fearless and Successful Personality in one of the most magnificent selling campaigns that history ever placed upon its pages."[27] Far from being perceived as sacrilegious, the use of religion for public relations purposes was embraced by the public: Bruce Barton's *The Man Nobody Knows,* which posited Jesus as a great executive, his parables as effective advertisements, and suggested that, were he alive today, he would be a successful public relations man, topped the best-seller lists for all of 1925 and 1926.

Bingham's reappearance at this late date in the trilogy is significant. He shows up as Dos Passos is using his strongest ammunition to blast away at ineffectual or morally corrupt forms of discourse. Doc Bingham is both one of the most amusingly sleazy characters in the trilogy and, perhaps, the character with the greatest rhetorical skill. For example, when he first meets Mac, his young employee in *The 42nd Parallel,* Doc Bingham eschews log-cabin imagery and instead uses Progressive Era slogans of modernity and liberation: "Oh, religion, what crimes are committed in your name. I'm an agnostic myself. . . . No sir, my God is the truth, that rising ever higher in the hands of honest men will dispel the mists of ignorance and greed, and bring freedom and knowledge to mankind" (*FP*, 55). Bingham's ability to use effectively such a wide range of rhetorical styles has the result of somehow cheapening all the styles. If the progressive talk of the importance of education and freedom from prejudice is a coded sales pitch, if Shakespeare (whom he quotes incessantly) can so easily be used to advertise the self and to drown out debate, and if Jacksonian rhetoric is a cover for Barnum-style hucksterism, then it is clear that none of this speech is inherently strong enough to withstand abuse by its speakers. Bingham is one of Dos Passos's most effective characters in that he is granted such a great facility for slippage. The comic effect of his appearance lightly makes the serious point that no speech is sacred and, more importantly, that "virtuous"—that is, culturally or politically sound—rhetoric can easily be put to nefarious uses and thus should never be taken for granted. The fact that Bingham has, of course, no such virtuous past as he claims in his patent-medicine-king guise calls into question the soundness of this rhetoric to begin with: Was the image of America painted now by Bingham ever an accurate one, or has it always been as much of a lie as it is now in the mouth of this con artist? One thing is clear, however, and that is that the rhetoric of patriotism is now particularly liable to exploitation.

We see this patriotic rhetoric being used to its fullest extent when Moore-house and Savage go to Washington to try to fight the progressive legislation that would put Bingham and others like him out of business. Disputing the value of the pure food legislation, J. W. says,

> Once government interference in business is established as a precedent, it means the end of liberty and private initiative in this country. . . . What this bill purports to do is to take the right of selfmedication from the American people. A set of lazy government employees and remittancemen will be able to tell you what laxatives you may take and what not. Like all such things, it'll be in the hands of cranks and busybodies. Surely the American people have the right to choose what products they want to buy. It's an insult to the intelligence of our citizens. (*BM*, 505)

Moorehouse's ease in turning the language of Jacksonian Democracy to commercial uses is disturbing. It's not necessarily that this linguistic corruption is anything new—as James Harvey Young points out in his essay "Patent Medicines and the Self-Help Syndrome," "Learned physicians also lost caste, along with members of other educated professions, during the cultural climate associated with Jacksonian democracy. As leaders of opinion lost this traditional role, each common man had to decide for himself."[28] It is this Jacksonian tradition that Moorehouse is exploiting in using terminology like "liberty," "private initiative," and "government interference," as well as in questioning the right of "experts" to make decisions for common people.

As one of his lobbyists says, "all these so-called pure food and drug bills are class legislation in favor of the medical profession. Naturally the doctors want us to consult them before we buy a toothbrush or a package of licorice powder" (*BM,* 506). Thus these reactionaries are managing to use the language of the class struggle to oppose legislation that will regulate quacks. Similarly, when Moorehouse resumes, it is to speak to the American mythology of individualism: "The tendency of the growth of scientifically prepared proprietary medicine has been to make the layman free and self-sufficient, able to treat many minor ills without consulting a physician" (506). Thus the reader is not surprised when his lobbyist tells the assembled company that "Mr. Moorehouse is about to launch one of the biggest educational drives the country has ever seen to let people know the truth about proprietary medicines. . . . He will roll up a great tidal wave of opinion that Congress will have to pay attention to. I've seen him do it before" (506).

A puzzling and important question here is why Dos Passos has situated this debate over pure food and drug legislation in the late twenties when in fact it took place much earlier, in the first decade of the century. Public outrage, sparked by the publication of *The Jungle,* fueled the furor, which culminated in the 1906 passage of the Pure Food and Drug Act. Indeed, the muckraking attacks on the patent medicine industry to which Moorehouse refers were undoubtedly those written by Samuel Hopkins Adams, which appeared in twelve articles published in *Collier's* in 1905 and 1906. Critics have certainly pointed to the compression of time that Dos Passos employs in order to most effectively intertwine certain events in the lives of his characters. Barbara Foley, for instance, while documenting the distortion of time that Dos Passos uses in describing events in his characters' lives, sees this as a device that does not intrude on the historicity of the trilogy. "Clearly," she writes, "Dos Passos prefers to distort the time it takes for a fictional character to marry, have children, and achieve or ruin a career than to tamper with the dates of strikes and executions."[29] Foley is surely right about the careful attention Dos Passos generally pays to the dates of historical events. And yet, in the patent medicine section of *The Big Money,* rearranging history is precisely what Dos Passos does.

Given the "historical" nature of the trilogy, and given the importance of historical events such as the Great War and the Sacco and Vanzetti case in the text, it is particularly striking that Dos Passos would have moved such an important event as the fight over reform legislation twenty years into the future in describing it. In doing so, however, he gains in rhetorical ammunition what he loses in historical accuracy. The great debate over patent medicines that took place in the early years of the century was won, at least in some sense, as the result of Upton Sinclair's publishing *The Jungle.* As James Harvey Young writes, antinostrum measures, prompted in large part by the publication of Samuel Hopkins Adams's series of articles in *Collier's*, had little chance of gaining passage into law. Although the 1906 Pure Food and Drug bill had passed the House, it was destined to die in the Senate: "Lobbyists for interests fighting restrictive legislation were checking out of their hotels and leaving town. A reporter learned from a leading House Republican the decision to keep the bill from coming to debate during that session." It was only after publication of *The Jungle* had roused the public that passage of the Pure Food and Drug Act was assured. Meat sales declined by 50 percent, and "When an investigation revealed that Sinclair had not overdrawn the case, the President insisted that Congress act to insure clean meat and pure food for the American people."[30] Thus Dos Passos has turned what was one of the great reform triumphs into a victory for the opposition. Incidentally, in so doing he manages to ignore the ability of the muckraking novel to effect social change. By pitting Moorehouse's advertising speech directly against that of the reformers, he can demonstrate the power of the public relations men to overcome even the most truthful and well-meant speech.

However, in his portrayal of Bingham, and in his manipulation of the historical events surrounding the passage of the Pure Food and Drug Act, Dos Passos raises some disturbing questions. He, after all, has the same facility with rhetorical styles as does Bingham, his fictional creation, and if Bingham, through his use of different forms of discourse (progressive, religious, Shakespearean, etc.) cheapens all forms of discourse by turning such speech into advertisements for himself and his products, is Dos Passos so different? Is he, perhaps, simply a savvier, more ironic Moorehouse or Savage, manipulating history to further his own cause?

What he offers his readers in Bingham and Moorehouse is a portrayal of the triumph of style over substance, of cynicism over deeply held moral beliefs. And in his depiction of Mary French he shows his readers how even the most fervent reformer will ultimately be rendered powerless.

The Failure of Reform

Mary French is a character with an honorable reform lineage: She comes from the small mining town, Trinidad, where Agnes Smedley's heroine, Marie Rogers, grows up in her autobiographical novel *Daughter of Earth*. However, Mary French, a doctor's daughter, is born into a very different class from Marie Rogers, the daughter of a miner. Although Mary is influenced by seeing the work her radical father does among the miners, her own radicalism is partially literary in its origins. It may not be stretching matters too much to suggest that Dos Passos implies that her interest in radicalism is an outgrowth of her childhood literary interests. Her favorite occupation as a child is to listen to her father tell her stories "about the old days and miners and prospectors and the war between the sheepherders and the ranchers" (*BM*, 128). Literature is initially a way for her to escape an unhappy childhood: "Mary would run away from the table in tears and throw herself on the bed with a book . . . she'd start reading, hardly able to see the printed page through her tears at first, but gradually forgetting herself in the story in the book" (128). From "The Hound of Heaven" she graduates to *The Theory of the Leisure Class*. From "The City of Dreadful Night" she moves on to *The Promise of American Life*.

> On the train she read Ernest Poole's *The Harbor* and reread *The Jungle* and lay in the Pullman berth that night too excited to sleep . . . thinking of the work there was to be done to make the country what it ought to be, the social conditions, the slums, the shanties with filthy tottering backhouses, the miners' children with grimy coats too big for them, the overworked women stooping over stoves, the youngsters struggling for an education in nightschools, hunger and unemployment and drink, and the police and the lawyers and the judges always ready to take it out on the weak. (133)

Initially, at least, we see reform literature as having the power to change lives, to motivate its readers to take radical action. However, as Mary French's life progresses, we see this literature and, indeed, radical language in general losing its meaning and diminishing in effectiveness.

Like Marie Rogers, French becomes a reporter. Unlike Marie, however, Mary's career as a newspaperwoman is short-lived, as it quickly transpires that the paper she works for has no interest in printing the truth about labor conditions: "Well, young lady," her editor tells her as he fires her, "you've written a firstrate propaganda piece for the Nation or some other parlorpink sheet in New York, but what the devil can we do with it? This is Pittsburgh" (*BM*, 153). Thus commences her career as a publicist for various radical causes, a career in which we see her working only for broken strikes and lost causes. Moreover, and consistent with Dos Passos's portrayal of women throughout the novel, French's radical work defeminizes her; just as the "feminine" women in the novel cannot manage to be radical, so the sole radical woman in the trilogy cannot be successfully "feminine." From almost the moment she takes her first job as publicist for the Amalgamated in Pittsburgh, "her clothes were in awful shape, there was no curl in her hair" (154). Few of the men she falls for are interested in her, or manage to stay interested for long; the only man she has a long relationship with is George Barrow, the labor scab. It seems impossible for her to be both feminine and radical.

Because it is often illegal to produce, distribute, or even own radical texts, and because there are almost no forums in which radical language can be heard, the use of radical discourse is always dangerous and disempowering for the speaker. For example, in her early days as a publicist, Mary French "couldn't sleep for the memory of the things she'd seen, the jailings, the bloody heads, the wreck of some family's parlor, sofa cut open, chairs smashed, chinacloset hacked to pieces with an axe, after the troopers had been through looking for 'literature' " (*BM*, 155). And when Gus Moscowski, the first radical who spurns her, is arrested and sentenced to five years in prison, it is for the crime of distributing radical leaflets.

By the time she is working on the campaign to save Sacco and Vanzetti, language becomes a meaningless jumble of words to her rather than a means of communication:

> She came back one afternoon and found G. H. Barrow sitting at her desk. He had written a great pile of personal telegrams to senators, congressmen, ministers, laborleaders, demanding that they join in the protest in the name of justice and civilization and the workingclass, long telegrams and cables at top rates. She figured out the cost as she checked them off. She didn't know how the committee could pay for them, but she handed them to the messengerboy waiting outside. She could hardly believe that those words had made her veins tingle only a few weeks before. It shocked her to think how meaningless they seemed to her now like the little cards you get from a onecent fortunetelling machine. For six months now she'd been reading and writing the same words every day. (*BM*, 460)

Thus language itself becomes devalued. Its value, literally, is measured only by the amount of money it will cost to distribute, and not by its power. Terms like justice and civilization have been coopted by public relations men and thus rendered meaningless. If even French herself is not moved by the rhetoric of radical politics, how can anyone else be? How can this language move people to action? If the slogans of radical politics have become as interchangeable as the standardized fortunes from a penny machine, it is hard to imagine that they can be put together in new and fresh ways. The effect of this rhetoric is deadening rather than invigorating, its tingling effect wearing off in a matter of weeks. With this passage Dos Passos effectively writes Mary French off as a potentially powerful speaker. We have not seen her language achieve anything other than to get her fired from her newspaper job.

Of course, the pamphlet that Dos Passos himself wrote to save the two anarchists was finally as ineffectual as all the telegrams that Barrow sends out. But whereas Dos Passos went directly from working on the failed campaign to save Sacco and Vanzetti to beginning the *U.S.A.* trilogy, in which he would redefine radical discourse, Mary French cannot claim the same measure of success. The last project on which we see her working is a cataclysmic 1928 strike by western Pennsylvania miners, described by Communist leader William Z. Foster as one of the longest and most bitter in the history of American labor, which resulted in the shattering of the union for years to come.

Given the failure of every rhetorical form but the most despicable, the language of advertising, what is to be done to further a vision of America that is both just and stirring? If poets are involuted, reformers ineffectual, journalists silenced or cynical, radicals likely to obliterate language altogether through overuse of tired slogans, and if public relations men alone are endowed with the tongues of serpents, it is difficult to see where hope for change lies. Fortunately, Dos Passos provides us with a clue.

Many commentators, among them, especially in his later years, Dos Passos himself, have seen *U.S.A.* as an attempt to resuscitate the "old words" of American democracy and rescue them from the hands of such master manipulators as Moorehouse. As Camera Eye (50) asserts, "America our nation has been beaten by strangers who have turned our language inside out who have taken the clean words our fathers spoke and made them slimy and foul" (*BM,* 468). David Vanderwerken, most notably, claims that "the *U.S.A.* trilogy focuses unceasingly upon the theme of the misuse of the 'old words.'"[31] Though there are passages, such as the one quoted above, that do reveal a reverence for these "old words," it is also true that many of the pronouncements made by Dos Passos on this subject were made in the fifties and sixties, when he had altered his political views considerably. Above and beyond Dos Passos's aim to rescue American rhetoric from the wrong Americans, *U.S.A.* is one long attempt to fashion a new kind of American rhetoric.

Inventing the Novel for a Nation in Crisis

As Alfred Kazin points out in his introduction to the 1969 New American Library edition of *U.S.A.,* the biographical subjects whom Dos Passos treats with most respect and enthusiasm are inventors, either those, like Steinmetz, who invented things or those, like Veblen, who invented ideas. "What Dos

Passos created with *The 42nd Parallel,*" writes Kazin, "was in fact another American invention. . . . we soon recognize that Dos Passos' contraption, his new kind of novel, is in fact . . . the *greatest character in the book itself*" (*FP,* xi). Indeed, *U.S.A.* is, in large part, an advertisement for itself: Having exposed the poverty of conventional radical discourse, the futility of poetry, the ineffectuality of the muckraking novel, and the unbelievable strength of the most banal advertising slogans, Dos Passos leaves his readers with one possibility for hope. By portraying—through a collage of newspaper headlines, capsule biography, stream-of-consciousness memoir, and conventional narrative—the failure of all other forms of radical and artistic discourse to effect positive change in America, Dos Passos throws down the gauntlet to his contemporaries, setting his production and its new form of discourse as example and himself as exemplary author.

However, having spent hundreds of pages denigrating American advertising as such, Dos Passos is loath to resort to standard techniques in promoting his own work. Having shown his readers how to critique the successful slogans of a Moorehouse or, more amusingly, a Bingham, Dos Passos uses a sophisticated approach to trumpet the merits of his own trilogy. He does not, like the public relations men he condemns, debase great literature or national sentiment to sell his product (though he is occasionally willing to distort history to make his point). Dos Passos shows his readers how clichés are manipulated by advertising men, but he also celebrates those men who are willing to turn their backs on the comfort of received ideas in order to create something genuinely new, something that will change the course of history. And, in the course of the trilogy, Dos Passos never lets his readers forget how innovative his own form is: He leaves a place for himself beside that of the inventors he glorifies.

The capsule biographies in the trilogy include a few politicians such as Theodore Roosevelt and Bob La Follette, a couple of political writers and journalists like John Reed and Randolph Bourne, and a couple of performers, Isadora Duncan and Rudolph Valentino. However, the vast majority are inventors, including both those whom Dos Passos views favorably, like Luther Burbank and Charles Proteus Steinmetz, and those who are given less flattering portraits, like Thomas Edison and Frederick Winslow Taylor, creator of the Taylor System of Scientific Management. Whether or not he lionizes all of these inventors in every particular, the net effect of studding his narrative with biographies of persons (with the exception of Isadora Duncan, all men) whose works transformed some aspect of American society is to stress the transformative possibilities afforded by new ideas. Taylor's system doubles assembly-line productivity; "Steinmetz jotted a formula on his cuff and the next morning a thousand new powerplants had sprung up and the dynamos sang dollars and the silence of the transformers was all dollars" (*FP*, 334). The inventors are granted a complexity and depth that Dos Passos rarely allows the characters in his narrative. We learn about Taylor's insomnia, his impatience, his good tenor, his puzzled honesty in the face of the greed of the manufacturers who hired and fired him. We learn about his short temper and his breakdowns, his nightmares and his practical jokes. It is hard to pinpoint a single character in any of the narrative sections who is permitted these kinds of quirks or contradictions. Thus, while Dos Passos maintains a cool narrative distance from Dick Savage, J. W. Moorehouse, Eleanor French, and the other characters he profiles, the reader views the biographical subjects both more intimately and more reverentially.

Interestingly, the only other portions of the trilogy that come close to the capsule biographies in warmth of tone are the Camera Eye sections, which furnish an intimate portrait of a young boy's consciousness—a boy who shares many biographical particulars with Dos Passos himself. The Camera Eye sections are full of the emotions ("you were scared") and the textures of childhood ("the smell of melons filled the whole room" [*FP*, 50]). Similarly, the capsule biographies eschew the detachment of the ongoing narrative in favor of a kind of sympathetic lyricism: "Luther Burbank had never a thought of evil" (102), Dos Passos tells us, as he presents a picture of the innovator, "full of his dream of green grass in winter everblooming flowers everbearing berries"; it is hard not to be beguiled by the hopeful visions of the nurseryman. Similarly, Dos Passos writes of Eugene Debs that "under the smoke a fire burned him up, burned in gusty words that beat in pineboarded halls; he wanted his brothers to be free men" (51). This, like a Camera Eye section, is a portrait that places the reader in close proximity to its subject. The autobiography of the Camera Eye sections stands in close and in some ways equal relation to the capsule biographies. The net effect is that the life of the Camera Eye subject can be read in the same way as the life of one of the inventors; the stylistic similarities invite comparison between the two.

Having thrown the achievements of other inventors into relief, Dos Passos seems loath to hide the light of his own literary invention under a bushel. The table of contents for each volume calls attention to the unusual structure of his text: Each Newsreel section and each Camera Eye section is titled and numbered; biography subjects are announced in capital letters. Since these sections are often just a few pages long, and rarely longer than twenty pages, it is impossible for a reader to get absorbed by the plot, as one might while reading a realist novel, and forget that *U.S.A.* is, after all, a constructed narrative. And the section entitled "U.S.A.," which precedes each volume of the trilogy, in celebrating "the singsong fade of a story, the gruff fall of a sentence," reminds us that, although "U.S.A. is a group of holding companies . . . U.S.A. is a set of bigmouthed officials with too many bankaccounts," it is language, finally, that can define a nation: "But mostly U.S.A. is the speech of the people" (xx). The *U.S.A.* that Dos Passos offers us, however, is far from naturalistic American speech. He has taken our discourse apart, analyzed it, and rebuilt it. The resulting document, while incorporating many forms of American discourse from the popular song to the newspaper headline, from the advertising slogan to the protest telegram, has its own entirely new form.

Although the conspicuously labeled sections of *U.S.A.* are highly experimental, the trilogy is designed for accessibility. It is a book that can be read by a variety of Americans. Just as Dos Passos shows us, in the "U.S.A." section that opens each book, many forms of American speech, so he offers us, in the trilogy as a whole, something for many kinds of readers. His novel is not only innovative in form; it is a profoundly democratic invention. High modernists may be beguiled by the stream-of-consciousness narratives of the Camera Eye sections or by the Newsreel montages of headlines, song snippets, and politicians' speeches, but a reader need not be schooled in the techniques of the avant-garde in order to appreciate the work. The featured character of one narrative section will appear in another character's section; characters removed from one another by virtue of geography or class background meet, employ one another, fall into bed together, fight, experience unrequited passion for one another—in short, engage in all the activities of conventional characters in conventional novels. At times the characters of *U.S.A.* seem to inhabit a particularly lurid soap opera world, and someone who reads the trilogy to find out what happens next in these characters' lives will not be disappointed: There is ample payoff in the tragic affairs, business successes, suicides, and meteoric rises in status of low-born characters to satisfy the most jaded reader of popular fiction. The "low" elements of the narrative sections— the healthy doses of sex and violence—are an incentive for the reader not particularly taken by "high" art, that is, modernist technique, to continue on through the text.

Yet, though Dos Passos may incorporate crowd-pleasing techniques into his trilogy, he never lets his readers forget the difference between *U.S.A.* and the novels that have preceded it. And though his novel may be accessible to the general reader, it is more than anything a novelist's novel, a work, especially, for the radical writers of the Depression. In *U.S.A.,* Dos Passos addressed the fears and frustrations of his literary colleagues: the rage at the corruption of language and the misuse of history by the public relations men of the twenties, at the inadequacies of the newsreels, at the inability of radical discourse to save the lives of Sacco and Vanzetti or of modernism to reach a wide audience—the failure of art, finally, to make a difference in American life. More importantly, with his flamboyant, sprawling, funny invention, he showed his colleagues how to turn stale American rhetoric on its head, how to create a new literature that would both enrage and entertain readers. For *U.S.A.,* in giving readers a new way of looking at their recent national history, offered writers a new way of writing the American story.

CHAPTER THREE

BOYS WILL BE BOYS

Farrell Examines
Working-Class Manhood

John Dos Passos may have offered a blueprint for the new novel, but he failed to address the question of who exactly would be reading this radical literature. Although publishers were offering prizes for the best proletarian novel of the year, it was difficult not to notice that sales of these novels were not strong. It would be up to James T. Farrell, in his *Studs Lonigan* trilogy, to address the problem of proletarian readership and to point out that the idealized spitting, swearing working man envisioned by Mike Gold and other proletarian writers could not possibly read "highbrow" novels and preserve his masculine self-image.

What the Proletariat Reads

By the time James T. Farrell published *A Note on Literary Criticism* in 1936, American writers had for several years been deeply embroiled in the debate over how best to produce class-conscious art. And as the arguments raged on over such issues as the political suitability of using the inner monologue (it "is too closely connected," wrote D. S. Mirsky in *New Masses,* "with the ultra subjectivism of the parasitic, rentier bourgeoisie, and entirely unadaptable to the art of one who is building socialist society"), it became clear that there was another, related, issue that demanded the attention of proletarian writers: very few people, let alone members of the working class, were reading their books.

In his 1934 *Saturday Review of Literature* article, "What the Proletariat

Reads," Louis Adamic, a critic hostile to proletarian literature, reported the results of a year-long survey, which showed that, in fact, workers had very little interest in the literature addressed to them by the radicals of the period. Among those he quotes in the article is a "rather intelligent worker" who wonders:

> Dos Passos, by the way: why does he write so queer? I read "1919" which everybody seems to rave about when it came out, and man, it was like solving puzzles from start to finish. Some of the things I solved were interesting and true, I don't say they weren't; but why should a writer want to turn reading into a game? Why should I spend a week or two puzzling over a book? Why shouldn't they write so that a fellow who isn't altogether dumb could understand things right away? Do they want to make me feel stupid and humble before their genius, or is that art?[1]

This unidentified (and possibly apocryphal) worker was not alone in his concerns. As Henry Hart pointed out in his address to the first American Writers Congress in 1935, sales of proletarian novels tended to hover around one or two thousand copies, with even an exceptionally successful work like Cantwell's *Land of Plenty* selling only three thousand copies. And, as he concluded, "Sales like these mean that the bourgeois publishers are going to begin to refuse to publish our novels."[2]

Farrell, whose volume of literary criticism is in large part devoted to an attack on what he terms "the school of revolutionary sentimentalism," as embodied most famously by Michael Gold, was himself deeply involved in the ideological struggles surrounding the "proletarian literature" movement. Farrell's discussion of Marxist aesthetics attracted a great deal of attention in left-wing literary circles, its publication sparking a debate that raged for weeks in the columns of the *New Masses*. It could be argued, however, that Farrell had already published his most convincing critique of leftist literature in a work that not only raises the "proletarian novel" to new heights of sophistication but is also deeply concerned with the issue of working-class readership. That work was *Studs Lonigan,* Farrell's first trilogy of novels, published between 1932 and 1935.

Like most of the dozens of novels that would follow the trilogy, *Studs Lonigan* was based on a class, and a neighborhood, that Farrell knew very well. In his introduction to the Modern Library edition of the trilogy, he wrote that his attitude toward Studs "is essentially a simple one. 'There but for the grace of God go I.' "[3] The grandchild of Irish immigrants, Farrell was born in 1904 into a working-class neighborhood on Chicago's South Side. When he was three, the pressures of poverty and too many children forced his parents to send Farrell to be raised by his maternal grandparents, with whom he lived until he was twenty-seven. Although he was raised only three or four miles from where he was born, James was separated from his siblings and parents by a vast cultural chasm. In the Daly household, which included an aunt and uncle in addition to his grandparents, Farrell grew up with indoor plumbing and steam heat, and here it was made clear to him that he would not have to end up a teamster like his grandfathers and father. Thus Farrell, shifting uneasily in his youth between the poverty of his parents and the genteel strivings of the Dalys, and later working as a gas station attendant to put himself through the University of Chicago, was perfectly positioned to write about working-class cultural life from a stance neither of the comfortably dispassionate observer nor of the engaged insider.

The Problem of Working-Class Culture

There are some obvious correspondences between *U.S.A.* and *Studs Lonigan,* both in their tripartite structure and in the time span they cover, each ending just as the Depression sets in, each increasingly experimental in technique, each obsessed with the nature of the American Dream and its dissemination through journalism and popular culture. However, whereas Dos Passos's characters are intentionally representative of American citizenry as a whole—they come from a wide range of socioeconomic classes and ethnic backgrounds, are geographically scattered, and participate in the great events of the day—Studs Lonigan inhabits a claustrophobically small world comprising the two neighborhoods in which he and his family live at different times, and his activity is largely restricted to drinking, whoring, and painting houses. His attempts to participate in the public life of his time are both ugly and futile, as we shall see. Although the authors of both novels employ seemingly similar experimental techniques, especially the newsreel device, and share an obsession with mass culture, Dos Passos offers us a view from the top, showing us through characters like Moorehouse, the great ad man, the tools that are used by the ruling class to manipulate mass opinion. What Farrell demonstrates, on the other hand, is the effect on hapless individuals like Studs of the mass culture created by men like Moorehouse. It is fitting, somehow, that Moorehouse and Studs Lonigan are born in the same year, for as one rises to greater wealth and power through his ability to manipulate the image of the American Dream, the other loses all his money and ultimately his life in an attempt to emulate the characters in the mass-media fantasies he both devours and, at least in his imagination, inhabits.

Studs Lonigan, the trilogy composed of *Young Lonigan, The Young Manhood of Studs Lonigan,* and *Judgment Day,* can be seen as a challenge to the proletarian writers like Gold and Clara Weatherwax (author of *Marching! Marching!*) who were writing rousing stories and novels about an energetic and often lovable working class. Farrell's trilogy follows William ("Studs") Lonigan, the listless and unlovable son of a lower-middle-class Irish Catholic contractor in Chicago, from his junior high school graduation in 1914 to his untimely death, months before his thirtieth birthday, in 1929. Along the course of his journey Studs experiences no great revolutionary conversion (as do characters such as Mac the Wobbly and Mary French in *U.S.A.*). Nor does he, unlike characters in so many other radical novels of the thirties (*Grapes of Wrath, The Land of Plenty, The Disinherited*), get involved with the labor movement (the one character who dares to be a unionist, the father of Andy Le Gare, a peripheral member of Studs's gang, is blacklisted and forced to leave Chicago). Solidarity among Studs and his friends exists only for the sake of oppressing those weaker than themselves, usually members of ethnic or racial minorities. Excepting the lone appearance of a Communist parade at the very end of the trilogy, when Studs is offstage dying, there are no scenes of unity among men and women, blacks and whites, Italians and Irish. And, although there is a *Judgment Day,* there is no redemption. Thus *Studs Lonigan* stands as a reproach to writers guilty of sentimentalizing the proletariat, as well as an object lesson to those writers who naively assume that members of the working class are ready to join arms in a common cause. The American working class, Farrell seems to be saying, may be a tougher nut to crack than had been assumed.[4]

Although it may be instructive to pinpoint the stock elements and scenes, present in other leftist novels, that are missing from *Studs Lonigan,* it is even more important to note what Farrell does include in his trilogy. What Farrell offers us is no less than a critique of the masculinized, idealized proletariat so lauded by Gold and other radical writers. By examining the relationships between cultural consumption and gender roles, Farrell seriously challenges the class and gender stereotypes adhered to by Gold and his allies and, in the course of doing so, powerfully addresses the issue of why Studs and others of his class are not reading the novels of Gold, Weatherwax, Cantwell, and others. Although *Studs Lonigan* has often been seen as a critique of mass culture, it is perhaps as much an embrace. By showing us the power and importance of art in Studs's life as well as its deadening effect, Farrell in effect dangles Studs, and other laborers like him, as a prize just out of reach of the proletarian novelists. If Studs spends so much of his leisure time reading books and magazines and listening to music, one might well ask, why are they not proletarian novels that he is reading, why not radical magazines, why not songs of protest that he listens to?

In fact, it is not so far off the mark to say that, when Studs is not drinking, whoring, or beating up on those weaker than himself, he is consuming or discussing art. Even in the pool hall where he hangs out, discussions about literature are commonplace:

> "Well, Conrad's a classic," Mose Levinsky, poolroom intellectual, said.
> "What is a classic? Define it," said Big Syd.
> "A classic is a book that lives."
> "Now take a book like Robert Herrick's *The Common Lot,*" said Big Syd.
> "It's a good book, but it isn't a classic," said Mose.
> "Say, you guys act like you thought you were too good for the human race," said Red Kelly, passing them on his way from the can.[5]

Although the poolroom boys all seem to consume culture at the same rapid clip as does Studs, they all, save perhaps isolated "poolroom intellectuals" like Mose, operate under a sometimes overt stricture: To read too much, to become too educated, is to betray one's class, to feel superior to the human race. This is apparent in the first pages of the book, when Studs's sister speculates that he is reading in the bathroom. "Why, Frances, how dare you accuse him like that!" is his mother's enraged response.[6] The notion that too much education is hazardous is voiced at many points, as by Studs's father, for instance, who tells him that "Maybe you're better off without an education, and a lot of book-learning. It might make you into a high-hat snob like it did Dinny Gorman. You don't need an education like that to be a success. I didn't" (*YMSL*, 53). If this belief were widespread, it would obviously limit the time working-class families spent sitting around the dinner table discussing the latest proletarian novel.

Another set of strictures on cultural consumption comes from the Roman Catholic church. When a renowned priest, Father Shannon, comes to preach, his message is chiefly concerned with "modern authors whose books perfume the vilest of sins" (*YMSL*, 351). He is not afraid to name names, and among the authors that he mentions is Sinclair Lewis, whose books Studs's sister has been reading: "What books do I mean? For one, there is a scurrilous novel, *Elmer Gantry,* a book that belongs in no decent household, a book that no self-respecting Catholic can read under the pain of sin, a book that should be burned in a garbage heap" (352). It is unclear whether Studs's sister Fran continues her proscribed reading. However, Father Shannon's message, that reading dangerous books by writers like Nietzsche and H. L. Mencken can lead to having dangerous thoughts, is one that Studs and his friends embrace: After hearing the sermon, they pressure the owner of a local restaurant into firing a Greek waiter who is translating Walt Whitman into Greek and has been overheard discussing Heine, Nietzsche, and Lewis.

Not only does Studs read and go to the movies constantly, he identifies with the heroes of the drugstore novels and gangster movies he consumes. After seeing an adventure movie set in Alaska, he imagines himself as Yukon Lonigan. After reading a dime novel or seeing a gangster film, he becomes Lonewolf Lonigan, stickup man. Thus Farrell, by presenting us with a protagonist who yearns to be a fictional character, who sees his life as a series of performances, and whose most coveted role is that of the two-fisted, spitting, swearing working man, not only echoes Pirandello's "character in search of an author" (or, for that matter, Walter Mitty) but prefigures the slippage between reality and textuality that we commonly associate with postmodern works. Additionally, he raises questions about the constructed nature of that working-class masculinity so strongly endorsed by other radical writers of the time. For, as Paula Rabinowitz notes of the period's radical art, "The prevailing verbal and visual imagery reveled in an excessively masculine and virile proletariat poised to struggle against the effeminate and decadent bourgeoisie."[7]

Tough Guys Don't Read

Among the epigraphs that Farrell selects for *Young Lonigan,* the first volume of the trilogy, is a question from Frank Norris: "A literature that cannot be vulgarized is no literature at all and will perish." *Studs Lonigan* is itself a record of one boy's deliberate vulgarization of himself, as he attempts to become a masculine cliché modeled on the generic characters of tough-guy magazines, books, and movies. In a sense, part of the appeal of Studs is that of a backstage movie magazine; we get to be present at the creation of Studs's role as the star of the movie he imagines his life to be, watching as Studs selects the gestures and words that will best suit his macho persona. As the fourteen-year-old Studs boasts to himself in a Paul Bunyanesque monologue, delivered for his own benefit, "I'm so tough that you know what happens? Well, bo, when I spit . . . rivers overflow. . . . I'm so hard I chew nails" (*YL,* 9). What gives the work its ironic as well as its tragic edge is Studs's inability to reduce himself fully to the one-dimensional man he longs to be. Another dimension to that irony lies in the fact that the masculine image that Studs is trying to project so closely resembles the image of Mike Gold's ideal proletarian.

In his notorious 1930 attack on the Humanism of Irving Babbitt and Paul

Elmer More, Gold defined the terms on which, for many radical writers, the battle between proletarianism and bohemianism (read modernism) would be fought. Contrasting the "aristocratic Humanists" and "fairy-like" Thornton Wilder, with his "little lavender tragedies," with the more masculine leftist writers, Gold honed his sexually essentialist view of the working class.[8] As he wrote in a letter in the July 1930 issue of *New Masses,* Humanism "was responsible for the flowering of a 'fairy literature.' Nursing a 'mad jealousy' because they had been 'deprived of masculine experiences,' the Humanists denounced in writing what they secretly envied. 'A word like sonovabitch and a good healthy spit in the gutter knocks these men over, but I am sure they would exchange their whole unhealthy stale lives to be able to swear resoundingly and to spit like a man.' "[9] Indeed, the model proletarian writer whom Gold described in a 1929 essay for the *New Masses* entitled "Go Left, Young Writers!" would be a "wild youth . . . the son of working class parents. . . . He is a Red but has few theories. It is all instinct with him."[10] Rather than study literature, this young man would simply produce an eruption of literature "in jets of exasperated feeling." While Gold's rhetoric may have been the most overblown, he was far from the only leftist writer to nurture a cult of masculinity. Jack Conroy, in Gold's defense, wrote that "The stale Bohemian writer, recognizing the vigor of the new proletarian literature, sadly contemplates his own wilted phallus, and howls that the Goddess of Pure Art is being raped by barbarians."[11] By no means all radical writers followed in the footsteps of Gold and Conroy in positing a healthy, virile proletarian literature in contrast to the impotence and/or homosexuality of "bohemian" literature, which was associated with bourgeois decay. However, this attitude was prevalent in leftist circles. Not only, thus, were proletarian writers and their art masculine, but the proletarian characters within these books were fairly bursting with testosterone. Workers in radical novels, and especially union men, seemed often to follow in the footsteps of Dos Passos's Mac, the tough, love-'em-and-leave-'em Wobbly of *U.S.A.,* or of Edward Dahlberg's hard-living *Bottom Dogs.* Yet the unexamined gender categories of *U.S.A.*—the hard, active men and the grasping, apolitical female consumers—are shown in *Studs Lonigan* to be anything but organic, are shown, in fact, to be quite literally constructed.

Before we get into an analysis of the text, however, a word on class categories seems advisable. Walter Rideout, in defining *Studs Lonigan* as a proletarian novel, describes it as belonging to that "major group of proletarian novels, those concerned with middle-class decay." Paul Rabinowitz similarly sees the brutal sex within the book as conforming "to the prevailing gendered aesthetic categories that link the bourgeoisie to sexual perversity."[12] However, this strict identification of Studs with the middle class seems to oversimplify matters and to obscure the important link in the novel between gender and class. Although Studs is often described by critics as lower-middle-class (and as such vulnerable to the "decadence" and "effeteness" of the petit bourgeoisie), class identities within the novel seem not only fairly fluid but also inextricably connected to issues of gender.

This connection between class and gender had already been drawn in texts ranging from the advertising memos of the 1930s to the novels of the previous generation, such as Dreiser's *An American Tragedy* and Norris's *McTeague.* Think for a moment of the way Trina, in *McTeague,* is the one responsible for her crude husband's gentrification:

> Gradually the dentist improved under the influence of his little wife. He no longer went abroad with frayed cuffs about his huge, red wrists—or worse, without any cuffs at all. Trina kept his linen clean and mended, doing most of his washing herself and insisting that he should change his flannels—thick, red flannels they were, with enormous bone buttons—once a week, his linen shirts twice a week, and his collars and his cuffs every second day. She broke him of the habit of eating with his knife; she caused him to substitute bottled beer in the place of steam beer; and she induced him to take off his hat to Miss Baker, to Heise's wife, and to the other women of his acquaintance.[13]

Manners, personal hygiene, and the consumption of upscale beverages are all part of the feminine domain. The signs of gentility are understood and enforced by women and are counterpoised to the rough, "natural" masculinity of the predomesticated male. Norris, indeed, seems to take malicious glee in lingering over each kitschy detail of the McTeagues' living room, from the matching pictures bearing the titles "I'm Grandpa" and "I'm Grandma" hanging on either side of the mantelpiece to the knitted worsted tidies hanging from the back of each chair. And yet Norris is up to more than a bit of spiteful class comedy here: After McTeague's marriage, Norris notes, "he began to observe the broader, larger interests of life, interests that affected him not as an individual, but as a member of a class, a profession, or a political party.... But most wonderful of all, McTeague began to have ambitions—very vague, very confused ideas of something better—ideas for the most part borrowed from Trina."[14] Thus it is not just that Trina is getting her husband to change his linens more frequently; she is in fact imbuing him with class consciousness and with the desire to rise. It is not simply that she inhabits a separate sphere or that she is a woman who is domesticating her mate.

In *Sister Carrie,* too, it is Carrie Meeber who is acutely conscious of class and its signifiers: "She made the average feminine distinction between clothes, putting worth, goodness, and distinction in a dress suit, and leaving the unlovely qualities and those beneath notice in overalls and jumpers." Even though Carrie at first must fulfill her class ambitions through linking herself to wealthier men, such as Drouet and then Hurstwood, it is she, rather than they, who is most aware of the possibilities for ascension, just as within Hurstwood's family it is his wife and daughter who are most interested in bettering their class standing rather than he himself. Hurstwood himself is necessarily conscious of class distinctions in his job as a manager and modifies his greetings according to "a finely graduated scale of informality and friendship, which improved from the 'How do you do?' addressed to the fifteen-dollar clerks to the 'Why, old man, how are you?' which he addressed to those noted and rich individuals who knew him and were inclined to be friendly." However, these distinctions are made from professional necessity; after he is forced to leave his job, in his life with Carrie it is she who becomes increasingly more genteel, he who takes to wearing ragged old clothing around the house. It is not just that Carrie is materialistic, or that the factory work she must initially do is unpleasant—more than that, she eschews the working-class culture of the factory, which she experiences as "hard and low" and "common," in favor of a more genteel existence.[15]

Both in the novels under discussion and in the advertising wisdom of the 1930s, women do more than simply shop for groceries, clean the house, and raise the children—it is they who are responsible for the class uplift of the family. As Roland Marchand observes in his chronicle of American advertising from 1920 to 1940, "Advertisers recognized that consumers would rather identify with scenes of higher status than ponder reflections of their actual lives. In response, they often sought to give products a 'class image' by placing them in what recent advertising jargon would call 'upscale' settings." The consumers who thus sought to uplift themselves were by no means ungendered, however: "As one ad in *Printers' Ink* succinctly put it, 'The proper study of mankind is man . . . but the proper study of markets is woman.'" "Style" goods, whether they be colored bathroom fixtures or designer watches, were designed with upwardly mobile customers in mind. This was clear in such trends as prepackaged ensembles, whether of writing paper, silverware, or camera equipment. "The ensemble, properly authenticated by an authoritative source, offered the consumer 'an education in good taste' and a defense against social disapproval." And "women were viewed as virtually the sole buyers of 'style goods.' To incorporate style into a product was to give it a 'feminine appeal.'"[16] Thus, both in real life, at least as perceived by the American advertising industry, and in fiction, we see class ambitions inextricably linked with femininity. (We also see in *Studs Lonigan* the solemnity with which this targeted audience views its commercial seduction. When Studs's brother has the temerity to mildly parody a radio jingle, Mrs. Lonigan reproves him: " 'Martin, they have to have money for the radio, don't they, and I think you should appreciate what you get for nothing and not be making such mean remarks. I think it's nice of people and business men to spend good hard-earned money in these days so we can hear all the wonderful things we do hear over the radio, without you making fun and belittling,' his mother nagged.")[17]

This class division by gender clearly operates within the Lonigan household. While Studs's sisters aspire to greater things, he himself paints houses for a living. It is not as though any member of the Lonigan family has a very secure foothold even among the ranks of the petit bourgeoisie. Studs's parents are both the children of peasant immigrants who have managed to gain a fairly tenuous hold on gentility. Even within the immediate family of old man Lonigan, Studs's father, there is one brother who is a motorman, another who is a sailor, one who is an unidentified working man, and a sister who is a prostitute. Studs's acquaintances are for the most part working-class. The father of Weary O'Reilly, Studs's nemesis in his gang, is a teamster. Andy Le Gare's father belongs to a labor union. There are a few fathers who have made good: old man O'Brien has his own small coal-delivering company. Red Kelly's father is a cop. These families all hover uneasily between classes, but the culture of Studs and his friends is by no means that of upward mobility. Studs and his friends, when they get old enough, work as laborers. Very few attend high school, and fewer complete it. They have no dreams of professionalization, and Studs's own aspirations are to be a boxer or, perhaps, a gangster of some kind. Because class identities are so nebulous within this book—Farrell himself has noted that many critics have seen Studs as representing the proletariat[18]—it is difficult to pinpoint Studs as either a proletarian or a member of the middle class.

As in *McTeague,* class itself is gendered within the novel. Studs's sisters are somewhat intent on achieving middle-class gentility: Fran attends formal dances and encourages Studs to join her, and she wants to cure Studs's younger brother of his uncouth language by sending him to a "refined private school" (*YMSL*, 136). (It should be noted, however, that his sister Loretta makes good by marrying a bookie, which hardly seems like a solid middle-class occupation.) However, Studs and his brother eschew anything that smacks of gentility. At the formal dance to which his sister invites him, Studs reflects that "Hell, it was all artificial. They were all trying to put on the dog, show that they were lace-curtain Irish, and lived in steam-heat" (282).

This cultural division extends to the kinds of books that the Lonigans read: When Fran reads books by authors like Sinclair Lewis it is as part of her middle-class aspirations: "*She said she was not taking them seriously. She only read them because a couple of her girl friends who thought they were sophisticated were reading them, and she had gotten them to look at, only so they wouldn't be able to think that she was old-fashioned, or not up to the times in things*" (*YMSL*, 342). Culture for Fran thus involves "keeping up with the Joneses." As Joan Shelley Rubin writes, advertisements for ventures like the Book-of-the-Month Club were precisely designed to play on the kind of anxiety that Fran experiences: " 'What a deprivation it is to miss reading an important new book at a time everyone else is reading or discussing it,' the club's 1927 brochure announced, reminding potential subscribers that neglect of the latest books meant loss of 'fine camaraderie.' "[19] Yet Studs, as we have seen, shares no such aspirations. To read such books is to become a "high-hat," a snob—someone, perhaps, who is less than a man. Studs's culture—the culture of pool halls, taverns, and brothels, of little money, much violence, and a resentful nativism—aspires to the tough masculinity Gold so reveres. In describing the construction of Studs's stereotypically macho identity, Farrell undercuts the notion of this machismo as an inherent quality, showing it instead to be behavior which is learned at a tremendous cost to the spirit.

When we first meet Studs, it is in that most classic of adolescent green rooms—in front of the bathroom mirror, where he is prepared for yet another performance, his grade school graduation:

> He faced the mirror and stuck the fag in the right-hand corner of his mouth. He looked tough and sneered. Then he let the cigarette hang from the left side. He studied himself with satisfaction. He placed the cigarette in the center of his puss, and put on a weak-kneed expression. He took the cigarette out of his mouth, daintily, barely holding it between his thumb and first finger, and he pretended that he was a grown-up mama's boy, smoking for the first time. He said to himself:
> Jesus Christ!
> He didn't know that he bowed his head when he muttered the Lord's name, just as Sister Cyrilla had always taught them to do. He took a vicious poke at the air, as if he were letting one fly at a mama's boy.
> He stuck the fag back in his mouth and looked like Studs Lonigan was supposed to look. (*YL*, 8–9)

As he will do throughout the novel, Farrell alternates between a clinical inspection of Studs as a product of his environment—by, for instance, noting his unconscious Catholic mannerisms in such a way that creates a complicit relationship between Farrell and the reader—and a presentation of Studs's attempts to mold himself as a generic tough guy. Studs, when he is feeling proud, identifies with "Bronco Billy, or Eddie Polo in the movies" (*YL*, 8). And already in this passage we see Studs trying out different versions of masculine behavior, including ones associated with homosexuals, and then lashing out at the "mama's boy" within himself, as if to eradicate it and replace it with the hypermasculine, tough version of himself—"like Studs Lonigan was supposed to look." It is worth noting that the "Jesus Christ!" which escapes from Studs's lips is somewhat ambiguous: It is unclear whether he is angry with himself, uncomfortable with his poses—or perhaps he enjoys trying out different forms of sexual and class identities. The "grown-up mama's boy" holds the cigarette "daintily," in a way that is refined and femi-nine as opposed to gangsterish or lower-class (his first pose). We will see Studs assuming these various identities, and rejecting any but the most rigid version of himself, again and again throughout the trilogy, and our sympathies are engaged as we keep seeing him shutting down possibilities for himself. There is certainly something comic about the scene, but its implications are sad indeed. We see this clearly when, following his lapse into reflections on Lucy Scanlan, the girl he admires, he "goddamned himself, because he was getting soft. He was Studs Lonigan, a guy who didn't have mushy feelings! He was a hard-boiled egg that they had left in the pot a couple of hours too long" (8). Thus readers are in the position of wanting to discourage Studs's "masculine" behavior and encourage what he himself identifies as "soft" or feminine. His acceptance of only the narrowest of self-definitions, one based on the tough-guy ethos of popular culture, dooms him to a life of dull failure. And yet his humanity, which he so insistently quashes, keeps us hanging on through 1,100 pages of street fights, gang-shags, drunkenness, vomiting, and generally churl-ish behavior on the part of Studs and those who surround him. As Donald Pizer notes, "We see clearly the potential for 'good' in him which he himself fails to understand, and we thus accompany him through the largest portion of his life with the painful recognition that his failure in self-knowledge is contributing to his self-destruction."[20] Throughout the trilogy we see the conventional sex roles, as embraced by Studs and his friends, as being severely limiting and dehumanizing. In a typical scene Studs, now a young man, spends an evening with his friend Paulie and Paulie's new bride. Studs's first reaction is covetous; he sees Eileen only in terms of property: "Studs envied him, because she was his girl, his woman, and she slept with him, undressed in front of him, and he could do whatever he wanted with her body" (*YMSL*, 75). However, as the evening progresses, Paulie ignores his wife, who seems capable only of talking about what she wants to buy. The drama of the evening occurs when Paulie assaults a man for staring at Eileen's calves, exposed as she sits on a park bench. After Studs has helped him beat up the man, Paulie turns on his wife: "Any time you sit like you were then, showing off everything you own, there'll be trouble. My wife ain't acting like a whore in a public park when I'm around" (79). The progression from consumer discussion to physical violence takes but a few minutes—there are few representations of heterosexual relationship that do not revolve around an acquisitive woman and a brutal man.

Interestingly enough, the one person to whom Studs feels comfortable expressing his feelings is a lesbian, Helen Shires. "She was a square shooter, and she understood things" (*YL,* 76). In his early years, at least, Studs feels comfortable exposing his less macho side to her: "If he tried to sip a soda with a spoon before anybody else, they would laugh at him" (76). Helen is the only person before whom Studs does not feel the need to perform. With Helen, a natural athlete, Studs can let down his guard: "They . . . gave each other a good match, and they trusted each other and knew there was no cheating, so they could go ahead and play, not having any squabbles or having to talk and chew the rag a lot" (79). With Helen, who does not easily fit the gender categories to which Studs is accustomed, he can discuss his interest in Lucy Scanlan, which he can never admit to anyone else. He can talk about religion and explore his changing feelings about himself. "Sometimes, with Helen, he could talk more, and say more of what he really meant, than he could with any other person" (80). With Helen, too, "He felt soft inside, as if his feelings were all fluid, all melting up and running through him like a warm stream of water" (80). And yet these feelings are threatening—Studs cannot tolerate them for long: "He didn't know what he ought to say. He hurriedly glanced across the street" (80). Studs has difficulty maintaining the relationship, even though he wants to, and when, years later, he encounters Helen again, he struggles against his own inability to view women as more than conquests: "Might date her up at that and make her; she probably could be made, and every jane a guy made was another notch in his belt. But he liked her, and wished they could be as they used to be" (*YMSL,* 168). Even though he sees her as sexually undesirable, "He wanted to talk about old times, and have them just naturally talk about themselves, and maybe about Lucy" (167).

It is the gay characters in the book who reveal the instability of Studs's aggressively heterosexual stance: When, on a visit to his old neighborhood, which is now primarily black, Studs is propositioned by three gay black men, "He was momentarily tempted to take a chance out of curiosity. Self-disgust rose, changing his mind. He turned and told them to blow. They laughed, and he walked on, hearing their voices and laughter behind him, feeling that he was being talked about. It was almost as if he were being humiliated, undressed, in public, and he hastened" (*YMSL*, 387). Not only does this encounter threaten his sense of self, it also puts him in the position of the women who are vulnerable to the commentary and lewd proposals of Studs and his gang. For a minute Studs is at the mercy of those he and his friends customarily victimize: blacks and gays.

As in Studs's sexually ambiguous bathroom posing, there is often a strong affiliation in the novel between homosexuality and genteel, or middle-class, behavior—just as there is between femininity and upward mobility. For example, Leon, a middle-aged gay man living in Studs's neighborhood, is a music teacher by profession and tries to seduce Studs by offering him free piano lessons. "Fine music can make a life beautiful" (*YL*, 72). What Leon is offering him is the opportunity to become "cultured," to play music more sophisticated than that of the movie houses. However, this offer is entirely presented as an exchange—Studs's heterosexual identity in return for cultural elevation into the middle class. "We'll be all alone, and there won't be anyone to bother us, and we'll be free," Leon tells him, "for our first lesson" (73). Needless to say, Studs does not take Leon up on his offer, since to do so would severely compromise his masculine, working-class image.

A Character in Search of an Author

It is instructive to note that most of the sexual encounters of the book have a strong homoerotic subtext to them: Studs's first sexual experience is a "gang-shag" (a group encounter involving many boys and one willing female) with the neighborhood "bad girl," Iris, and afterward he reflects that "It didn't help guys to understand girls any better, and after it Iris didn't understand him any better, and it didn't scarcely last a minute" (*YL*, 191). However, as unsatisfactory as it may be as an experience of male–female intimacy, it is necessary as a bonding experience between the boys in his gang: "when the guys said they were going to Iris', he couldn't have run out. He'd had to do it" (189). Actually, the most common sexual situation in the trilogy is that of the gang-shag or of a group visit to a brothel. As Eve Sedgwick notes in a somewhat different context, Studs's culture is one in which "male-male desire became widely intelligible primarily by being routed through triangular relations involving a woman."[21] It is as though Studs and his friends are having sex not with the woman involved, who seems unimportant, but with one another. As Kate Millett writes of Henry Miller, "the reader is given the impression that sex is no good unless duly observed and applauded by a ubiquitous peer-group jury. . . . His strenuous heterosexuality depends, to a considerable degree, on a homosexual sharing."[22] In fact, as we learn through the angry comment of one woman with whom Studs has a gang-shag, "I pity any woman who'd get the idea you're a good time. Say, you don't even know how to jazz" (*JD*, 251). But then, perhaps "jazzing" isn't the point: What takes place behind closed doors is irrelevant compared to what occurs in the public, men's arena.

The performative quality of the sex in the trilogy is reflective of the performative aspects of all of the rest of Studs's life. Studs, as Ann Douglas has pointed out, is a character whose life is conducted as a long-running performance: "He incessantly imagines what others are thinking of him: are they admiring, preferably envying him—or scorning him? The principle of comparison is the closest thing he has to an idea."[23] And the comparisons Studs makes are usually not between himself and his peers but between himself and fictional characters.

Farrell structures the novel in such a way as to highlight this quality: From grade school graduation to neighborhood football match, from masses to initiation into a Catholic men's organization, most incidents in the book revolve around rituals of one sort or another. Thus there are unlimited opportunities for Studs to measure himself against fictional characters of one sort or another. And this identification with the heroes of movies and books is by no means incidental to the plot. Indeed, it is important in many ways, from Studs's brutal interpretation of masculinity and his resulting loss of humanity to his final financial debacle.

At the beginning of the first volume of the trilogy, *Young Lonigan*, Studs wants to be either an outlaw like Jesse James or a pioneer "and go out to fight Indians and build log cabins. He would have had a swell time, pot-shotting Indians, rescuing girls like Lucy from them, and from smugglers and hold-ups" (78). His fantasies, thus, are strictly in the American grain: He wants to have a mythic role in American history. As he gets older, in fact, he will work harder to achieve what he sees as heroism through participating in historical events. Yet every attempt of his to do so will be doomed to failure.

Farrell was a Trotskyist, not a Communist Party member, and yet it is interesting to note that Studs's insistence on seeing himself as part of canonical American history seems to foreshadow the Communist Party's Popular Front efforts to align itself with the American tradition. As Irving Howe and Lewis Coser note, "Communism became 'Twentieth Century Americanism'; Washington and Lincoln, the progenitors of modern progressive sentiments; Jefferson, the ancestor of those 'Americans who are fighting against the tyranny of Big Business with the revolutionary spirit and boldness with which he fought the Tories of that day.' "[24] Communist leaders themselves were pulled from the margins and pointedly positioned right in the mainstream of American history. As party leader Robert Minor wrote,

> It was in the springtime of 1776 and Thomas Jefferson may well have been driving his one-horse shay . . . with a draft of the Declaration of Independence in his pocket, when a certain boy, just turned 21, stepped into a recruiting station in Dinwiddie County, Virginia. He gave his name as Littleberry Browder and was sworn in as a soldier of the Continental Army of General George Washington.[25]

Had he lived into the late thirties, it seems plausible that Studs could have been attracted to the appeal of this "Americanism." For Studs, even as he lies on his deathbed, is haunted by hallucinatory images of George Washington—and throughout his short life he is hobbled by his ineffectual attempts to be a true hero in the American grain. For example, when an underage Studs attempts to enlist in the army during the First World War, he muses that "After he became a hero, and everybody knew of him, the story of the stunt they were pulling would be remembered and they would all be telling it. . . . Well, he would become a hero. . . . He would!" (*YMSL*, 12). However, his "heroic" stunt consists of stealing a bicycle with his friends in order to steal bananas, stuffing himself with said bananas and water in order to gain enough weight to enlist—and then unheroically vomiting profusely and showing up at the recruitment station only to be told by a sergeant to "G'wan home, children, and get your diapers pinned on" (21). Thus his "heroic" attempts are literally sick-making, and his attempts to be masculine—a macho soldier—end with his infantilization.

Although this attempt is comic, a later scene makes more ominous Studs's "heroic" impulses to participate in the life of his times. This occurs during the Chicago race riots of 1919, when Studs and his gang perceive themselves as the bold defenders of white Chicago. Conflating the mythology of white supremacy and that of baseball heroism, Studs boasts that, "when he cracked a dinge in the head, the goddamn eight ball would think it had been Ty Cobb slamming out a homer off Walter Johnson" (*YMSL*, 73). And yet, despite the gang's grandiose boasting and determination to kill large numbers of blacks, "They only caught a ten-year-old Negro boy. They took his clothes off, and burned them. They burned his tail with lighted matches, made him step on lighted matches, urinated on him, and sent him running off naked with a couple of slaps in the face" (74). Clearly, the desire of Studs and his friends to be "heroic," to participate in important historical events, is something that less racist, less bloody-minded readers would wish to suppress. Additionally, the gang's longing for large-scale, historically significant mayhem can only be enacted on the pettiest of scales—as the torture of a small child. It is notable that in this case, as elsewhere in the novel, the political solidarity and concerted action of Studs and his friends are used for ends completely unlike those of the ennobled strikers in novels such as Robert Cantwell's *Land of Plenty*, not to mention, of course, the united Wobblies of *U.S.A.* Whereas a character like Dos Passos's Mac will travel to Mexico and experience solidarity with his foreign comrades, Studs and his friends unite in order to throw pepper in the eyes of Jews, torture animals, and arrange for the firing from his job of a Greek radical. Here, working-class solidarity is shown in a menacing light—it would be far better for all concerned if the pool hall gang confined themselves to individual pursuits and eschewed group action.

This type of repetition—an incident occurring first as comedy and then as tragedy—is seen in Studs's identification with the gangsters he sees in movies and reads about in pulp novels. When as a boy, for instance, Studs has an argument with his father, he takes his rusty gun and runs away. It is here that he has what one might term an existential moment: "He couldn't remember ever having felt like he did now, with only his feeling of being alone, as if all the loneliness of the night and the sky were inside him, crushing out everything else" (*YMSL,* 57). But he immediately connects this feeling of being alone to his literary experience: "It was a snaky feeling like maybe some one would have, or Robinson Crusoe might have had, being alone on a desert island" (57). However, this literary imagining is then transformed into a moviegoer's gangster fantasy: "He had burned all his bridges, and gone from everything, and he was a man alone forced to fight by himself, an enemy of society, a burglar and a robber—well, he would be one after he pulled off his first stickup" (57). Unfortunately for him, his career as the gangster Lonewolf Lonigan is truncated, since he cannot manage to behave like his heroes in the films he loves. When he first attempts a stickup,

> The realization that it was just like a movie holdup flew through his brain.
> "Don't . . . m-move . . . or I'll . . . drrr . . . drill you."
> The victim smiled with self-possession.
> "Son, you'd better put that toy away!"
> The gun fell. He turned and ran lickety-split down the alley, hearing diminishingly, the echo of hearty laughter. (*YMSL,* 60)

In this instance, he can go home safely, and no harm is done—except, perhaps, to his mythic self-image. It is in a later incident that we see how truly damaging are the effects of his identification with the heroes of the gangster movies he loves.

When the twenty-nine-year-old Studs, who is weakened from pneumonia and thus less likely than ever to be able to pull off feats of gangsterish daring, sees a tough, up-and-coming hood, Joey Gallagher, on the screen, his life is transformed. "If he could have busted into something big that way, he'd be much better off today. But Studs Lonigan wasn't Joey Gallagher" (*JD*, 64). However, although Studs is aware of how futile and unreal his imaginings are, he cannot keep from identifying with the hero of the picture:

> His mind became like a double exposure, with two reels running through it. He saw Joey Gallagher as the hero, and he saw himself in Joey Gallagher's boots, and Studs Lonigan and Joey Gallagher together leaped up the career of gangdom's adventurous ladder to fame. They hijacked. They spoke with crisp, hard words, and with barking gats and tattooing machine guns, bumping off friends and foes, letting nothing get in their way. Ah, that was the kind of a guy Studs Lonigan wanted to be, really hard and tough. . . . Why hadn't Studs Lonigan lived like that? (65)

Studs's fear that he has, after all, "no guts" is what leads him to walk out of the movie theater and invest all of his savings in bad stocks. It is this decision that enables him to think of himself as not so different from the gangster-heroes he idolizes on the big screen: "He viewed himself as a gambler, a chance-taking fool, prepared to face the risk of losing all the money he had saved for years and to drop it with a game smile on his face. . . . Hell, you never got anywhere unless you took a chance, and that was Studs Lonigan all over, he counselled himself" (*JD*, 72). The rest of the novel details the slow collapse of the Imbray stocks in which Studs has invested and his corresponding loss of faith in the "big men" like Solomon Imbray, whose power Studs had hoped would protect him. It is in the final volume, too, that we see the full immersion of Studs in mass culture—and that we more thoroughly see the effects of the newsreels that Dos Passos documented on the audiences for which they are intended.

Dos Passos, in *U.S.A.*, presents dozens of Newsreels that are very similar to those we see Studs watching. For instance, in Newsreel XLVI we see a montage of popular songs, newspaper headlines ("BANKERS HAIL ERA OF EXPANSION," "PROSPERITY FOR ALL SEEN ASSURED"), advertisements, and an editorial snippet, presumably on the subject of Sacco and Vanzetti: "these are the men for whom the rabid lawless, anarchistic element of society in this country has been laboring ever since sentence was imposed, and of late they have been augmented by many good lawabiding citizens who have been misled by the subtle arguments of those propagandists" (*BM*, 49). What we miss, however, is the response of the audience for whom this work is intended. In what seems both an homage to and an advance on Dos Passos's technique, Farrell in *Studs Lonigan* lets the reader into the minds that this material is intended to convince.

Just before viewing *Doomed Victory*, the gangster picture that influences Studs to make his foolish investment, Studs and his moviegoing companions settle in for the newsreels. "The thing I like best about news reels is that they're short" (*JD*, 52), confides Studs to his friends, and with that the three of them settle in to watch the insipidly cheerful "news." The first feature is about a program to reduce the surplus of eggs: "Out on the coast these days, business clubs and fraternal organizations are doing some novel fighting against the bogey of Old Man Depression. And is it fun, boys! I'll say it is!" (53). This program, which turns out to be a giant egg fight, is reported in grotesque, warlike detail by Farrell. "The laughter in the theatre increased at the sight of a wobbling fat man, surrounded by enemies who subjected him to a merciless fire of eggs, spluttering and staining his white clothing. . . . In a closeup, the fat man bawled like a baby, his hair matted, egg shells clinging to his face, his double chins dripping egg yolks" (53). By zooming in on the sadistic "fun"— the tears and childlike nature of the fat man, his powerlessness in the face of an onslaught by a phalanx of enemies, the details of his pain—Farrell makes the reaction of the crowd, and of Studs, seem that much more insensitive: "Studs leaned forward, laughing. Wished he was in a fight like that" (53). There seems to be little difference, really, between this "amusing" group assault on a single helpless victim and the enjoyment that Studs and his friends have taken in torturing animals and ganging up on Jews and African Americans. The militarism of the next cut—a film of navy bombers, presented as "Uncle Sam's latest bid for supremacy of the skies" (54)—seems perhaps ominous but not yet of a whole with the first piece.

However, the presentation that follows this one, on the attempts of a group of scabs to break a strike, is reported in a manner that is so incongruous with the actual events shown that it is apparent even to this audience. The brutal assault of police on strikers is reported by the announcer "in the same tone as if he were describing a heroic hundred-yard run on a college gridiron" (*JD*, 54), and yet the images presented reveal that "A fleeing man in overalls was clubbed by a policeman, and as he fell groggily forward, a special deputy smashed him on the shoulder with a truncheon. He lay face forward in the center of the picture, blood oozing from his head, and the struggling crowd surged over his body" (55). The sadism of the egg fight, the celebration of military might, and the brutality of the police toward the strikers present an image of the violence lurking just beneath the surface of American life. The correspondence between the egg fight and the attack on the strikers is made nearly explicit not only by one of the brutal cops, who seems aware of the performative nature of this violence—"one full-faced policeman turned to smile into the camera" (55)—but also by the announcer, who describes the latter as "not the best form of sport" (55). Although one of Studs's friends is moved to sympathy for the strikers—" 'Poor bastards,' Pat mumbled" (55)—this is a very limited form of political awareness. Studs reacts not at all to the predictions of bankers that the Depression will soon be over—"We are again on a solid footing, and we shall see, in the next six months, another commercial upswing" (59)—although this optimism runs directly counter to his own experience. And his only comment on a staged funeral for "Old Man Depression" is to note that "The Queen of Optimism" riding in the parade is a "swell-looking dame" (55). Studs cannot understand why some "damn fool" in the audience is hissing Mussolini, since "Mussolini couldn't hear it" (56) and, all in all, is happy when the newsreels are over so that the movie can begin.

He may think that the newsreels are just filler, but it is clear that they have a profound impact on him. Weeks later, he compares the sticks with which neighborhood kids play war games to the realistic mock weapons of Italian boys in the Mussolini training films he has seen: "And maybe Mussolini was smart, all right. It might be good for this country to give kids the same thing, training them, because when they grew up, if they were needed for war to repel a foreign invader like the Japs or the Russian Reds, they'd not go into it green" (*JD*, 72). The Fascist training dovetails perfectly with Studs's own boyhood fantasies. In fact, it is easy to see how all of Studs's worst impulses—toward sadism, war, and, in a lesser way, zeroing in on the "swell dame" but not questioning the meaning of a funeral for Old Man Depression, which he knows for a fact is far from dead—are nourished by the content of the newsreels. It is not hard to see how Studs's values are shaped and reinforced by his viewing experience, and yet, at the same time, it is clear that Studs and his fellow moviegoers are reluctant to question for a minute the content of the on-screen propaganda even when it is directly contradicted by either the images on-screen, as in the case of the strikers, or by their own experience. (If Old Man Depression is dead, why is Old Man Lonigan having such a tough time making ends meet?)

Studs seems numbed by his immersion in mass culture, which Farrell presents as being antithetical to thought. When Studs is troubled by thoughts of his own mortality, "He couldn't stand this, and he quickened his steps to get home and read the newspaper, listen to the radio, do anything to get those thoughts out of his head" (*JD*, 172). To read, ironically, means to avoid self-reflection of any kind. And even when Studs is reading the newspaper, he is incapable not only of drawing any political conclusions but of reading stories that are related to political issues. As he reads a headline that says "MUS-SOLINI PLANS CORPORATIVE STATE," he guessed Mussolini was a smart man but flipped to the funnies (178).

Perhaps it is only his short attention span that will prevent him from becoming a fascist. Yet it will also prevent him from gaining any political knowledge: "He skipped the account of farmers rioting with guns and pitch-forks, and avidly turned to one next to it. Sixteen-year-old girl found unconscious in forest preserve. Did a guy pulling such a stunt get anything worth the effort?" (*JD*, 356).

And yet Farrell does finally allow a small loophole, a glimmer of possibility for the radical novelists trying to capture the hearts and minds of the proletariat. This occurs as a milder version of Studs is meandering along the street, weakened by pneumonia and upset about his caddish, overly macho behavior toward his fiancee: "even if he was in the right, he needn't have been so goddamn mean to her. Yes, he was kind of sorry about it" (*JD*, 215).

> He stopped at the window of a book store and rental library, looking from a stack of greeting cards to books piled up and spread around the window, with their bright jackets, reading the titles, *Lumber, Jews Without Money, The Women of Andros, The Crystal Icicle, Iron Man, The Mystery of Madame Q, Arctic Quest.* Sometime he might rent one or two of the books they had and do a little reading, he reflected, turning away from the window. (216)

It is notable that Studs becomes interested in these books only at a point in his life when he seems to be rethinking his macho behavior. Musing on his fight with Catherine, his fiancee, "He could see her, begging forgiveness at their next meeting, while he was aloof, just to teach her a lesson" (215). This certainly sounds like the old, tough-guy Studs talking. And yet what follows is very different: "But he probably wouldn't act that way, because he wanted the scrap patched up" (215). It is precisely when Studs has shed his role as the tough worker that he becomes interested in the books of Michael Gold and Edward Dahlberg, the proselytizers of radical literary machismo. When Studs is behaving like the spitting, swearing worker these writers idealize, he cannot be enticed by such literature: To read a serious book would be to betray his class or his gender. It is only a more androgynous Studs who is ready for the proletarian novel.

MEET THE SISTER AND AUTHOR OF "MY SISTER EILEEN"

RUTH McKENNEY JOINS NEW MASSES STAFF

NEW MASSES

AMERICA'S
INDISPENSABLE
WEEKLY

There are 10,000,000 middle-class Americans – doctors, lawyers, teachers, small business men, etc.–who would find *New Masses* stimulating and indispensable to a complete understanding of their own situation today. The same is true of *I Like America* by Granville Hicks, which gives such a splendid picture of America and the role of the middle class. Of these we believe 20,000 are immediately potential readers. We ask your cooperation in reaching these 20,000 quickly. First, become a regular subscriber yourself. Second, bring this offer to the attention of your friends and urge them to become subscribers too—remembering the while that America can be anything which enough Americans want to make it.

Communists are funny people! This amazing discovery burst on an unsuspecting world about the time Robert Forsythe made his appearance in *New Masses*. Now along comes Ruth McKenney to add fresh proof that a twinkle in the eye is no impediment to a leftist's vision. The adventures and antics of the McKenney girls, as related in Ruth's book *My Sister Eileen*, have added considerably to the bearability of heat waves and other summer crises, and put the book on the best-seller lists.

But Ruth has her serious moments too. Don't forget, she is the girl who scooped McNaboe, Hearst and Dies last spring with her intimate, authentic expose of the Communists and how they work, published exclusively in *New Masses*. And her second book, soon to appear, is a tome about Akron and the rubber workers there.

Here is your answer to every friend who likes *New Masses* but thinks it is "so serious," and another jolly good reason for getting yourself and all your friends on the regular subscription list. Hurry up and sign the coupon—for beginning with September, the laughs are on us!

NEW MASSES

I Like America

Drive for 20,000
new subscribers

FREE—A copy of I LIKE AMERICA by Granville Hicks with one year's subscription to *New Masses* (52 weeks—$4.50)

NEW MASSES I LIKE AMERICA DRIVE
NEW MASSES, 31 EAST 27TH STREET, N. Y. C.

Enclosed is $4.50 for which please send NEW MASSES for one year (begin with Sept. 20 issue), and a FREE copy of Granville Hicks' I LIKE AMERICA to:

NAME _____

ADDRESS _____

CITY _____ STATE _____

OCCUPATION _____

6 MONTHS' SUBSCRIPTION $2.50 (WITHOUT BOOK)

1. "Communists are funny people!" proclaimed the text of this *New Masses* back cover. Ruth McKenney moved easily between the worlds of popular culture, proletarian literature, and modernism. Courtesy of the John Carter Brown Library at Brown University.

2. The Federal Theatre Project maintained an extensive research staff for their Living Newspapers. Here is a research shot of a tenement, used as background material for *One-Third of a Nation.* Courtesy National Archives.

3. The set of *One-Third of a Nation.* Courtesy National Archives.

4. The tenement in the Hollywood version of *One-Third of a Nation*. Courtesy MOMA film stills collection.

5. By contrast to the Living Newspaper, the film version of *One-Third of a Nation* stressed romance. Courtesy MOMA film stills collection.

6. The directors of the Federal Arts Projects saw their mandate in broader terms than mere entertainment. Here, "paintings by children of 'One Third of a Nation's People'" are featured in a theater lobby, drawing attention to the link between the slum conditions on stage and work done by actual slum children. Courtesy National Archives.

7. Living Newspapers mediated between individual tragedy and larger socioeconomic causes. Here, a mother in *Triple-A Plowed Under* explains to a policeman that she was forced to kill her starving baby. Courtesy National Archives.

8. In another scene from the play, the effects on consumers of rising prices are dramatized. Courtesy National Archives.

9. *Triple-A Plowed Under.* The Living Newspapers presented an inclusive vision of America and Americanism. Courtesy National Archives.

10. Ordinary Americans are afforded extraordinary stature in *Triple-A Plowed Under*. Courtesy National Archives.

11. This Federal Theatre Project children's play, *Revolt of the Beavers,* raised the hackles of conservative congressmen who objected to its radical content. Courtesy National Archives.

12. As the director of the Federal Theatre Project, Hallie Flanagan brought artistically innovative and politically radical living newspaper productions to millions of spectators. Courtesy National Archives.

CHAPTER FOUR

FAMILY HISTORY AND POLITICAL IDENTITY IN HERBST'S TREXLER TRILOGY

James T. Farrell wrestled with the problem of gender and cultural identity in his trilogy. Although he critiqued working-class manliness, he did not address the problem of how a working-class woman might become radicalized. Josephine Herbst not only accomplished this task but, by bridging Dos Passos's concern with the radical writer and Farrell's focus on the reader, offered a blueprint for transforming readers into writers. Herbst, however, never attained the celebrity of Farrell and Dos Passos. Consider the words of her biographer, Elinor Langer:

> Imagine, for a moment, that you are Josephine Herbst. For ten years you have devoted yourself to a grand reconstruction of American history at least as ambitious as the comparable trilogies of your friends John Dos Passos and James T. Farrell, yet unlike those works, which gradually attain the hallowed status of classics, yours is never mentioned.[1]

Josephine Herbst's career through the 1930s followed a course common to many radical writers. Born in Sioux City, Iowa, in 1897, she moved to Greenwich Village in 1920, already radicalized, in order to lead the life of a writer. Her first literary job was as a reader for a group of magazines, including the *Smart Set,* supervised by George Jean Nathan and H. L. Mencken. She continued her literary apprenticeship in Germany and in France, where she knew Hemingway, Nathan Asch, and Robert MacAlmon; published her first novels,

Nothing Is Sacred (1928) and *Money for Love* (1929); and embarked upon a career as a radical journalist. She wrote about the Scottsboro Boys for the *New Masses* and about the farmers' strikes in Iowa for *Scribner's*. She returned to Germany in 1935 to write about Hitler's rise for *The Nation* and the *New York Post*. Not only was she an active journalist, but she published short stories in many of the literary journals of the thirties, including *Contempo*, where her fellow contributors ranged from Farrell, Dos Passos, and James Rorty to Ezra Pound and William Faulkner, and *The Magazine*, where she shared an issue with Elizabeth Bishop, William Carlos Williams, and Caroline Gordon. And, of course, she published the trilogy that was to be her most enduring literary monument. In his *New Masses* review of *Rope of Gold* (1939), the trilogy's final volume, Edwin Berry Burgum wrote of Herbst's "conspicuous distinction among novelists of the left: that she takes as her unit of action, not the factory or the strike or the town, but the family."[2] In her trilogy, composed of *Pity Is Not Enough* (1933), *The Executioner Waits* (1934), and *Rope of Gold*, Herbst would enter the debate that raged, throughout the decade, in the pages of radical and mainstream literary journals on the nature and manufacture of radical fiction. Whereas Dos Passos uses his trilogy to demonstrate the defeat of radical and literary discourse by the discourse of journalism and, especially, the language of advertising, and Farrell explores, in his trilogy, the problems of developing a working-class audience for the proletarian novel, Herbst devotes her trilogy to a radical task that falls outside the purview of both Dos Passos and Farrell.

From the Kitchen to the Picket Line

Herbst opens up her definition of politics to include a whole new class of people—women. Dos Passos's women are avid consumers whose political action, if such it can be considered, consists largely of preventing their husbands and lovers from gaining access to radical material that would distract them from money-making pursuits. Although Farrell goes far toward questioning the gender categories to which Dos Passos and Gold so rigidly adhere, his female characters seem chiefly interested in marriage and status. Herbst's female characters are, by contrast, fully autonomous. In her trilogy, we follow three generations of Trexler women through their struggles for survival and greater understanding. Unlike the female characters in *U.S.A.* and *Studs Lonigan*, the Trexler women don't see marriage as their only possible goal. "Don't be stupid and shut your eyes and imagine that the only things in life worth while come from men and what people call romance," Anne Trexler Wendel, who is happily married, cautions her daughters.

Beyond simply granting subjectivity to women, however, the Trexler trilogy provides a virtual how-to manual for the radicalization of women. By ratifying women's domestic experience as political, Herbst challenges the separation of the personal and the political: She demonstrates how inevitably suffused the personal is with the political, and vice versa. Herbst's female characters become radicalized through learning to understand their family's experience in larger political terms. Much of this education comes by poring through the treasure trove of family papers that fill the family attics in the trilogy. It is this political usage of what are traditionally private documents—the family letters and clippings that the Trexlers preserve—which suggests a feminist solution to the problem of ratifying the "invisible" experience of women. Herbst's critique is as much class-based as gender-based, however. Because their class-based analysis is based on personal experience, her working-class female characters can produce meaningful works of radical documentary. By contrast, middle-class radicals, whose knowledge of working-class life is shallow, intellectual rather than experiential, and tinged with class guilt, are unable to escape their pasts in order to see the present clearly. In effect, Herbst provides a critique of the radical writer that parallels Farrell's critique of the proletarian reader.

The trilogy, which ranges back and forth through time, documents the brief rise of the Trexler family and its long, slow decline. The events of the trilogy are based heavily on those of Josephine Herbst's own family, and as Langer amply documents, she quotes her own family papers, often verbatim, to document the events she narrates.[3] *Pity Is Not Enough,* which covers the years 1868 to 1896, concerns the generation of Josephine's mother, named in the trilogy Anne Trexler. Anne's brother Joe goes south to try his luck as a carpetbagger, where he is made the fall guy for larger interests (a favorite theme in the trilogy) and slandered in the newspapers (several long, libelous articles are included in their entirety in the novel). Later, Joe's attempts to make his fortune panning gold in the Black Hills lead only to insanity. In some sense, Joe comes to this particular bad end because he takes the stories of American success too literally; even as a young man he draws inspiration from *The Life of Daniel Boone.* It is his whiny, selfish, unheroic younger brother, David, who really strikes it rich in the goldfields—not by actually digging gold but by selling government flour at vastly inflated prices to the starving miners. In this volume we see Anne marrying Amos Wendel and moving with him to Iowa to begin a life of rural poverty. As in the other volumes of the trilogy, the narrator's identity is unclear, and chronology itself is fluid. We have glimpses of Anne's daughters growing up and discovering their legacy through the old family letters (which are extensively quoted throughout the text of the novel), and we have a final glimpse of them as, grown up and living in Seattle, they long to join in the general strike of 1918.

The second volume, *The Executioner Waits,* covers the lives of the Trexler descendants from 1902 to 1929. We see David increasing his fortune from the World War, we see the IWW rising and falling, we see Anne's daughters growing up, struggling to make their livings as their family income drops, and marrying, and we see short set pieces covering political events, such as strikes, in the United States between 1932 to 1934.

The final volume concentrates on the dissolution of Anne's daughter Victoria's marriage to Jonathan Chance, a ruling-class scion turned radical organizer, and Victoria's own development into a journalist. It is in this volume that the struggles of radical writers, and particularly radical female writers, during the Depression are most directly addressed.

The masculinization of the proletariat, at least within the proletarian novel, that Farrell critiqued in *Studs Lonigan* proved exclusionary for Herbst and other female radical writers. If, as understood by Mike Gold and other powerful (male) leftist writers of the period, the favored representation of a radical worker was to be emphatically masculine, it would be difficult for the housewives, seamstresses, and other female characters of Herbst and other women writers to be hailed by Gold et al. as revolutionary models. The masculine ideology that Dos Passos embraces and Farrell deconstructs in their respective trilogies had the effect of shutting women writers out of the Marxist literary conversation of the 1930s. In Tess Slesinger's *The Unpossessed,* based on her experiences working at the *Menorah Journal* with Michael Gold, she describes a situation in which the radical women are consistently shut out of the men's talk and are defined primarily in their roles as wives of the men who are founding the leftist magazine. However, for all their lip service to radical ideas, Slesinger's women for the most part do not challenge the prevailing fictional stereotypes of women as emotional, apolitical consumers: The narrator of *The Unpossessed* sees her role in marriage as that of a refuge for her husband, who in turn reserves great contempt for the women in his life who "had come to him stupidly offering comfort, offering love. . . . if he were once to give in, to let their softness stop his ears, still the voices that plagued him this way and that, they would be giving him not peace, but death; the living death of the man who has consented to live the woman's life and turned for oblivion to love as he might have turned to drink."[4]

Slesinger's milksops are a far cry from the tough-minded women of Herbst's trilogy. The narrator of *The Unpossessed* is "amoeba-motherly" and wishes to be acknowledged by her husband and thus to herself by "the softness of her, the woman-ness of her." And though Slesinger is often mentioned in the same breath as Herbst, Slesinger still presents her female protagonist as consumer rather than producer, in the style of other writers of the period—as Margaret's husband Miles watches her pass the greengrocer's where she usually shops, "he felt the link existing between a woman and her market."[5]

Herbst, as a response to this exclusion, redefines the meaning of politicization, opening up its terms to include women as political subjects whose journey to radicalism—and to becoming radical writers—may occur on different terms than their male counterparts. It takes Victoria the better part of three volumes to start writing documentary texts of her own: The process of becoming a journalist, for her, entails both becoming fully autonomous and being able to see her own past in political terms. In general, however, the trilogy is an archivist's dream, studded as it is with all kinds of "found" texts. Throughout the trilogy we are privy to all of the written documents concerning the Trexler family, from newspaper articles on Joe's perfidy in Georgia to love letters from each generation of the family. Much of the work, indeed, traces the relationship of each member of the Trexler family to these documents, relationships that vary from that of Anne's sister Catherine, who becomes obsessed with the old family letters to the point where she develops brain fever and dies, to that of Victoria, who uses the family documents to gain an understanding of herself and her family as part of larger political and historical trends in America.

A Muckraking Heritage

The politicization of Herbst's women characters is linked to their reading of newspapers and, ultimately, their involvement as political journalists. Journalism, and most particularly the writing of political exposés, becomes the road to activism for Victoria Chance. While many radical writers of the thirties may have felt vaguely indebted to the turn-of-the-century muckrakers for the education in documentary techniques that they provided, Herbst makes the lineage of the thirties writers and their muckraking predecessors explicit.

If the muckraking novel of the Progressive Era is the thesis, the modernist novel of the twenties the antithesis, then the documentary novel of the thirties is certainly the synthesis of the two. Though Herbst and Dos Passos come out of a modernist tradition, they are equally indebted to the muckraking journalism that in some ways was the direct forebear of the documentary novel of the thirties. Some critics of the thirties recognized the potential of the muckraking movement and longed for its return. C. C. Regier, for instance, mulling over the devastation of the Depression in his 1932 volume, *The Era of the Muckrakers,* noted that

People are beginning to ask a fundamental question. Has capitalism failed? . . . We want to know; and before we can know much we must have the facts; and how can we get the facts except by further honest and scientific exposure? It would almost seem that before we can have another intelligent progressive movement we will have to have more muckraking.[6]

Though the investigative skill of such muckrakers as Ida Tarbell and Lincoln Steffens would be admired by the writers of the thirties, equally significant to them would be the effortless slide between journalism and literature accomplished by so many writers, most famously, of course, Upton Sinclair. Just as Herbst would blend fact and fiction in her trilogy, so the muckrakers of the first decade of this century, particularly those writing for *McClure's Magazine,* moved easily from journalism to fiction and back again. In essence, the muckraking novel was directly derivative of the journalism of the period. Many of the prominent novelists of the period, such as Sinclair or David Graham Phillips, had their start as journalists. However, the genre-crossing of the muckraking novelists did not necessarily translate into self-conscious literary experimentation, as witness the novels of Sinclair and of Jack London.[7]

All radical writers of the thirties could take a page from the muckrakers' book by combining different genres (as did, most famously, Dos Passos) or by using the tools of investigative reporting (as did Steinbeck, for example, in *The Grapes of Wrath*). However, the work of the muckrakers took on special significance for radical female writers of the thirties, many of the most prominent of whom, including Mary Heaton Vorse, Martha Gellhorn, Ruth McKenney, Josephine Herbst, and Meridel Le Seuer, worked as journalists. Unlike many of the radical writers of the thirties, including Michael Gold, Jack Conroy, and Dos Passos, the muckrakers had focused a great deal of attention on the plight of women. Many of the muckrakers were women, some staunch feminists, and their stories dealt with such topics as the poor conditions under which women labored. In a 1910 article for *McClure's* entitled "Working-Girls' Budgets,"[8] Sue Ainslie Clark and Edith Wyatt documented the pitifully inadequate salaries for which working-class women labored in department stores, and Rheta Childe Dorr, an active suffragist, worked side by side with, and then described the plight of, women factory workers in her 1910 book, *What Eight Million Women Want.* Dorr's book was written from a position with which Herbst would no doubt have been sympathetic—the desire to treat working women as subjects rather than objects—a position which was itself a reaction to a highly successful 1903 volume, Marie and Bessie Van Voorst's *The Woman Who Toils,* which had claimed to tell the working woman's story. Though the Van Voorsts had indeed made brief visits to a few factories, they made no attempt to use the workers' own voices or to tell their stories; the work lacked both empathy and accuracy.[9]

Although many writers of the thirties, male and female, used the techniques of muckraking in their novels, it would be left largely to radical women writers of the period, including Herbst and Lauren Gilfillan, to reflect self-consciously on the ways in which becoming a journalist could be a tool for political empowerment. Journalism held a pivotal place in women's fiction of the thirties, in part because women often saw the process of becoming a reporter as a chance for greater freedom in a world in which there weren't many opportunities for them. Just as women in earlier centuries tended toward new forms such as the novel rather than more established genres like verse drama, the lack of historical models for documentary and journalism made it easier for women to carve out roles for themselves. From fictional characters like Henrietta Stackpole in *Portrait of a Lady*—the free-wheeling journalist who escapes the confines of marriage and ladyhood to traverse continents—to muckrakers like Ida Tarbell, whose exposés of Standard Oil were so influential, female reporters were able to live and work in untraditional ways. Like the settlement house workers of the Progressive Era, these reporters were free to travel to places where women, especially middle-class women, would not normally be welcome—whether these places were the wars covered by Martha Gellhorn in the thirties or the factories covered by muckrakers like Rheta Childe Dorr in the early years of this century. In fact, the transgressive journeys of many of the women who went where respectable women had no place—to the homes of tenant farmers, to bread lines, even to lynchings—were financed by Harry Hopkins's Federal Emergency Relief Agency, the New Deal's first version of welfare. Indeed, Agnes Smedley's autobiographical protagonist, Marie Rogers of *Daughter of Earth* (1923), in many respects an important predecessor for the women writers of the thirties, is a reporter, as would be so many female characters in women's novels of the thirties.

Perhaps the most notable example of these novels is Lauren Gilfillan's *I Went to Pit College* (1934), which concerns the growth of a young woman's political consciousness through her work as a reporter covering a mining strike. What differentiates the narrator of Gilfillan's novel from the women characters, especially Victoria, of Herbst's trilogy is that, whereas Herbst's characters are teetering on the edge of poverty themselves, Lauren Gilfillan's narrator is a young woman with a degree from Smith College who recounts in wide-eyed detail her descent into the life of the miners—an enterprise she treats as a masquerade ball. For example, when she first comes to stay with a miner's family, she conceals her identity and in the morning undergoes a careful toilette in order to fit in: "I took up a hand mirror and some eye shadow and drew blue circles around my lashes. Now my face looked like Yren's. In the filtered light, my face glimmered pale and pinched. Yes, that was the way Yren looked. I had an air of poverty and hunger. Oh, yes, and—I had nearly forgotten. I took all my money and several checks from my purse and folded them into a money belt, which I buckled around my waist under my dress."[10]

The Uses of the Familial Past

Herbst's young women characters, whose political understanding tends to be hard won, would have nothing but contempt for Gilfillan's slumming narrator. In fact, there is an extended discussion in the trilogy concerning who is entitled to be a spokesperson for workers. As one might imagine, members of the middle class out for "experience" are low on the list. From the first pages of *Pity Is Not Enough* we are caught up in the generally difficult lives of the youngest generation of the Trexler girls, who will by the trilogy's last volume be grown women struggling for personal and political survival in the depths of the Depression. Although becoming an investigative journalist may be an important route to female empowerment, in that it is a means of escaping traditional roles, gaining autonomy and mobility, and doing important political work, it is a path that requires a great deal of preparation. The first and most important step in the process is the ability to understand personal history in political terms. Thus the experiences of Anne Trexler Wendel, mother of Victoria, who will become a reporter, are eventually understood by her daughters as fitting into a larger framework of American history.

Although the events of the trilogy begin in 1868, its opening, narrated by one of the Trexler girls,[11] occurs in the basement of the Iowa farmhouse where the girls grow up, when "At least once during the cyclone season, Anne [Trexler] Wendel and her four girls raced through the pouring yellow rain to the cellar. . . . Down there, they huddled around and Anne brought out to still their terror old Blank and his fits, the dead and gone Trexlers and Joe, the most generous brother, poor Joe."[12] Natural disasters are matched with a narrative of personal disaster: "The day the cotton wood snapped off short and fell heavy as a horse upon the roof, cracking the plaster off the upstairs room and sending the mirror off the wall to break for seven years bad luck, that day, she let it out for the first time that Joe had run away" (*PINE*, 1). And yet, Anne Wendel's personal mythology of the glorious past prevents her from being able to tell the truth about her brother: " 'He was the finest man, always wore the best clothes. He had the most charming manners, was generous to a fault,' and so she shut us out once more from learning why Joe ran and why he was poor Joe" (2). The Wendels are a family always on the brink of financial disaster: "A bad year for crops. It was always a bad year. Too hot, too wet, too dry, too much Republicanism, the Democrats were ruining things. Flowers were hard to raise in that baked soil" (2).

As things go from bad to worse financially, Anne uses family nostalgia as a weapon against the present:

> She made an island of her past and climbed aboard with all her dead and gone and took us children too, clinging and listening, fascinated and scared of the rushing water around us and she had to sit there on that island and see us overboard and sink or swim according to our nature and the chance. The year Amos Wendel lost his business and all the other years of ups and downs, she had her island and we had it too. (*PINE*, 3)

As their poverty worsens, Anne comforts herself not only with her familial past but by identifying with a larger tradition of American literature. She would "paste up Emerson on her pantry door that whosoever owned the land, the horizon belonged to that one with the soul to see it" (4). (Later on, we will see the danger as well as the comfort of identifying too closely with canonical American texts, as Joe sets off into the world with his copy of the autobiography of Daniel Boone, unaware that this work, unlike the work that Herbst herself is writing, can in no way be used as a model for living.) The more the girls find out about Joe, the more they wonder whether his story, their family story, does not belong to the wrong kind of narrative: "we were ashamed a little, silly it sounded and not quite there, like a play with too much shooting in it" (4). Yet, when they discover the documentary sources detailing the family mythology, their perspective changes: "but one day we found a clipping in an old pocketbook hanging to a rafter in the attic and then we didn't feel that way any more" (4). What is intolerable to them in Joe's story when it belongs to family mythology seems different when the story is recast in a public setting—this is, in fact, the first step that the Wendel girls will take toward understanding their private experience in a public light. This passage, the first four pages of what will be more than a thousand, in a sense provides the frame for the entire trilogy: Family secrets, whose concealment by some and discovery by others take a lot of time and energy, are a source of comfort, a bulwark against the difficulties of the present—a present in which one has few choices. For "If Amos Wendel had made a go at his business Anne Wendel, who was a Trexler, might not have dug so deeply in her past, fishing up stories for her children" (116). It is only when they are seen in documentary perspective, ultimately as part of a larger political truth, that they provide the vehicle for personal and political liberation—that they enable the family members, women, to become political agents.

In fact, what we see are three possible models for women dealing with the documentary materials of their family past: Anne Trexler Wendel, her sister Catherine, and Anne's daughter Victoria. Anne Trexler Wendel cannot move beyond a fascination with family history for its own sake. Rather than placing the events of her family in a larger historical context, she sees only their personal significance—stories from a past richer and more enthralling than the grim present of foreclosures and job losses. These stories provide a refuge not only from the outer world but even, initially, from her family members— "as we grew older we tried to worm it out of her why he was poor Joe" (*PINE*, 3). It will be left to her daughters, particularly Victoria, to draw the connections between the personal and the political. Her struggle to find a larger political meaning from these documents will finally end, years later, far from the clay cellar of her childhood, in Victoria's thought that her mother "had died with an attic full of things too good to throw away, with bags of letters hanging from the rafter like beheaded corpses as if the written words of the dead somehow pledged the family to immortality" (*RG*, 169). It is the effort to keep the past from being personally overwhelming, from being private baggage, and instead to make some social use of it, gain some larger understanding from it, that will become Victoria's mission.

The dangers of this obsession with the family past first become apparent in Anne's generation. Against a background of her brother Joe's Horatio Alger–like rise in the world and his subsequent fall, precipitated by, significantly, newspapers that use planted information to discredit him, we see the struggles of women to break free from the home and escape to a larger world of ideas. In Joe's rise and fall and in the difficulties of the women who are left at home we see both the failure of the pioneer model for male individuality and the failure of the domestic ideology to which the Trexler women are expected to conform. Women are pulled inward while men are pulled outward by narrative.

We see Joe's desire for adventure fueled by his reading of Daniel Boone, after which he "wrote his brother that such a life would be the sort for him hunting and fishing alone for years surrounded by none but the savage Indians, escaping from them like Daniel Boone, fighting and never being hurt" (*PINE*, 7). Once he does make his escape to work with the carpetbaggers down south, Joe finds that he—or, initially at least, his boss—has entered the public sphere via the newspapers. Though the references to his boss are anything but flattering—"With his hands to the elbow in the State Treasury Mr. Carpet Bagger Bullock can well afford to be sumptuous and to dine and wine, and feast and flatter the men who have done his bidding on the floor of

Congress" (30)—Joe ignores this version of documentary reality (at his peril, it later turns out) in favor of pursuing his version of the American Dream, fashioning himself carefully with the help of Daniel Boone and an etiquette book he purchases. "A proud well dressed man generally does everything well. It takes a man of wit and pride to wear a well fitting suit of clothes. Wellington said his dandy officers were his best officers" (31). His reliance on American mythology and myths of upward mobility, coupled with a willful ignorance of what is actually going on around him, will prove to be his downfall. "Perhaps he could write poems too" (53), Joe thinks, but like Dick Savage, the Harvard poet of *U.S.A.,* he will find that his poetic dreams, his etiquette books, his references to Cato, will avail him nothing. Joe's downfall will be charted in the pages of the newspapers, however, and it is here that his sisters and mother will read accusations against him for swindling, will see him becoming the fall guy for the carpetbaggers originally derided in the pages of these same papers.

It is the publicizing of what was once simply a private matter—the details of Joe's life—that will pull the Trexler women out into the public sphere. The life that Joe leads stands in stark contrast to the alternative that his sisters must choose, "in that house where Injun Blank never for a minute let him forget he was a poor relation" (*PINE,* 7). In a sense, Joe and his sisters are inhabiting—or trying to inhabit—very different narratives. Anne and Catherine and their mother are trying to live in a world like that of the domestic novel of the nineteenth century, exemplified by *Wide Wide World,* whereas Joe, one might say, wants to inhabit a Horatio Alger story. Neither form of narrative proves adequate to the experience of the Trexlers.

It is not just the Trexler women, of course, who are forced to live lives of relative confinement. Some of the most poignant moments in *Pity Is Not Enough* occur in the portrayal of Lenore Blondell, one of the text's many intellectual women who suffer because they have no place to go. Lenore, a southern woman who is in love with Joe but cannot compete with her good-looking sister, finds that a good female mind is completely irrelevant in the absence of beauty. Lenore can feel superior to her sister, thinking that Lucy "Never read a book" (65), and yet know that this is beside the point, that she herself "would always be helping others all her life" (65). It is in the later exchange of letters between Joe and Lenore that we see more clearly the inadequacy of women's lives lived by proxy. Joe, shivering through an unsuccessful winter in the goldfields, writes to Lenore of his world travels: "I climbed the perilous peak of Teneriffe until blood oozed from my lips and great globules formed along the arteries that I might for a moment behold a world of solitude. Oh how solemn and grand. I worked for months in the ruins of Herculaneum and Pompeii as well as a short time on the Tiber that I might supply my mind with information of an interesting nature" (222). Lenore must live vicariously through these imagined adventures. More pathetic still, somehow, is her friend Margaret who "said it was the best thing that had ever happened to her in all her life to be allowed to see the letters Lenore received from her friend" (223).

As Joe begins to lead an increasingly troubled, though exciting, public life, the women of the family have a harder and harder time trying to inhabit a domestic narrative like that of poor-relation Ellen Montgomery in *Wide Wide World*. Anne is distracted not only by events in the family but by her awareness of disturbing intellectual currents in the larger world: "Perhaps Darwin and his ideas were poisoning the air; one of the teachers at the school had tried to tell her this but she couldn't help being fascinated by the new theories" (*PINE*, 150). Her introduction to new ideas is simply making her aware of how unsatisfying the atmosphere of pure domesticity is for her. Although "she stayed home instead cutting out clippings from papers about duty and the home and womenly women . . . she found it hard to keep her mind on these things that had nothing to do with the life that was secretly going on around her" (150) After reading disturbing accusations against Joe in the newspaper, Catherine "tried to take an interest in her scrapbook but an editorial on 'Hospitality' and another on 'Restraint' seemed stupid and she wondered why they had ever interested her" (85).

As Joe is forced to flee his public life, where every train ride he takes is charted in the newspapers, and retreat to the total anonymity of a changed identity, complete with a phony name, Catherine, in particular, tries to make the opposite journey into a wider world, a move that is near impossible because of her gender: As her landlady tells her, "you'll put your eyes out with too much reading. Just wait, when you are my age, you'll see what little good it does you. The men don't like women to know too much, my dear, you'll be cheating yourself out of a husband one of these fine days if you don't watch out" (*PINE*, 144).

In many ways Catherine's story serves as a cautionary tale of what happens when women use the family narrative as an end in itself rather than as a means to a greater understanding of the world. Rather than looking outward, making the political connections that her nieces will later do, Catherine turns away from politics and inward to the purely familial: "She collected all of her father's diaries and old letters and began reading them. She drew a family tree with all its branches. It gave her a feeling of stability to draw that tree and to make the branches with the good fine stout old names" (*PINE*, 145). She writes to distant relatives for stories of her father, and "the honor they gave her father made Joe's trouble easier to bear" (145). And yet, it is this excessive pride in the family past—along with its counterpart, shame in the documents relating to the family present—that will eventually kill her. It seems that the Trexlers, even at this early stage in their history, are incapable of letting go of any documentation relating to themselves: Catherine first gets the opportunity to read damaging documents about her brother when the police find Joe's trunk, which is full of letters and newspaper articles about his troubles, and threaten to throw him into prison if he doesn't buy them off.

It is thus that the trunk gets sent to the family—and thus that Catherine becomes finally overwhelmed by the family shame. For her, the trunk is a Pandora's box, and when she finally opens it she is, as is traditional, sorry: "*The Evidence Taken by the Committee of the Legislature to Investigate the Management of the State Road.* Printed on cheap paper, about a hundred pages. She turned it over carefully to put off finding out the truth. There were many clippings in her scrapbook about truth" (*PINE*, 157). The "truths" of domestic literature—the homilies that she has collected in her scrapbook—have little to do with the documentary "truth" which she is both drawn to and repelled by. She is uneasy, too, with the idea that what is printed about her brother in official documents may not be accurate: "She could not rest until she read the entire report but even now she was telling herself that one man's testimony wasn't to be swallowed whole. Perhaps he was one of those who had tried to get Joe into trouble. As soon as she thought of this, she grew quiet in her bed and felt calm and happy" (160). Yet the power of official documents—whether government testimony or newspaper reportage—is too strong to withstand. She cannot stand to see the Trexler name in this context: "Trexler. On all those stones at the Blue Church and in the old Lutheran graveyard. The plain gray stones. Trexler. Here lies a Trexler. Honest, peaceable Trexlers" (160). The disparity between her previous image of the family and what she reads in the papers in Joe's trunk is too much for her, and reading the papers becomes an addiction: "The dark hot attic was two floors above her and even in the kitchen she could feel the trunk like a hot magnet drawing her up through the very ceiling. Twice she put the iron down and ran up the stairs, her hand on the attic door. But that was weakness, no she would not give in, it was like a vice, it did not show strength of character" (162). The only way she can cope is by burning the documents; however, in destroying the family history, she herself is destroyed, and she collapses in the attic of brain fever, from which she will never recover.

Catherine's inability to come to terms with her family history is repeated in the inability of her sisters to represent her death accurately: "When they talked at all, they told separate stories, Hortense out of her own need for some special romance, that Catherine had died because she had loved and expected to marry a man already married, and Anne that her sister had studied too hard trying to pass her examination" (*PINE,* 166). Thus Hortense recasts Catherine's story as a sentimental novel, and Anne as a cautionary tale against the dangers of becoming a female intellectual. However, Anne's daughters may be able to understand Catherine's story in a different way: "the two younger girls were raw and unsettled in their way of living. Then, this material of Anne Wendel's telling reinforced their struggle and as the debris of bills and worries climbed higher around them, a kind of anger surely mounted in them, still helpless children, who did not want to die" (167). The Wendel girls are unwilling to become martyrs to the family past, but they are unable themselves to resist the pull of family history: "When Amos Wendel finally failed in business, the attic was the hardest spot to tackle. The two younger girls helped their mother all they could with the job of packing and they thought it was about time some of the old papers were burned instead of cluttering up bags and boxes. Somehow they began to read one old letter and then another and for hours they sat there piecing together the dead and gone. Papa's failure got a little faint with all the other failures and successes and the deaths and births crowding in the heat and dimness of one small attic room" (201). At this point, they can only use the family letters as their mother can—as a way of contextualizing the problems of their nuclear family within those of their extended family.

As well as offering consolation for present pain, the family documents will take the place of romantic fiction for the girls: "so much heartbreak in the attic, stored in old letters, gotten out on rainy days, relished because in Oxtail there wasn't even a theatre that amounted to much . . . of course there were the movies, but it wasn't a substitute for real life."[13] The Wendel girls' absolute indifference to mass culture stands in stark contrast to Studs Lonigan. Rather than being drawn to Hollywood's fantasies, the Wendel girls revel in the specificity of their familial past. The girls have a strong sense that they can enlarge themselves as romantic heroines by identifying with tragic female characters in the family past: Musing on her Uncle Aaron's mistress, who had died giving birth to his child, Victoria thinks: "who could help feeling sometimes more like the lovely Mrs. Ferrol, victim of love, than Vic Wendel, a working girl. There was a kind of terrible satisfaction in that kind of unhappiness that no one could explain" (*EW,* 125).

It is only at the very end of *Pity Is Not Enough,* when their mother's brother Aaron is dying, that they begin to see their family history as part of a larger political picture:

Once [Anne] sent Victoria some old papers that had been in Uncle Aaron's office about Joe, because Victoria had been named for him. The Wendel girls poked through them and came on a yellowed newspaper with an account of the Haymarket Riot and the hanging of the anarchists and their silent defense.

It was raining that afternoon and very quiet in the girls' room. They shivered vigorously reading the words of the dead men that leaped at them alive and vigorous after so many years. Seattle in wartime seemed dead. The words carried over the years, they suddenly wondered what that paper had meant to Uncle Joe and they began to talk about him and to feel that the paper had a relation to themselves. (289)

It is this leap from the personal to the political that brings them out into the larger world—just as, on the verge of insanity, it has been Joe's reading about the Haymarket anarchists, rather than any of the tales he has spun for Lenore Blondell, that affect him: "the words seemed to stick in his very skin. When he got up and walked around the room, they were as alive as human voices" (286). Once they begin to see their own family past as political, they can themselves begin to imagine entrance into a larger world: "Now in their bones the Wendel girls felt alive and as if they had a clue to living. They were ready to burn all the old papers but Victoria said that would be a shame to do that to poor Joe. They argued every night with the boarding house people and wished they were on the inside of the strike and got excited about all the news of troubles and wars in the world" (290).

This politicization of the personal is mirrored in Herbst's own structuring of the novel; she liberally quotes old family letters word-for-word, quotes newspaper clippings about her relatives, even uses the real name of the man who abandoned her mother when she was young.[14] One could argue that all writers use autobiographical material in their fiction, yet Herbst goes one step farther. In the final volume of the trilogy, she even incorporates examples of reportage she wrote for *New Masses*, attributing this work in the novel to Victoria Wendel Chance.

Public Events, Private Lives

As Victoria and her sister Rosamond move outward into the public sphere in the second volume, the public sphere also begins to invade the private. We see this perhaps most clearly in an episode in which Bill Haywood and other members of the IWW visit the town of Oxtail to hold a convention. For Victoria, "The excitement of the I.W.W. about to meet was much more real than John Gason's opera glasses" (*EW,* 125)—Gason being a suitor of Victoria's mother in her youth. And at this point, the next part of Victoria and Rosa-mond's political education will literally take place at the kitchen table, as they sit at a neighbor's house with their father and the visiting radicals, who teach them new songs: "The Wendel girls were mortified not to know the words. 'Let's sing it again,' said Vicky. 'Then we can learn it'" (147). Thus the girls are initiated into a new form of political discourse, as they sing "Casey Jones went to Hell a-flying. / 'Casey Jones,' the devil said. 'Oh, fine; / Casey Jones, get busy shoveling sulphur— / That's what you get for scabbing on the S.P. line'" (149). The domestic sphere becomes a site for the Wendel girls' political education. And their sense of belonging to a larger American history can now begin to free them from the shame of poverty in a way the family narrative never could: Remembering an occasion on which her sister Nancy, still a child, was snubbed by the wealthier girls in town, Vicky reflects that

> The swells had swept by the two girls from the wrong side of town and none of Mamma's stories of her family and their exploits could cover the discomfort. Only Ed and a street full of Wobblies singing and making things uncomfort-able for these first families could wipe out the past. (155)

Moving beyond an identification with the family past to identification with radical workers proves empowering for Vicky. As she begins her journey toward becoming a documentarian in her own right, however, she learns that history can be used and misused. Particularly in her relationship with reporter Lester Tolman, we see her examine and discard a number of ways of using, and representing, history. As we move on through the trilogy, we see several characters, but especially Victoria, engaged in a debate on the uses of history in narrative and on the relationship between fact and fiction.

Male journalists, or many of them, are presented as being untrustworthy, since they tend to use their presence at historical events to further their careers or as material for seduction. As Anne Wendel reflects when her daughter Rosamond gets involved with a married journalist, "All Corny Stebbins' talk about Pancho Villa and the war in Mexico where he had been a correspondent didn't pull the wool over Anne Wendel's eyes and hide the fact that he was a man not to be trusted" (*EW,* 29). Interestingly enough, these journalistic seductions compare favorably in Rosamond's mind to more literary compli-ments: She thinks about this while "rubbing a slight bit of rouge on her cheeks that were so like the Blessed Damozel of Dante Rossetti. The one thing she had liked about that fellow Bruce at Wisconsin was his way of linking her to other things. 'You look like the Blessed Damozel,' he said, 'leaning out of heaven,' . . . But how tinny all those words had seemed at last" (35). There is no way that fiction can compete with the "real life" that Rosamond, in particular, is always waiting to begin, and which she feels to a great extent barred from by virtue of her gender. Later, Victoria will experience a kind of shame at letting herself be swept away by the experience of reading literature:

> While she had been in tragic suspense over *The Brothers Karamazov* her father's life had been fraying to pieces and she had been so cut off from the living world as to feel only irritated as he sat silent at the evening meal, his eyes struggling to meet his wife's, grateful for the bread passed him as if he had not earned it. Shut in within her little world, she had not seen her father and his comments on the weather had been only boring and inane. "If this keeps up the crops will be ruined," might have been an empty phrase. (*RG*, 15)

Once again, fiction pales next to fact. Thus Herbst proposes her own type of documentary fiction as an alternative, one that can not only compete with but also enrich the reader's understanding of contemporary events, that, instead of shutting the reader within her little world, can open her up to the possibility of meaningful political action. Within this model, the novel, rather than being a privatizing experience, can be a liberating one, with the potential to galvanize readers to act collectively.

Journalists tend to be timid. Barney Blum, for instance, with whom Victoria is close, considers himself a Socialist but is unwilling to proclaim his beliefs openly: "Socialism wasn't made in a day. And even on the Bulletin, he worked stuff in. It counted to get even a line across, he argued, picking up the evening paper as it lay on the restaurant table, the headlines roaring at him. His own small lost line with the double meaning was hidden somewhere. He turned pages" (*EW*, 43).

They also tend to blame their failure to be more political on the demands of women and of family life. Corny Stebbins, Rosamond's married lover, uses his private past journalistically: "his own past with its continual intrigues with women made good copy when he was talking with the boys" (*EW*, 173). However, Corny "said that if he hadn't hamstrung himself with a wife and kids, nothing could stop him from jumping into the labor struggle" (173). His solution? "Someday he was going to write a novel about it" (169). It is clear, of course, that even this nod toward the world of fiction is nothing but lip service; the trilogy is littered with failed (male) novelists, from the assembly line worker at Vidischis', the Detroit literary salon, to Victoria's husband, the modernist-turned-organizer Jonathan Chance. In at least one instance we see, as we have in *U.S.A.* and *Studs Lonigan,* upward mobility as being both destructive of individual dreams and inextricably linked to feminine aspirations: This occurs in the case of the Rabelais-reading tool bench operator, who "was an expert worker and [who] liked to think that someday he could use words with the same precision as tools" (178) and who is one of the few working-class artists in the trilogy. Like the other men in the trilogy, this man's novel-writing project will eventually fall by the wayside: "His book had slowed up, he was not so much interested in it any more. His girl was putting ideas in his head about being somebody, about getting up in the world and not just squatting at Ford's all his life" (220).

It is these cautious men who will be the first to lose what integrity they have. In the thirties, Barney Blum, after a muckraking story on conditions in the fishing industry in Alaska, "had for some unknown and mysterious reason sold out Sandino. . . . he rose in the estimation of his paper and sailed firstclass for Europe. The last Victoria had heard, he was foreign correspondent in Rome, not exactly taking a shine to Mussolini but uncertain, full of onthe-onehand This and ontheotherhand That" (*RG*, 42). Thus the muckrakers are not necessarily committed to anything more than a headline-grabbing story that will further their own careers.

Of course, the newspapers themselves support the moneyed interests. Just as the publicity that Anne's brother Joe had received in southern newspapers aided his downfall, so the newspapers of Oxtail are quick to propagandize against the IWW: "run them clean out of town. They are the riffraff of humanity, refuse to work and are leeches and parasites" (*EW*, 115).

Yet the man who will marry Victoria, Jonathan Chance, a rebel from a wealthy family, starts his life as a correspondent for a Detroit paper. The reporters with whom he surrounds himself, more than one of whom harbors a dream of writing a great novel, are curiously apolitical: "the prime subjects of the day escaped them. None of them allowed the League of Nations to divert them from Rabelais or from a discussion of the importance of Mr. Cabell on which they were divided. The Spartacans in Berlin met defeat, Rosa Luxemburg was drowned in the Spree, and Karl Liebknecht shot in the back, and the young men at Vidischis' continued to eat their salami and to discuss arts and letters" (*EW*, 178).

It is here that we first encounter Lester Tolman, the journalist for whom Victoria will later work, a man who at this point of his life is "determined that if his life of Balzac were not published he would commit suicide" (*EW*, 179). For Tolman, as for the other journalists, the suffering of others is no more than a scenic backdrop. The sole meaning of conditions in Weimar Germany for Tolman is that "it's wonderful. Took a train to Dresden from Berlin, cost him a dime. Went to the Rhine from Berlin. A quarter. Lives in the best hotels, buys Rhine wine at every meal. One dollar. What a lucky break" (258). Hearing this, Rosamond's husband is taken aback but thinks that "He might think the same if his mother's folks were not all the time writing about the schrecklichkeit and how every day the Egg was leaping to the sky in price, something way beyond them" (259). Yet, for Tolman and his friends, the suffering of the Germans is simply not worth noticing.

If the muckrakers come off badly (at least as exemplified by the sell-out Barney Blum), the modernists come off worse. As the representative modernists of the trilogy, awash in discussions of Gertrude Stein, Ezra Pound, and T. S. Eliot, Tolman and his cohorts exhibit a complete indifference to the suffering of those around them. Tolman, in the same letter in which he notes that German girls are prostituting themselves for postage stamps, cheerfully mentions that "In Munich he was in the center of artistic life . . . spent evenings in the homes of American painters, who, suddenly valuta wealthy, hired whole orchestras for all night parties where orgies went on behind palms and a German with a Harvard accent talked seriously about an incredible little pansy who was trying to push over affairs in the south" (*EW*, 294). Any revolutionary notions on the part of these young men seem divorced from their real conditions: Jonathan, who likes to consider himself quite a radical, relies on monthly supplementary checks from his wealthy father, as does Tolman and as do the others. Tolman is at this point still a literatus: "Tolman said the old realism was dead. The old language was dead. The old literature was dead. It was all dead. People like Joyce were creating a new world of language" (340). Herbst's modernists in general, and Tolman in particular, share the reprehensible traits of Dos Passos's Richard Savage, the Harvard-educated poet, who is a compulsive aestheticizer with no human sympathy. Like Dos Passos, Herbst critiques the modernists while using many of their techniques, albeit adumbrated with a healthy dose of documentary and radical politics.

As a woman, Victoria is excluded to a certain degree from both the journalistic and the literary discussions: As Tolman pontificates about Pound and Joyce, "She felt on the outside, a domestic woman pouring drinks" (*EW*, 342). As Victoria and Jonathan spend more and more time with artists and journalists, we meet a wide array of talented, intelligent women who are subordinate to male artists and writers. There is Victoria herself, with her job at a publishing house, where she is told that she would soon be promoted to an editorship but is instead "fired for a reason that Mr. Ravenwood considered good and sufficient. He wanted to oblige a young friend, a handsome boy from Princeton" (274). There is her friend Cora, the assistant to the little dark thoughtless man who traded on his ability to paint and had this really talented girl running around wiping his brushes, arranging his shows, meeting his friends until she had walked out one day quietly about her business but not to leave him, just to earn money so they could have the good food he liked and she could buy a new mattress as the old one hurt the middle of the back. (277)

When she returns one day to find "some outlandish powder and one of those terribly bright lipsticks" (277), Cora leaves, and she and Victoria take comfort, as Victoria's mother has always done, in the past: "They sat huddled over a table avoiding reference to the lipstick and powder and indulging in their childhood pasts" (278). Deprived of power and security in their own lives, subject to the whims of the men for whom they work, it is still easier at this point for the women to take refuge in the domestic past that is incontrovertibly their domain, a realm that cannot be invaded by men. It will be a long struggle, and a painful one, before women can claim the public domain as their own. As Victoria reflects, "Men often enough thought that they alone were human, that little girls were quiet eggs waiting for the great moment. Most of her early heartaches had come from not being a quiet little egg" (46).

Even though Victoria may have a hard time penetrating the public realm, it is her access to the private past that enables her eventually to become an effective writer. Because she herself has a working-class background, she lacks the shame and discomfort experienced by Jonathan and other ruling-class radicals. Jonathan, who allows himself to be supported by his father's money well into adulthood, cannot help but feel embarrassed about his necessarily false position in regard to his own radicalism: "When his father's check was late, he hated the position he was put in, necessitating a wire or meechy letter" (*EW,* 184). The guilt caused by this disjunction between his class background and his political beliefs makes it impossible for him to reflect on his origins. We see this as he and Victoria go through packages of his childhood possessions and photographs of old lovers: "The Alabama boys would be heading into Talapoosa county now. He picked up the packages, tying them together with quick resolute fingers. 'Let's get started,' he said in a voice that seemed, in its finality, to have called the last train from a station about to be abandoned" (*RG,* 29). It is Jonathan's difficulty in reconciling his personal past with a political present that leads to his blockage as a writer, for as Victoria tells Tolman, "He hated his past and he couldn't seem to make friends with the present" (124). He will be able to do useful political work as an organizer of farmers, certainly, but will be incapable of translating his own experience into terms that can move others to action. Although Victoria, as a woman surrounded by men who would prefer that she be a "quiet egg," has not yet begun to work as a writer, she has access to a wealth of narratives from her familial past which will eventually make it possible.

The trilogy's critique of radical culture is thus as much class-based as gender-based. It is not just that Victoria and other women are barred from full participation in the cultural life going on around them because they are women, but that the men who are getting involved in radical culture have little experience of the workers about whom they write. Victoria gets a job typing a proletarian play by one of the Hollywood writers who "had moved into old farmhouses and installed improvements that were an eyeopener to natives who had struggled along with the old pump and an outdoor backhouse for generations" (*RG,* 62). As she complains to her husband,

> "It's fishy. It stinks. I tried to tell him Jim Barclay didn't talk like that. He makes him talk like an organ-grinder."
>
> "Jim went to highschool. And he's an educated man. Does he think union organizers are wops?"
>
> "I don't know what he thinks, and I don't want to. But he's got two bathrooms." (90)

Clearly, it will be difficult for wealthy writers to write convincing, let alone useful, radical works. The modernist dilettantes of the twenties have jumped on the bandwagon of revolution: "Even frivolous women like Mary Godey held parties for the benefit of the Scottsboro boys at which men and women with good jobs talked glowingly of 'throwing themselves into the class struggle' as if it were a tropical sea" (*RG,* 118).

Naturally, Lester Tolman is not slow to refashion himself in a new, radical mold. When Victoria runs into him in early 1934, he is full of hair-raising stories about political repression in Germany. Rather than regaling Victoria with anecdotes about modernist celebrities, he talks about his suspicions that he was being pursued by the German police:

> It gets you. I'll never know if they had their eyes on me or didn't. It comes to the same thing, I suppose. You wake at night and think you hear steps coming up the stairs, you hear the rustle of someone outside your room. You go on the street, stop to look in a window, and a man stops too. You don't know who he is, you begin to turn gooseflesh, you think he's following you. You cross the street and turn suddenly, ha, there he is, picking his teeth. You turn cold all over, you begin to whistle, you saunter slowly with your hands in your pockets, your heart pounding. Hell, he can't touch you, you're an American, but the next

minute you remember the Englishmen they picked up. You know names. Addresses. You whirl at the corner, pretend you are losing your hat, he is gone. (*RG,* 125)

Although it seems unlikely at best that the opportunistic Tolman has actually been involved in political activity in Germany, he has managed to transform his experience—or his suspicion that he was experiencing something—into a terse narrative worthy of a Hollywood spy movie. Even if one didn't suspect him of trivializing the experiences of real political activists by his breathless autobiographical drama, it would be difficult to view charitably his use of his own presence during the burning of the Reichstag, the story of which he relates to Victoria when they meet: "They were standing on a New York street but the Reichstag had gone up in smoke and fire. The heavy glass dome had crashed and the tunnel of fire had shot up to lick the trees, the sky, the stars. Red had tinged the city; loud blows had sounded late at night on quiet doors" (*RG,* 127). Now, Tolman is horrified at the remembered behavior of Americans who, "in what now seemed to Tolman a callous triviality, were talking about skiing at Partenkirschen" (127). Obviously, the preoccupations of these insensitive Americans are not far from Tolman's own in the letters he had sent home to Victoria and Jonathan. But now he is deeply into his role of committed activist and eyewitness to history, a role he will use to further his journalistic career.

Like so many other of the (male) reporters we meet throughout the trilogy, Tolman's reportage of political events will benefit not the people whose experiences he is narrating but only himself. When Victoria gets a job on a magazine as Tolman's assistant, she must listen to his story over and over again: "he told over and over about his terrible night in Berlin and added many details as time went on. Sometimes through the opened door of his office she could hear his voice saying 'and the glass dome fell' so that the horror of that night, terrible and true, seemed to become diluted with the histrionics of Tolman's voice" (*RG,* 161). This is a cheapening of history and an ignoble use of documentary, something of which even Tolman himself becomes aware. "I have told that story once too often, Lester Tolman thought, as he heard his voice mechanically repeat, 'And the glass dome fell.' He stopped, ashamed at the degeneration of a tragic event to an anecdote" (214). Even Tolman has moments of shame. Despite this, he will continue cynically to use his anecdote to impress equally cynical audiences: "Mr. Pettibone . . . knew all he needed to know about that business in Berlin. This romantic young man was after all representing a very influential magazine; therefore sound" (215). It will be up to Victoria to make meaningful use of her reportage.

Typically, her first experience on the road is not as a reporter but as Tolman's assistant while he reports on the condition of American farmers. Victoria has grown up in Oxtail, Iowa, has watched her father's farm implement business collapse, has herself been living among farmers in Pennsylvania for the past several years. Tolman, by contrast, is shockingly ill informed, yet this does not stop him from assuming a tone of command:

> Lester began to talk about his nerves and to refer to Victoria as his secretary in a pompous commanding voice when talking to government officials. He liked nothing better than drawing up his chair for a good long talk and was continually surprised at the intelligence of the farmers as if he had expected them to be Fiji Islanders. He was somewhat handicapped by not knowing wheat from rye and being uncertain as to the process that determined a steer, but as his notes grew in volume, he cheered and said they would do some great pieces. (*RG,* 244)

Victoria, who must stay in her gender-defined role of secretary, is forced to stand by and watch the story be butchered by Tolman, a man who lacks even the most basic sensitivity to the suffering experienced by the farmers whose lives he is attempting to document: "The trip was reducing Lester Tolman to a state of dependency hard to put up with. He demanded whole-wheat bread where they had nothing but rye, asked for beer where there was milk" (259). It is only when Lester's personal relationship with an actress becomes so stormy that he is incapable of working that he gives Victoria the chance to write the article.

Ironically, it is Lester who takes on a traditionally female role in letting his romantic relationship interfere with his work, while Victoria chooses to work even as her marriage crumbles. The decay of the Chances' marriage forms a backdrop to Victoria's emergence as a journalist. Her mother "had never breathed such foolishness as that she must choose between a 'career' and marriage" (*RG,* 47), but Jonathan, despite his radical politics, cannot quite accept a wife who lives on the same terms as he himself does. Although Jonathan "had even persisted in certain light affairs since his marriage as if to test his wife's capacity for enduring love" (196), he cannot tolerate Victoria's single affair with an exiled leader of the German Communist Party (with whom, significantly, she becomes involved through the process of telling him stories about her past; there have been so few men in her life who really wished to listen). And although Jonathan resents Victoria working to meet a deadline on the night they are reunited after her trip west, it is he who had first departed for his own western trip, one she had asked him to postpone.

"Jonathan answered with a peculiar coldness that he ought to be able to go where he was most needed" (242). After Victoria writes her first story, Jonathan embarks on a relationship with the woman for whom he will leave her. Despite the intensity of Victoria's loss, it is hard not to feel that she may be better off without the petulant Jonathan, who resents his wife's inability to take his defection gracefully: "although he already thirsted for a sight of Leslie Day's face, he was reminded that he had begged Victoria 'not to mind' when he came in the door and she was most certainly and heartily minding. She would not even do that one small thing for him" (302).

A Journalism That Matters

With her marriage in ruins, Victoria departs for her first real assignment, a study of the sugar industry in Cuba. It is here that all the threads of the novel will come together, that Victoria will be able to reconcile her family's past with the historical present, and that she will be able to produce the kind of meaningful documentary that has proved impossible for the middle-class men in the trilogy. The contrast between her incisive, risk-taking, politically effective journalism and the kind of hackwork done by so many of the trilogy's journalists will be highlighted by the presence and actions of the ubiquitous Tolman.

Unlike Tolman, who is "curiously at home" (*RG*, 364) at the American legation, Victoria is frustrated by the pat answers she receives from official sources. She is relieved because "At last Victoria Chance had broken through the ring of United States government employees with their charts and figures, rosebuds and patronizing, through the circle of Cubans in white suits and briefcases to the workers who drifted into the office of the radical paper, Trabajadores, to tell their stories" (358). However, Lester Tolman is perfectly happy to let Ed Bland, the Batista-supporting, racist American attaché, take him to lunch and to see "a real rhumba, not the cheap stuff put on for tourists, but the genuine article, very secret and in fact a religious rite" (365). Lester Tolman, though he may despise it, exists comfortably within the old-boy network of powerful middle-class or upper-class men, a network Victoria is both excluded from and has no desire to join.

> Lester Tolman cursed himself for being a damned fool and playing around when there was work to do. His head bulged like a balloon and he thought of the night before. Bland had taken him to see a "real rhumba" in a shack on the outskirts where a tawdry altar with tinny vases of paper flowers attempted a religious background for a rite that was just dull nonsense, evidently cooked up for suckers. (387)

Tolman may be intellectually contemptuous of this nonsense, but this is just a form of self-hatred for the man he is: His contempt does not prevent him from undertaking a foolhardy trip back to the suburbs to find the rhumba dancer. For Tolman, paid sex with a dancer who works for a tourist racket is about as close as he will get to understanding Cuban culture. Victoria, on the other hand, in her independence from the comfortable supports to which Tolman clings, and in her newfound, albeit unchosen, freedom from entanglements with men, has the courage to follow the guerrillas into the mountains. "Jonathan had gone off into some dark world. Kurt [her German Communist former lover] was in jail. The fires the Realengo men had lighted on their mountains began to seem real to her, as if she had seen them" (*RG*, 361). Although Victoria is in many ways more alone than she had been in years, she draws strength from memories of her family. She is thus simultaneously creating her own first documentary and gaining greater understanding of the family documents and narratives on which she has been raised. As she begins to dig more deeply into the story of the Cuban sugar strike, as she starts to question the official assurances of growing prosperity and to listen instead to a wealth of Cuban voices, her past comes back to her: "At night she gave in to the powers of darkness and lay on her bed as if stunned, asking herself why everything came too late, why the vacation she and Jonathan had needed so badly had come when it could no longer heal; heard again her mother's voice, when dying, rich and tender with longing. . . . In the morning she got out of bed and ate her roll and coffee, sustained by the voices that were waiting, even at that moment, to pour themselves into her ear" (339). There seems to be little difference in strength and importance between the voices in her head and those of the Cubans whose stories she will record. In fact, both the voices of the Cubans and those of her long-dead family members will help her move beyond the pain of her failed marriage and into a new realm of personal freedom and will give her the courage to make the arduous journey to the hideout of the guerrilla leaders. However, Lester, who has always lived safely, who will always be more comfortable speaking to the American flacks than to the Cuban strikers, cannot accept the idea that Victoria has struck out on her own: When he finds out where Victoria has gone, that she is taking some personal risk, he upbraids his informant: "When's she coming back? I don't like it, I can tell you. Her husband will blame me" (366).

Yet Victoria, alone with the strikers, can take care of herself. As she climbs the mountain to the guerrillas' hideout, on a horse "not at all like the swift running pair that used to take her father and herself and her little sister Rosamond over the Iowa roads to distant farms" (*RG*, 370), the past comes flooding back. She thinks of her Uncle Joe, the carpetbagger:

She thought of him now as, step by step, they mounted higher and higher and of the pony that the Indians had shot from under him when he stole into the Black Hills hunting gold, and of the love letters she found when her mother died that a girl Uncle Joe had loved wrote him from Atlanta, Georgia, where he had got into a jam with a lot of fancy politicians so long ago. All the lives of all the people she had known joggled and pressed as if they were beams of light. (371)

Able to live with her past, and unafraid to move into a larger political present, Victoria finds herself liberated from her personal pain. As she approaches the mountain hideout of the revolutionary leaders, "It was a high fine day and she thought with astonishment of her trouble that she had grown accustomed to as a malignant disease with which one must live and finally die. It had not vanished but was as remote as the view of the sugarmills they were soon to see from the turn in the path that corkscrewed through such perilous rocks to little plateaus of safety. A light giddy happiness without rhyme or reason seemed pouring into her from no other source than the sun" (370). Her belief both in the cause of the revolutionary Cubans and in their ability to take the island back from the sugar interests empowers her and sets her apart from Lester Tolman, who thinks that, "Lordalmighty, he wanted to see the Cubans get a decent break for once in their lives but he was a realist. He just happened to know the cards were stacked against them" (390). Thus, when Lester has a chance to interview Batista, he can do nothing afterward but get so drunk that he nearly forgets what Batista has told him, feeling that since the strike is doomed there is no point in staying sober: "There's nothing new. I told you he'd use force and he will. He has already. He's jailed everybody he can. . . . If the strike isn't broken now it will be in a day or so. Force, dear girl, force. Papa love mama" (393). Tolman's getting drunk is the ultimate gesture of futility, since it makes him completely incapable not only of gathering information but of informing the strike leaders of the danger they're in. Lester's unwilling-ness to hope and his lack of Victoria's ability to build relationships with workers doom him to a life of ineffectual cynicism, just as Jonathan's guilt over his own past and his inability to reconcile himself to the present will mean that his own work as an organizer for the Party will boil down to

Talk. Would he never break free of it? . . . For some men talk and the routine of organization begins to seem like death. His feeling of guilt about the many vacillations in his life had made him harden his doubts into acceptance of whatever was assigned him. . . . A fellow like Williams gets kidnapped; Rudd takes his life in his hands and goes on the trail. For better or worse, that was the life he wanted. Instead he was only the dressed-up doorkeeper, opening the door for the rich ladies. (399)

When, finally, we see Jonathan in attendance at a Washington soirée of recently radicalized intellectuals and wealthy society women, it is hard to feel that he has come very far from his early days at Vidischis' in Detroit, and we must agree with him that "Perhaps men like himself were doomed never to become men of action. Only yearners in that direction" (*RG*, 397). It is only Victoria, whose acceptance of her family past and use of it as a political education enable her to become an effective journalist, who will be able to accomplish what Lester and Jonathan only dream of. As we see Victoria for the last time, she has just gotten Jonathan's final send-off. At this point, she can integrate all of the elements of her life, from her present pain and the political crisis she is documenting in Cuba to the memory that opens the trilogy, of listening to her mother reveal the family past while she and her sisters crouch underground, listening as the "slimy caterpillar crawled around us to the south and north, writhing from tree to house, biting corners from barns and nipping tops from silos" (*PINE*, 2). Dazed from the pain of Jonathan's rejection, she thinks that

> A storm was soon coming and would soon break and she must hurry home and shut all the doors and windows. When the storm broke they would have to crouch in the cyclone cellar as they did long ago. Before it came she must hurry and send all the notes she had promised Lester. . . . She sat down and began hammering the typewriter keys. It was like an antidote to poison, the harder she struck the keys, the quieter she became. (*RG*, 403)

The stories of her childhood inform her furiously written notes on Cuba, and it is this final merging of past and present, the use of the personal past for empowerment in the political present, that makes it possible for her to write the kind of journalistic accounts of which Lester Tolman and the other (male) journalists in the trilogy will never be capable. The fact that Victoria's family experience is not extraordinary, that she is not a woman cast from a heroic mold, makes it possible for readers to identify, to think back to their own family stories, to find political meaning in the domestic details of their own lives. For, as Victoria muses as she sits in a bar in Cuba, flooded by memories of the past, "In fact, the family history had some pitch in it, no more, not as much as most family fortunes" (*RG*, 361). We are left with the implication that many readers might, through immersion in their family history, find their own sources of strength to shape the narrative of their times.

Perhaps the greatest strength of the Trexler trilogy is this interplay between past and present, between childhood memory and the documented realities of the familial, as well as the public, past. In this trilogy, which is itself a meditation on the uses of history, Herbst by no means privileges "hard" facts over the twilight state of memory: It is, above all, Victoria's opening herself up to the flood of memories that enables her to find the strength to move out into the public world. Like *U.S.A.*, the Trexler trilogy relies on modernist and journalistic techniques while portraying many examples of failed journalists and bankrupt modernists. Though the Trexler trilogy encompasses a great span of time and space in its portrayal of the Trexler family, it is finally an intimate work and a hopeful one. Whereas Dos Passos ends his trilogy with the image of the radical journalist Mary French overwhelmed by words and by the ineffectuality of radical discourse, Herbst's final vision of Victoria Chance is triumphant—this despite the vicissitudes of Chance's personal life, and despite her sometimes bitter knowledge that shoddy journalism is often what gets printed, that modernists may care more about imagery than about human suffering, and that even proletarian literature may be most successful in its prettified Hollywood version. While what Dos Passos learned best from the modernists were their flashier techniques, such as stream of consciousness and pastiche, Herbst uses the modernists' concern with the subjectivity of memory to delve deeply into character, while never neglecting the world outside her characters' heads: It is those half-remembered stories of her mother's, whispered in a storm cellar while the winds battered the house, that will give Victoria Chance the strength to plunge into the howling storm outside.

CHAPTER FIVE

FINDING A COLLECTIVE SOLUTION

The Living Newspaper Experiment

Josephine Herbst opened up the radical novel to include women as subjects and even offered a model for turning readers into writers and activists, but she faced a problem common to Dos Passos, Farrell, and all the other radical novelists of the thirties. No matter how radicalizing a novel might be, it was designed to be consumed in private. It would take the Living Newspapers of the Federal Theatre Project to offer radical culture in a collective setting—and to enable those audience members to interact not only with one another but with the action taking place onstage.

In the late thirties, Josephine Herbst had two very different experiences working on the Living Newspapers that were the hallmark of the Federal Theatre Project. Although she was not working under the auspices of the government, she used the form that had become familiar to millions of theatergoers, basing her scripts on news events of the day and incorporating documentary sources such as newspapers and the *Congressional Record*. The first such attempt, which was successful, was written to be performed not in a theater but in an auto plant. The second Living Newspaper, written for the League of American Writers, would, for political reasons, never be produced. Both efforts exemplify the attractions and pitfalls of working in one of the most radical literary forms of the Depression decade. The most successful Living Newspapers were not, as might be expected, produced by Communist groups like the New Theatre League or workers' theater groups like the Blue Blouses, or by the Group Theatre, the Stanislavskian company headed by

Harold Clurman, Elia Kazan, and Cheryl Crawford, which was to produce some of the most memorable theater of the Depression era. Rather, the Living Newspapers—documentary, modernist plays that tackled such issues as the need for the passage of an antilynching bill or the problems caused by monopoly capital—were productions of the federal government. Between 1935 and 1939, when the Federal Theatre Project (FTP) was dismantled by Congress, the FTP produced dozens of Living Newspapers, many of them wildly successful, on subjects ranging from the history of syphilis to the problems of urban overcrowding. The Living Newspapers used documentary and modernist pastiche not only to represent American history on the stage but to demand political activism from the mass audiences who saw the productions. In short, these Living Newspapers attempted, and often achieved, the same kinds of radical cultural work as had Dos Passos, Farrell, Herbst, and other radical novelists of the Depression era. Though free from the commercial pressures most writers and theatrical producers faced, the Living Newspapers faced political pressures from conservative congressmen. Thus, as a successful Popular Front form, they also illustrate the difficulties of producing politically charged work under government auspices.

The Federal Theatre Project Begins

The Federal Theatre Project, created in 1935 as one of the three principal Federal Arts Projects (Writers, Art, and Theatre), was headed by Hallie Flanagan. She got her start in George Pierce Baker's theater workshop at Harvard;[1] received an early Guggenheim grant (1926–27) to travel through Europe and Russia, where she studied the theater of Stanislavski and Meyerhold; and became director of the Vassar Experimental Theatre in 1925. Her work at Vassar included a production of *Hippolytus* performed in ancient Greek, as well as productions of such modernist plays as T. S. Eliot's *Sweeney Agonistes* and the works of Pirandello and Ernst Toller. Steeped as she was in modernism, however, Flanagan retained a sensitivity to the political issues of the day. One of her more noteworthy productions at the Vassar Experimental Theatre was her adaptation of a Whittaker Chambers story, published in the March 1931 issue of *New Masses,* on the severe drought that had ruined many farmers the past summer. *Can You Hear Their Voices?* was a critical success, enjoying rave reviews from both *New Masses,* which lauded it as "the best play of revolutionary interest produced in this country," and the *New York Times.*[2]

Given this background, it was unsurprising that Harry Hopkins would pick Flanagan to head America's first national theater, which in the four years of its existence would produce a wide range of performances that would be seen by over thirty million people. Federal Theatre Project productions ranged from marionette and puppet shows to the *C.C.C. Murder Mystery,* developed specifically for workers of the Civilian Conservation Corps, from Christopher Marlowe to Thornton Wilder, from plays in Yiddish, German, and Spanish to circus and vaudeville, from the Federal Ballet to the Negro Playwrights Company. The FTP presented a Suitcase Theatre, bringing plays to audiences who for the most part had never seen a stage show before, and produced plays for the Oklahoma School for the Blind, where blind students performed for their classmates and teachers. From this sometimes dizzying array of productions, performed in every state of the union by state companies under federal supervision, one genre emerged which was to become the hallmark of the FTP: the Living Newspaper.

The Genesis of the Living Newspaper

Although the FTP Living Newspapers concerned American issues and tended to celebrate Americanness in an at times vociferous fashion, the form itself was far from indigenous, having originally developed in the Soviet Union during the 1920s in response to the Soviets' need to disseminate propaganda and public information. The government had few sophisticated tools with which to reach illiterate peasants with important information. The theatrical approaches to agit-prop (agitation and propaganda) that Soviet artists developed would provide future generations of politically conscious artists with the means to transmit radical ideas via accessible forms, such as street theater (used in the 1960s and today by groups like the San Francisco Mime Troupe) and polemical theater which, though staged on a proscenium, still broke down the fourth wall between audience and actors (see, for instance, that classic of American 1930s theater, Clifford Odets's *Waiting for Lefty*). Not all of these theatrical innovations, including agit-ships and agit-trains, were destined to be lasting forms, but the Living Newspapers not only survived but flourished, arriving in America after having spread to the workers' theaters of Germany.

Living Newspapers in their earliest form were simple affairs: Literate members of Soviet workers' clubs would get on the stage and read newspaper articles to their illiterate comrades. It was not long, however, before these performances evolved into something much more elaborate: Readers would wear masks, change costumes, shout slogans into megaphones. Eventually, songs, acrobatics, film clips, and dance were incorporated into the Living Newspapers. In their most developed form, they incorporated mass spectacles—usually reenactments of recent historical events—literary montages of poetry, slogans, and documents; theatrical trials, staged statistics, and mass declamations.

With the explicit support of the revolutionary government's policies on proletarian culture, the Living Newspapers became the most popular form within amateur proletarian theater between 1923 and 1928. Influenced by the cinematic techniques of Eisenstein and by modernist ideas of montage and pastiche, these early Living Newspapers also incorporated elements of farce in their attempt to instruct and persuade. For example, a Soviet workers' club production of *The Most Energetic Workers Fight against All Diseases* featured actors playing bacteria, diseases, and boils of all shapes and sizes and carrying signs condemning unsanitary conditions. The climax involved a duel between the energetic worker and a spirochete. This particular Living Newspaper was part of a national campaign to combat disease and was probably devised by one of the central agencies in Moscow for performance in clubs and in the repertoire of agit-trains.[3]

The American production on a similar theme may have had a somewhat more dignified tone (and perhaps may not have been quite as much fun) but was certainly concerned with some of the same material. A decade or so later the Federal Theatre Project would produce a Living Newspaper entitled *Spirochete*, an antisyphilis drama, based on research supervised by the surgeon general of the United States, Thomas Parran. *Spirochete* traced the disease from its arrival in America via Christopher Columbus to its treatment in the thirties. Like the Soviet production, the American Living Newspaper did more than entertain: During the Chicago production, audience members were invited to undergo a series of blood tests in a makeshift clinic that local health authorities had set up in the lobby of the theater. In the interests of public-spiritedness, two Roman Catholic priests and the daughter of a local health commissioner were the first to volunteer.

The difference between the two antisyphilis productions highlights the transformation the Living Newspapers underwent upon moving from the Soviet Union, through the workers' theaters of Germany, and finally to the United States—that is, from the wackiness of a Soviet actor duking it out with a giant microbe on behalf of the revolution to the good-citizen tone of a New Deal tool, used first to expose the outrages of American history and, later, as a consensus-building tool.

German workers' theater groups, operating under the auspices of the Communist Party, had been exposed to the Soviet Living Newspapers through the touring Moscow Blue Blouse group in 1927. Subsequently, they staged a series of Living Newspapers, which included scenes written by Ernst Toller, Bertolt Brecht, and the ubiquitous Mike Gold. Although it is difficult to be precise about who exactly brought the Living Newspapers to the States, there was in the late twenties and early thirties a flood of refugees from fascism, who founded a whole series of workers' theater groups, from the German-language Proletbuehne[4] to the Hungarian Shock Brigade. In addition, there was the indigenous Workers' Laboratory Theatre, later to become the New Theatre League. These groups discussed, sometimes heatedly, the function of agit-prop theater in the pages of *New Masses* and *Workers' Theatre;* the Prolet-buehne performed regularly for bread lines and strike meetings and worked closely with the Communist Party. The onset of the Depression energized the workers' theater movement: By 1934 there were over 400 agit-prop groups operating in the United States. Although productions such as the Workers' Laboratory Theatre's *Newsboy,* a twelve-minute montage play that employed fragments of a Kurt Joos revolutionary ballet, scenes from a Claire and Paul Sifton play on unemployment, as well as scraps of documentary, used some Living Newspaper techniques and were critically acclaimed, it was not until the WPA Federal Arts Projects began its massive public works program that the Living Newspapers became widely known outside of radical theater circles—that they entered, in fact, the mainstream of American culture.

Living Newspapers were a perfect form for the FTP for many reasons, not the least of which was the enormous number of people—playwrights, re-searchers, actors—needed to stage each production: Since the FTP was de-signed to offer relief to as many theater people as possible, what would have been a Broadway boondoggle became a practical way of employing the great-est possible number of relief workers. Furthermore, as Flanagan wrote, "we felt we should experiment with new forms, particularly since we wished to supplement rather than compete with commercial productions."[5] Freed from commercial pressures, although fettered by the suspicions of right-wing con-gressmen, the FTP Living Newspapers were often able to enact onstage the concerns which the radical novelists of the thirties described in print.[6] An examination of the Living Newspapers as modernist literature reveals their status not simply as New Deal artifacts, not just as an interesting sidelight to theater history, not even as an effective form of political expression, but as the answer to some of the fundamental literary and political questions posed at the American Writers Congress in 1935, and which authors like Dos Passos, Farrell, and Herbst address in their trilogies.

Modernism for the Masses

A comparison between the radical novels of the Depression and the Living Newspapers may seem like a stretch. After all, the FTP productions of Living

Newspapers, unlike the publications of the radical novels of the 1930s, are inextricably bound up with issues of New Deal politics. While an editor, a publishing company, and bookstore owners served as the few mediators between a novel and its audience, the Living Newspaper productions involved dozens, often hundreds, of actors, writers, and directors, all laboring under the watchful eye of the federal government. For political reasons, some Living Newspapers, such as *Ethiopia,* were never produced: This script, which featured a representation of Haile Selassie and incorporated speeches by Roosevelt and Mussolini, was canned before production on the grounds that a Living Newspaper should not be permitted to show a living head of state; the playwright Elmer Rice, who at that time was director of the New York division of the FTP, resigned in protest.

The quality and tenor of Living Newspapers varied regionally, depending on who was director of the FTP unit which produced them and what was the political climate in that area of the country; and they varied over time as the New Deal political objectives developed. The Living Newspapers under the FTP changed significantly over the years, becoming less radical and more devoted to advertisements for New Deal social programs.

Texts of Living Newspapers were also highly various, written as they were by many different people. At this point, because of attribution problems, it is often unclear who the writers even were—at a certain point many collaboratively written scripts began to be attributed to a single author, Arthur Arent. They covered topics ranging from the history of syphilis to the problems of flax production in Oregon to the influence of the movies on the way we think about our own romantic lives.

And yet, it is still possible to talk about the Living Newspapers as an effective answer to the questions that writers like Dos Passos, Farrell, and Herbst had been posing in their novels. At their best, the Living Newspapers represented American history to a mass audience in a way that not only enabled spectators to see how different constituencies had shaped the course of current events but also offered them ways to change the course of future events. They used modernist techniques to create an art form that would destabilize audience expectations while remaining accessible. They used documentary techniques in a way that enabled viewers both to understand the importance of journalism as a political tool and to critique the unscrupulous use of documentary by such sources as the Hearst newspapers and the newsreel corporations. The creators of the Living Newspapers, thus, addressed the deep ambivalence of Dos Passos, Farrell, Herbst, and other radical writers about the effectiveness of mass culture, of the comforting, expected forms that could serve to lull audiences into accepting ideas which they shouldn't. They demonstrated how to shake up audiences while remaining comprehensible and communicative.

Although there are many similarities between the Living Newspapers and the trilogies of Dos Passos, Farrell, and Herbst, there are also important differences. Generally speaking, the novels focus on individual struggle—how to become an effective political agent within the context of the American scene, like Dos Passos's Mary French or Herbst's Victoria Chance, or simply how to negotiate a tenuous survival while caught in the historical trap of the Depression, like Farrell's Studs Lonigan. By contrast, the Living Newspapers are largely uninterested in individual character: Typically, the economic system and American history play a more vivid role, in a sense, than any human character. The Living Newspapers tend to be less concerned with the question of how a given individual—whether it be Mary French, Studs Lonigan, or Victoria Chance—will survive or discover a meaningful identity for him or herself than with how America as a nation will at least survive and at best flourish. The trilogies of Dos Passos, Farrell, and Herbst ask pointed questions that challenge the prevailing forms of radical fiction: Dos Passos asks how to use the novel form to write persuasive political rhetoric, given the inefficacy or political unsuitability of the available forms of discourse; Farrell, how to write radical novels for a male, working-class audience immersed in mass culture and embracing a definition of masculinity that saw reading anything but pulp fiction as a feminine activity; Herbst, how to expand the audience for radical literature to include women.

The creators of the FTP Living Newspapers, like Dos Passos, Farrell, Herbst, and other radical novelists of the thirties, assume that a knowledge of history is necessary for an understanding of contemporary problems and, to this end, make use of documentary sources to provide this historical background. In the novels, the documentary underpinning was supplied by Dos Passos's Newsreels, the newspaper headlines read by Farrell's Studs Lonigan, and the family letters and newspaper clippings provided by Herbst. The scripts of the FTP Living Newspapers were based on research by an extensive staff of journalists and were furnished with footnotes. This stress on the use of documentary sources was explicitly mandated by the directors of the FTP, who, in the manual entitled "Writing the Living Newspaper" produced by the FTP for the benefit of its staff, wrote that

> Few bravura scenes have the convincing impact of an adroitly presented fact. Authenticity should be the guiding principle on Living Newspaper production. Let it be kept in mind that some of the most fascinating and also dramatic statements are to be found in the daily columns of the press. Assemble a wide,

firm foundation of factual material and upon this can be built the architecture of good theater.

Employing an existing cinematic metaphor, the authors went on to advise that

> The research department of any Living Newspaper group can well be likened to the lens of a camera. The sensitive film will present a picture only as effective as the potentialities of the lens—its sharpness, its accuracy, its depth of focus. Before the shutter is released the lens must be carefully aimed. And so, before any real progress is made in doing the script, the research department must have done the spade work.[7]

In fact, the staffs of the Living Newspapers were in many cases dominated by researchers: As Morris Watson pointed out in a *Scholastic* article, "As many as 400 research assignments have been given on a single subject, and the report on a single assignment frequently runs to 100,000 words."[8]

From the raw research material unearthed by this "spade work" would be created a drama that, rather than offering audiences "tales of small triangular love stories in small rectangular settings," would seek "to dramatize a new struggle—the search of the average American today for knowledge about his country and his world; to dramatize his struggle to turn the great natural and economic forces of our time toward a better life for more people."[9]

The Ideology of the Living Newspapers

Although the FTP pamphlet stresses the importance of offering audiences a lesson in economics and history in the interests of effecting social change, it explicitly denies that this lesson will be presented within a Marxist framework. "Federal Theatre, particularly in its Living Newspapers, is trying to create theater on other terms; to make it out of every day factual material; to dramatize the struggle not of two men for one woman, not of one psychological trait against another psychological trait in a man's soul, not of one social class against another social class."[10] This passage may have been included as a politically necessary salve to a suspicious Congress: Throughout its four-year history, the Federal Theatre Project was attacked by the Dies committee, or the House Committee on Un-American Activities, which charged that the FTP hired Communists and that it presented communistic plays to communistic audiences.

FTP pamphlets aside, it is by no means absolutely true that Living Newspapers and other Federal Theatre productions did not represent the struggle between one class and another. A quick look at a Federal Theatre Project play such as "Revolt of the Beavers" is enough to cast doubt on this official assertion. This was a children's production that generated a great deal of controversy over its depiction of a revolution in Beaverland, in which " 'The Chief' and his cohorts force the other beavers to supply the bark for a wheel that produces clothes and food. The chief and his pals are the only ones with blue sweaters, roller skates and ice cream. When the working beavers object, they are replaced by 'barkless' beavers. Oakleaf, an exiled beaver, a beaver professor, and two children organize a beaver club, and establish a new order where all things are shared by all."[11] It would be hard to get more class-conscious than this.

In fact, the instruction manual on how to write a Living Newspaper seems ideologically equivocal at best, for while claiming to eschew a class-conflict model of art, the authors of the pamphlet see the characters of their dramas as "the physical, human, manifestation of forces that are larger and more important than individual psychology. They are individuals whose psychology is, in fact, the very product of these forces." The forces to which the writers refer are not spiritual or emotional forces; rather, they are economic forces: "When we present a scene in a Living Newspaper of an individual committing suicide because of poverty and hunger are we putting before the audience a study of that individual's morbid psychology? Rather, we tell of the even more malign nature of the forces that motivated the act: unemployment, lack of proper relief, etc."[12] The characters of the Living Newspapers are thus individuals at the mercy of historical forces. However, they are also characters who often manage, during the course of the drama, to reimagine themselves as historical agents rather than historical victims.

Perhaps because of the radical qualities of many of the FTP productions—qualities which would all too quickly draw down the wrath of conservative legislators—the government employees in charge of the Living Newspapers were quite eager to stress their American (and implicitly nonradical) qualities. Arthur Arent, who supervised the writing of such Living Newspapers as *Triple-A Plowed Under* and *Injunction Granted,* wrote that "I find that the number of claimed birthplaces of this particular medium is exceeded only by the number of beds The Father of Our Country and the Wealthiest Citizen of His Time is supposed to have slept in." After running through the list of possible birthplaces for the Living Newspapers, Arent concludes: "I never seem able to locate anybody who saw [an earlier] one. Nor have I ever seen the script of such a production. And so, while admitting the possibility of a whole avalanche of predecessors, I deny their influence and, for the balance of the article at least, that will be that."[13]

Arent was not alone in his historical amnesia. Hallie Flanagan, the director of the Federal Theatre Project, was equally reluctant to dwell on the origins of the Living Newspapers. "Although living newspapers were sometimes compared by critics to the broad cartoons of news seen in London music halls or on Russian or German stages, they were not like them; to the best of my knowledge they did not resemble anything hitherto seen on the stage." Rather than draw a direct line between the FTP Living Newspapers and their Bolshevik antecedents, she chose to link the form to classical (and nonradical) sources:

> Of course, certain of their elements had been used, for like all so-called new forms the living newspaper borrowed from many sources: from Aristophanes, from the Commedia dell'Arte, from Shakespearean soliloquy, from the pantomime of Mei Lan Fang. Being a flexible technique and only in its beginning, it still has much to learn from the chorus, the camera, the cartoon. Although it has occasional reference to the Volksbuhne and the Blue Blouses, to Bragaglia and Meierhold and Eisenstein, it is as American as Walt Disney, the March of Time, and the *Congressional Record,* to all of which American institutions it is indebted.[14]

In soft-pedaling the Living Newspapers' revolutionary origins, and in presenting them as a form uniquely suited to American themes and audiences, Flanagan was skillfully deflecting the kind of accusations that the Dies Committee would later use successfully to shut down the Federal Theatre Project altogether: accusations that the Living Newspapers were subversive, un-American. Although these remarks may have been politically motivated—indeed, politically necessary—they also reflected a larger truth about the FTP Living Newspapers. For, in their modernist, documentary reworkings of American history and American issues, the Living Newspapers engaged many of the same questions about Americanism as did the radical writers of the thirties.

From Page to Stage

Although Dos Passos, Farrell, and Herbst reveal themselves to be deeply concerned with issues of American identity, the Living Newspapers, finally, would go a step farther. While the trilogies are challenging in various ways, they all allow readers some of the traditional rewards of literature, such as the luxury of identification with individuals and with individual perspectives. Living Newspapers, at their best, force audiences to consider the American dilemma as a whole. They do not permit identification with characters—in fact, they barely allow individuals to exist. They refuse to allow the fortunes of one group—be that group the farmers of *Triple-A Plowed Under* or the senior citizens of *Townsend Goes to Town,* a play about a then-current proposal for old-age relief—to be shown unlinked to the fortunes of another group, such as consumers affected by higher farm prices or young people forced to pay higher taxes to support pensions for their elders. Instead of individuals reading activist literature alone in private spaces, groups in public spaces would view the Living Newspapers, providing a built-in opportunity for exchange and debate.

That the very act of reading was a private one, and thus not particularly conducive to sparking exchange, was a problem of which some writers were keenly aware. As Georg Lukacs wrote in 1936, "The genuine writers of this period begin with an ardent wish to conquer the isolation of literature and the aestheticism, the artistic self-satisfaction and self-sufficiency which flow from it; and in their desire to make literature an effective force in the society of their time—which they take as given—they naturally look around for allies."[15] Victoria Chance, the protagonist of *Rope of Gold,* feels guilt at having become so immersed in *The Brothers Karamazov* that she failed to notice that her father's farm was going under. Josephine Herbst dealt with the problem of the isolated reader by working collaboratively with striking auto workers to create art that bore a direct relation to the problems they were facing.

In 1937 Josephine Herbst and Mary Heaton Vorse were commissioned by the *Daily Worker* and *New Masses* to cover the six-week-old General Motors strike then in progress. While in Flint, Michigan, the two women decided to write a short Living Newspaper for the entertainment of the sit-down strikers inside the plant. The title of the production was to be *Strike Marches On,* a reference, of course, to the slogan of the "March of Time" screen magazines which both Dos Passos and Farrell had incorporated into their trilogies. Like the Living Newspapers of the Federal Theatre Project, *Strike Marches On* would be a historically based, well-documented representation of a current political or social problem, combining modernist techniques, cinematic references, and even vaudeville to present its message to audiences that cut across class and racial lines. Although the Living Newspapers became most famous in this country through the productions of the Federal Theatre Project, nongovernmental productions, such as the one written by Herbst and Vorse, were not unique.[16] In fact, *Strike Marches On* was not wholly free of the involvement of WPA personnel: Morris Watson, managing producer of the FTP Living Newspaper unit, accepted an invitation to speak on behalf of the striking Flint workers and had an important job to do once he arrived at the plant.

Strike Marches On featured a cast of more than eighty auto workers and their relatives, playing themselves and others involved in the strike (Watson had to press a well-known activist into playing the part of the stool pigeon, as this was a role that almost nobody else was willing to shoulder). Watson's real work entailed persuading the cast to actually perform the play, which reached performance readiness around the time that the strike came to a conclusion, when most of the strikers were much more interested in returning to their prestrike lives than in acting. *Strike Marches On,* performed in the local union hall at the strike's victory celebration, played to capacity crowds.[17]

Although *Strike Marches On* was a great success, Herbst had less luck with the Living Newspaper she attempted later the same year. Jerre Mangione, who worked for the Federal Writers Project, was impressed by his frequent house guest's stories of covering the Spanish Civil War—enough so that he persuaded her to make another venture in the Living Newspaper genre. The result, a play entitled *The Spanish Road,* was written by Herbst and Nathan Asch for the purpose of raising funds for the League of American Writers, the organization which had, in 1934 (in preparation for the Communist Party's Popular Front strategy), replaced the Party's thirty John Reed clubs operating across the country. However, although the league was enthusiastic about Herbst and Asch's finished script, the local Theatre Union, an organization closely allied with the Communist Party, determined that the work suffered from "some basic ideological flaws" and demanded that the writers "clarify the message." Asch and Herbst accused the producer of trying to reduce the script to "a stupid propaganda vehicle reflecting a narrow Stalinist-Communist point of view." Eventually, production plans were shelved.[18]

There were good reasons for Herbst's attraction to the Living Newspaper form. Of course, all theatrical performances, by their public nature, provide a solution to the problem of novel reading's private nature, but the political and historical concerns of the Living Newspapers distinguished them from most other plays. Political dramas like Odets's *Waiting for Lefty* (1935) offer many of the same elements as a Living Newspaper: an explanation of a political situation, in this case the New York taxi drivers' strike; the use of many characters to illuminate the situation; and finally, a degree of audience participation at the end of the play, when audience members are asked to join in the strike vote. However, the Living Newspapers go beyond this model in their insistence on a historical perspective that is wide as well as deep. They offer a focus not only on individual characters but on entire groups of people. In *Triple-A Plowed Under,* the effects of farm subsidies are seen not only on farmers but on consumers, the unemployed, the affluent, country and city bankers, salespeople, sharecroppers. Living Newspapers also provide a historical overview, which they insist is necessary to understand fully the problem under consideration. The history in *Triple-A* reaches back as far as the First World War, and some Living Newspapers go much farther: *One-Third of a Nation,* a Living Newspaper about inadequate housing, goes back to 1705 to explain the roots of the problem. And whereas *Waiting for Lefty* has distinct, named characters, the Living Newspapers tend to feature archetypes.

Yet even as character is subsumed to situation, to historical tableau, as it were, the Living Newspapers do not maintain an ironic distance from their audiences. Because the plays contain documents, such as speeches or newspaper reports, that audiences have seen or heard elsewhere, the Living Newspapers, by decontextualizing or, rather, recontextualizing political or factual statements, encourage audiences to reexamine current events.[19] For example, a Supreme Court decision, when presented within the context of a detailed lesson on economics, may look very different to audiences who are not accustomed to thinking in sophisticated economic and political terms. Living Newspapers expect a good deal from their audiences: They demand a willingness to take on all the burdens of citizenship, to understand the history and political context within which decisions affecting the country are being made. Having done this, they sometimes explicitly demand action from their viewers: to vote, to write to Congress, even to form new political parties.

Issues of national identity are played out in a number of Living Newspapers; I have chosen to examine two that approach the same theme—the problems faced by farmers during the Depression—in very different ways. *Triple-A Plowed Under,* which was wildly successful, and *Dirt,* which remained unproduced, illustrate ways in which the Living Newspaper form can be used as political art in its best sense and ways in which the form can be used to whip up nativist hysteria. However, both plays reveal a deep concern with the meaning of American citizenship as seen in the light of American history.

Triple-A Plowed Under

Triple-A Plowed Under, first produced at the Biltmore Theatre in New York in March 1936, was one of the great successes of the FTP, and it represented as well a test of the form itself. As Hallie Flanagan writes in *Arena,* her memoir of her work on the FTP, the cast demonstrated a good deal of initial resistance to the project: "some of the actors complained that there was no plot, no story, no chance to build up a character, no public interest in the theme, 'Who in New York cares about the farmer, about wheat, about the price of bread and milk?' "[20] It was unclear that this experimental form would be able to engage audience (or even actor) interest, given that it was lacking the traditional structure of the Broadway play, which emphasized individual character development and private life to the general exclusion of public considerations. And, in specifically political terms, could theater be used to build a national identity, to get New York audiences to identify with the issues and problems facing midwestern farmers, a group separated from them by a vast geographical and cultural chasm? The answer, as it turned out, was yes. Flanagan and the actors "ended with a mutual agreement: the actors were to give us all they could through the first performance; if the play failed we were to drop all plans for future living newspapers." This turned out to be unnecessary. "From the time the reviews came out saying that in spite of faults *Triple-A* undoubtedly represented a new theater technique, the actors, like most converts to anything, became apostolic in their zeal."[21]

In general, *Triple-A* received positive reviews: In the *New Theatre* article, "A Worker Looks at Broadway," John Mullen wrote that "Until I saw the WPA show, I had the idea . . . that the only groups attempting to grapple with serious problems were the New Theatre groups and the Group Theatre. I take it back . . . the WPA show is so good that it makes your hair tingle and sits you on the edge of your seat."[22] Mainstream as well as radical publications reviewed the show favorably: The *Saturday Evening Post*'s critic noted that "It may be said for the skill and technique that with few and simple properties, by means of graphs and symbols, with a language as terse as newspaper headlines, and by a trick of offstage voices breaking in with ominous repetitions of a single phrase or a few words of explanatory text, the amount of suggestion sometimes evoked by a scene lasting two or three minutes was extraordinary."[23] The *New Yorker*'s Robert Benchley wrote that "The Living Newspaper has shown [that] a subject as statistical as wheat production can be put on the stage with considerable excitement and dramatic value."[24] Some reviews highlighted the political drama surrounding this theatrical event. It is clear from reading these just how controversial the play was. The *New York Times* critic set the scene in the opening lines of his review: "In an atmosphere bristling with tension, uncertainty and blue-coated guardians of the law, the Living Newspaper of the Federal WPA Theatre finally got its first edition 'on the street,' as it were." Referring to the censorship of *Ethiopia,* the reviewer expressed surprise that "no hand appeared from aloft against the showing of 'Triple-A Plowed Under,' which is obviously loaded with a charge of controversial dynamite." Praising the show as "hard-biting, necessarily sketchy but frequently brilliant," the reviewer concluded that "The Living Newspaper must be credited with a pretty sensational beat."[25] *Variety* reported "loud applause and hisses mixing in reception of the initial performance." Failing to understand that the Living Newspaper form eschewed star turns in favor of collective achievement, the reviewer complained that "There are few chances offered to display individual effort" and dismissed the play as "propaganda for the AAA."[26]

The play was written collaboratively by a group of reporters and dramatists, based on the outcome of a brainstorming session involving Joseph Losey, Arthur Arent, the newspaperman Morris Watson, and Hallie Flanagan. *Triple-A* considered the social and political implications of a recent Supreme Court decision on farm subsidies by examining the decision within the historical context of farmers' experiences in the twenties and thirties. Using modernist techniques and employing documentary sources, it provided the means for audiences not only to understand and empathize with the problems of the farmers but to see these problems in the context of a larger political mosaic.

Triple-A Plowed Under demands a great deal of its audience. Not only is the play highly stylized, but unlike most Broadway productions it features as a central character not a person but an entire nation, in which groups are forever pitted against one another. This is a nation in which a gain by one group means a loss by another, and in which the struggle to find a workable solution to this problem ends with a proposal for the formation of a farmer-labor party (a proposal then on the table by the Communist Party). Ultimately, the play is not about people but about an economic system. Unlike most plays, its most vivid moments are in speech; at times, *Triple-A* seems almost willfully to eschew the staples of drama. Thus the most potentially "dramatic" scenes—those of mob violence and strikes—take place in the dark or even offstage. Instead, onstage, audiences are presented with a complicated lecture on economic history.

The play opens with a scene that recalls the propaganda slogans so skillfully crafted by the Creel committee during the First World War—slogans very similar to those produced by J. W. Moorehouse in *U.S.A.* The Loudspeaker voice opens the play with a simple introduction: "Triple-A Plowed Under. (*Curtain rises.*) 1917–Inflation."

> *At rise red spotlight is on* SOLDIERS *marching in continuous columns up ramp placed upstage left. After a brief interval there is an increasing volume of marching feet. The entire scene is played behind scrim. Spotlight on three* SPEAKERS *and crowd of* FARMERS. SPEAKERS *stand on highest level, right. Some of the farmers stand on lowest level, right, and some at stage level, right.*

Even within these first stage directions, some things are clear. By playing the scene behind a scrim, individual characters are literally effaced, made abstract. Soldiers are represented not heroically but rather as a rhythmic force. The abstraction of the stage directions is mirrored in the text:

FIRST SPEAKER: Your country is at war.

SECOND SPEAKER: Your country needs you.

FIRST AND SECOND SPEAKERS (*together*): If you can't fight—farm.

FIRST SPEAKER: The fate of our country rests upon the farmers.

SECOND SPEAKER: Do you want our land invaded?

FIRST SPEAKER: Do you want your daughters ravaged by Huns?

WOMAN: Farmer, save the nation! (*Trumpet.*)

FIRST SPEAKER: The boys in the trenches need the men in the fields.

WOMAN: Farmer, save our boys.

SECOND SPEAKER: Every bushel of barley is a barrel of bullets.

WOMAN: Farmer, save democracy. (*Trumpet.*)

FIRST SPEAKER: Every hand with a spade is a hand-grenade.

WOMAN: Farmer, save our honor. (*Trumpet.*)

SECOND SPEAKER: Every man behind a plow is a man behind a gun.

WOMAN: Farmer, save civilization. (*Trumpet.*)

FIRST SPEAKER: Every head of cattle can win a battle.

WOMAN: Farmer, save our flag. (*Trumpet.*)

FIRST SPEAKER: Plant more wheat.

SECOND SPEAKER: Plant more potatoes.

FIRST SPEAKER: More corn!

SECOND SPEAKER: More food, more seed, more acres!

SECOND AND FIRST SPEAKER (*together*): More! More! More!

WOMAN: Farmer, save the world![27]

We start off here with a notion of Americanism based on the idea that the interests of all Americans are synonymous, that a man behind a plow is truly equivalent to, interchangeable with, a man behind a gun. The task of the play will be to reject this idea of what it means to be American and to replace it with another, more complicated version, to show the inadequacy of official sloganeering in nation formation and ultimately to espouse a more democratic version in which citizens come to reinterpret their history, using an analytic framework rather than a reliance on received ideas about history and current events, and to take responsibility for rewriting the future according to their own lights.

The hypnotic quality of the repetition, both in the increasing demands placed upon the farmer, from saving the nation to saving the world, and in the rhyming of the war propaganda slogans ("Every hand with a spade is a hand-grenade," etc.), serves to alienate the audience from the material. It diffuses the meaning and concentrates audience attention on the sound of the words, making it difficult to experience the emotional impact of the slogans. It is the belief in simplistic patriotic slogans that will lead the nation astray, and as the play continues, the poverty of slogans and of oversimplified explanations becomes clear.

In the next scene, announced as "The 1920's. Deflation" (11) by the Loud-speaker, an exporter tells a jobber that he can no longer ship his wheat because the Europeans are raising their own. "I'm afraid we won't ship more wheat to Europe unless they have another war," he says. The jobber responds: "That's a short explanation of a serious problem." When the exporter attempts to build an alliance between them by telling him that, "Well, anyway, you see why I can't take your shipment" (11), the jobber refuses to acknowledge that they are on the same side, that their interests are in any sense synonymous: "I don't see a damn thing" (11). This refrain, "I don't see a damn thing," is echoed in ensuing scenes by a country banker who cannot understand why a city banker is calling in his paper and by a farmer who cannot understand why the country banker is foreclosing on his mortgage. Simplistic explanations of the economic situation, most of them predicated on the notion, echoed by the banker to the farmer, that the farmer's poverty will be assuaged when "the big boys will begin to feel it, and maybe they'll get up another war" (13), are inadequate. As the farmer tells the banker, the human cost of such an enter-prise would be far too great, and besides, "by God, I wouldn't raise wheat for another war" (13).

Initially, the discussion is one in which sound and rhythm are more impor-tant than meaning. It is an argument for farm production based on a kind of emotional nationalism, one in which the war itself, for which greater produc-tion is being exhorted, is represented by nothing more ominous than march-ing silhouettes. The inflammatory propaganda slogans—"Do you want your daughters ravaged by Huns?"—are effective only if their auditors do not examine their content too closely. Though the feverishly patriotic atmo-sphere, enhanced by trumpets, may be effective in encouraging farmers to plant more wheat and corn, and may seem initially to be a display of Ameri-can unity, it is quickly shown to be based on a false premise. The poverty of these slogans is made clear in the second scene, where they are seen as inade-quate for smoothing over the class conflicts that we begin to see in evidence: The interests of the farmers are clearly not synonymous with those of the banker. In addition, the war, which we have seen only as a stirring exercise, about which we have heard no discussions of loss and bloodshed, is now seen to have been a debacle for the marching soldiers. As the farmer tells the banker, "Every day I get veterans asking for a handout, and not a one of them would go back to war" (13). Thus the vision of American unity with which the play opens is revealed, on closer inspection, to be a triumph of form over substance. Indeed, the entire play can be viewed as a deconstruction of those patriotic slogans which Dos Passos's advertising magnates so carefully construct and as a move toward a more nuanced understanding of American history and political events.

Indeed, it is in *Triple-A*'s effective use of the dramatic tools at its disposal—most specifically, in its use of many disparate voices to create a mosaic of possible viewpoints—that it differs most starkly from *Dirt*. Both plays document the development of the Farmers' Holiday Association, led by Milo Reno—a militant group formed for the purpose of holding grain, meat, and milk off the market until prices rose enough to cover the cost of production. To this end, members barricaded roads, stopped every truck bound for town, turned cattle loose, and emptied milk into ditches. Farmers' Holiday Association members refused to pay interest, debt, or taxes until Henry Wallace, the secretary of agriculture, responded to their demands and helped keep them from losing their land.

The violent protests of these farmers are documented very differently in these two plays, however. We can see this perhaps most clearly in a scene in which Milo Reno's rise and fall are enacted. *Dirt* dwells almost lovingly on the violence wrought by striking farmers. In contrast, *Triple-A* moves from a speech in which Reno lays out his five-point program for farmers to his perhaps less than heroic final appearance: "You can no more stop this movement than you could stop the Revolution of 1776. I couldn't stop it if I tried" (15), Reno declares, invoking iconic American images of revolution. And yet we quickly see how easily used this rhetoric is, and how insubstantial it can be:

Off stage voices shout, "Strike! Strike!" Follow RENO *with spot to stage left, where light comes up on* COMMISSION MERCHANTS *behind desk. Lights shift to left.*

SCENE FOUR-B

PRESIDENT OF COMMISSION MERCHANTS (*holding out contract and pen to* MILO RENO): Mr. Reno, I have here the terms drawn up by the committee of Commission Merchants. . . . We want you to call off that strike. . . . Will you sign? (*Pause.* MILO RENO *turns to where off stage voices are still rumbling "Strike! Strike!" He turns back, and signs.*) (16)

Not only does the play manage to effectively telescope a great deal of action into a single paragraph—in contrast to *Dirt*, and by way of explaining why *Triple-A* is roughly half the length of its counterpart—but it also manages to present a wide variety of ways to understand the situation. If *Dirt*'s natural forum is the soapbox harangue, *Triple-A*'s is the organizational meeting, a democratic institution in which everybody has an equal opportunity to speak and in which an array of views can be heard. Thus one speaker may declare that "We've been sold out! We've been cheated and robbed. Milo Reno declared a holiday for Milo Reno—not for us. Forget his crazy schemes!" (17). However, another speaker may point out that "talk is cheap. . . . Tons and tons of dirt are being thrown at Milo Reno. This is all a stunt to take your mind off the real situation—the milk situation" (18). Though his pleas to stick with Reno may eventually get him booed off the stage, his voice is at least heard. Farmers and audiences alike are presented with a chance to view Milo Reno's betrayal not in personal terms but as part of a larger economic picture—not as a question of character and honor, individual decision making, but as a minor act in a larger economic picture.

In fact, the speaker's suggestion that the vitriol being heaped on Reno is a ploy to distract attention from the crisis at hand has larger implications. It can be seen as a critique of the kind of art that focuses on character at the expense of the bigger picture, rather than examining how economic realities impinge on and change those stories. Again and again, the play refuses to glamorize or in any way romanticize the violence of the striking farmers; rather, it is depersonalized, deeroticized. When farmers overturn a milk truck, as they do as well in *Dirt*, we do not see the glee of the farmers, the pleading of the truck driver, the messy results of the incident. Rather, the episode takes place entirely in the dark, and the trucker's voice is not heard at all. The effect is one of businesslike efficiency: As the truck nears, as evidenced by its headlights,

SECOND MAN: Now! (*The* MEN *leap out from behind the boulder and rush off left. A single voice is heard off stage—clearly—with great but quiet determination.*)

VOICE OFF STAGE: Get down off that truck . . . (*There is a split-second pause.*)

TWO OR THREE VOICES: Dump the milk! (*From off stage is heard the ripping and smashing of boxes being hurled from the truck. . . . A moment of this and then one voice, clear and loud.*)

VOICE: Turn over the truck. Push! (*A moment . . . then the final terrific crash as the truck is turned over.*) (20)

It is as though the truck driver himself does not exist. He is certainly irrelevant in the larger scheme of things; in fact, his absence serves only to highlight the idea that this is a play about the problems facing America, not about individual experience. To focus on the terror of a trucker ambushed in the night would only distract from the larger points the play is making. A similar coolness is evidenced in the scene in which, as the Loudspeaker announces, "Farmers lose their land—their homes—unpaid mortgages are foreclosed; land is sold at public auction. The farmers take matters in their own hands" (21). Although the farmers who buy the farm of one of their neighbors for twelve cents may be able to do so only by forcibly preventing outsiders from making higher bids, the violence in the scene is implied, the threat softpedaled. As the auctioneer invites a stranger to make a real bid, the farmers spring into action:

(STRANGER *opens his mouth to speak. He starts to raise his arm. The* FIRST NEIGHBOR *grabs his hand.* THIRD NEIGHBOR *spins him around, tips his hat over his eyes and the two lead him off,* THIRD NEIGHBOR *speaking.*)

THIRD NEIGHBOR: . . . and when it rains around these parts, Mister, it pours. And you ought to see the pigs down to my place. It's the likeliest litter of little devils anybody ever seen. (*His voice trails off as they disappear off stage. The auctioneer's jaw sags. He looks at the* SHERIFF *and tries to catch his glance.* SHERIFF *deliberately turns his back and starts whittling.*) (23)

Indeed, the play moves quickly from these scenes of danger and possible violence to another meeting—this time of the Farmers' National Relief Conference. The secretary of the organization, whose speech is quoted from the *New York Times,* makes points that are reasonable, demands and suggestions that are based on a consideration of economic realities weighed against human needs. For instance, he says that "three-quarters of the farmers, which economists consider as surplus, cannot really be considered as such. Neither can they consider their crops as surplus when they know that there are millions of unemployed who lack the very things which they produce and cannot sell" (24). The speaker then brings forth an alternative method of viewing the situation, one which would allow for a consideration of both human and economic factors: "It was the recognition of this ironical situation which led the farmers of Iowa to give milk to the unemployed of Sioux City during the farm strike there" (24). This speaker's perspective is ratified in the next scene, in which the Loudspeaker points out that, "as our economic system now works, the greater the surplus of wheat on Nebraska farms, the larger are the breadlines in New York City" (25). The groups in this scene, consisting of a farm family on one side of the stage and a city family on the other, stand in contrast to the farmers and soldiers of the first scene. Instead of the false unity of the first scene, with its pretense that the interests of all Americans are synonymous, the second scene makes it clear that, while the two groups may be living in the same country and under the same economic system, they perceive their interests, not without justification, to be in opposition:

WORKER: We starve and they told us you had food in your fields.

FARMER: Food is in our fields but they told us you would not pay the cost of its harvesting.

WORKER'S WIFE: We had no money.

FARMER'S FIRST SON: We raised eggs and milk, and you wouldn't buy them.

WORKER'S FIRST SON: We had not the fifteen cents to pay.

FARMER'S FAMILY (*aroused*): Fifteen cents for milk?

FARMER: We only got three.

WORKER'S FAMILY (*shouting*): Fifteen, fifteen!

FARMER'S FAMILY: Three, three! (26)

In an earlier scene, presented without any comment other than the Loud-speaker's announcement that "Milk flows to market," we have seen a farmer being paid three cents for his milk by a middleman, who tells him to take it or leave it and then repeats the same comment to a consumer reluctant to pay fifteen cents for the same milk. This scene is nearly as brief as this description of it, and it appears immediately after the scene in which Milo Reno agrees to the demands of the commission merchants—in other words, five scenes previous to the one in which the farm and city families square off. The Loud-speaker does not intervene with any sort of editorial comment in the meantime—it is left up to the audience to ponder the effect that a middleman's pocketing of the twelve-cent discrepancy will have on the relationship between the two warring groups, as well as to consider the implications of such actions as the farmers' overturning of milk trucks.

What makes *Triple-A* such effective political theater is that it does not attempt to pander to the audience or to force-feed it any prefabricated ideological solutions. Rather, the play demands that audience members assemble the puzzle pieces themselves and come to their own conclusions. As the scene with the farmers and the city people continues, we finally move toward some kind of genuine common cause—not the artificially hyped patriotism of the first scene, in which differences are elided by propaganda slogans created from on high, referring to events entirely outside of the speakers' experience. None of the speakers have had their daughters ravaged by Huns or their land invaded, and yet these threats are the basis for their solidarity, in which "Every man behind a plow is a man behind a gun." Rather, when the farm family and the city family begin to use language that mirrors each other's, and when the scene reaches the kind of choral intensity effected by the play's opening scene, it is because the two families really do share a common experience: dire poverty:

> WORKER'S DAUGHTER (*wail*): I'm hungry . . .
> FARMER'S DAUGHTER: I can't go to school.
> FARMER (quietly): Food rots in our fields . . .
> FARMER'S SECOND SON: No money to ship . . .
> FARMER: No money to buy . . .
> FARMER'S WIFE: No money . . . (*Slight pause.*)
> WORKER: There is no work.
> WORKER'S SON: No jobs!
> WORKER'S DAUGHTER: No food!
> WORKER: We have been evicted from our homes.
> FARMER'S WIFE: And we from our land. (26)

Thus this American identity will be based on common suffering rather than an inflated national pride.

However, although it is becoming clear that workers and farmers share a common problem, they are still far from finding a common solution. The visceral experience of hunger may be enough for farmers and workers to experience a brief moment of solidarity, but until all groups can understand the economic linkages tying them together, and until all Americans represented in the play—the wealthy, the consumers, farmers, workers, and so on—can grasp the ways in which government action affects their lives, common action will be impossible. At the end of the scene quoted above, the farmer cries that "The wheat is better destroyed. I say, burn it!" (27), a cry echoed by his family, and the worker can only ask "Why?" It is intuitively ludicrous to a starving worker that perfectly good wheat should be burned; it is up to the text to explicate some fairly sophisticated relationships between cause and effect, between the establishment of the Agricultural Adjustment Administration (AAA) by Congress and the resulting government mandate to reduce acreage and curtail hog production and subsequent fluctuations in the stock market; between the new processing taxes on crops and the inability of a shabbily dressed man to buy a cup of soup for the same two cents he paid for it the previous day.

Triple-A, in order to remain theatrically effective while focusing on such conventionally untheatrical matters as hog prices and processing taxes, uses a range of modernist techniques. The play is willing to go to any lengths to teach its historical and economic message to a mass audience. Thus some presentations are graphic and nakedly didactic, such as projected maps showing acre reduction, which are screened as Henry Wallace finishes a speech explaining the new policy, and graphs depicting different-sized pigs representing different production years. All of these events are simultaneously explained by the Loudspeaker voice. Sometimes the lessons are dramatized by staged vignettes: After the Loudspeaker announces that "Triple-A pays four million dollars daily" (29), we see a meeting between a farmer and a salesman, who explains to his customer the impact of the new processing tax: "You get check for planting no wheat—planter pays more for bread of your wheat—you pay more for shirt of his cotton—that's where it comes from" (30). These explanations, which include stock market scenes demonstrating the effects of a drought on stock prices, weather reports, and sermons on the hardships wrought by the Dust Bowl, do not privilege the traditional staples of drama— emotional conflicts and terrible human problems—over explanations for the sources of these problems. Thus the play may depict a woman arriving at the police station with the body of her infant, whom she has killed because "I couldn't feed him. I had only five cents" (43), but this scene is sandwiched between a representation of the Supreme Court's decision to kill Triple-A and a scene depicting consumers rioting over higher meat prices (typically, the riots themselves occur offstage, after the scene's conclusion). The individual tragedy is presented only in terms of the group dilemma, and the understanding of one is possible only in the context of the other.

Whose America Is It?

Always, the question of who gets to define Americanism is crucial. As one of the commentators on the Supreme Court decision, Earl Browder, notes, "the reactionaries seek to turn both 'Americanism' and the Constitution into instruments of reaction, but neither of these things belong to them" (46). The play itself opts for a very inclusive model: In one scene, the preamble to the Declaration of Independence is projected in front of a scrim, while the heads of famous Americans, ranging from Browder to Thomas Jefferson, can be seen on the back of the scrim. Obviously, this definition of Americanness did not please all constituencies, and in fact it afforded an opportunity for the kind of interaction that was possible for audiences of and even participants in the Living Newspapers—and thoroughly impossible for readers of the trilogies. One actor who had rehearsed the words of Browder asked to be excused from repeating them. And on opening night, when the actor playing Browder was speaking, a veteran rose from his seat and began singing "The Star-Spangled Banner." However, the police in the back of the theater, who had been warned by a group calling itself World War Veterans to be on guard against Communist activity, misunderstood what was going on and promptly evicted the veteran. This incident provides a particularly vivid illustration of the ways in which Living Newspapers could involve audiences and actors in unexpected confrontations, as well as of the ways that definitions of what is American could collide. However, it was far from being an isolated occurrence: All through the production's run spectators seized the opportunity to voice their views. As Norman Lloyd, an actor with the Federal Theatre Project, remembers,

> A lot of people who saw that show had never been to the theater before. And they would talk back to the people up there. Most of all they would talk back to the Supreme Court justices . . . and if a justice got up to speak and someone in the audience didn't agree with him, that someone would shout him down.[28]

The text itself encourages a degree of audience participation. Its porousness is demonstrated most vividly at the end of the play, when spectators are invited to join in the meeting that is being held onstage. What we first see is essentially the dramatized transcript of a national convention of farmers meeting in South Dakota to draft a program. The scene soon opens up to include most of the characters from the play, from a man and a woman in evening clothes (seen in an earlier scene eating Beluga caviar and drinking fine wine) to unemployed farmers and workers to Secretary Wallace himself. The farmers at the convention can agree on a program to restore farm relief and levy higher taxes on the great industrial and financial interests of the United States, but the unanimity dissolves once all characters are present. Though a farmer and the man in evening clothes may agree that soil conservation programs must continue, a farmer may say that "Food prices must stay up," only to be contradicted by a woman, leader of a consumer strike group, who tells him that "Food prices must go down" (54). Even as the various interest groups clash, the text refuses to allow spectators to forget the interconnectedness of all groups. When one suffers, many others suffer:

FARMER: I can't buy that auto.

DEALER: I can't take that shipment.

MANUFACTURER: I can't use you any more.

WORKER: I can't eat.

VOICE (*over* Loudspeaker): There is now piled up in the banks a huge savings reserve, and it lays a basis for a new speculative boom—(*All look toward* Loudspeaker.)

MAN IN EVENING CLOTHES: Back to normalcy.

VOICE (*over* Loudspeaker): . . . Which may result in a far more disastrous collapse than any heretofore experienced.

MAN IN EVENING CLOTHES (*to woman with him*): The rugged individualism of our forefathers will solve the problem. (55)

It is clear that the simplistic solutions of the man in evening clothes, including reliance on the mythology of American individualism, will not do; a thorough understanding of the economic system is necessary. His insistence on rugged individualism is contradicted by an unemployed man who notes that "we need a State that permits no man to go hungry" (56).

Although many points of view are presented during this scene, individualistic solutions are depicted as ridiculous. We have seen enough hungry people onstage during the course of the drama to see the necessity for a solution that is inclusive rather than individual. In fact, at the end of the meeting the Loudspeaker delivers three news flashes on the decisions by several groups and by a congressman from Minnesota that a farmer-labor party should be formed. This is an answer that offers an opportunity for those with common class interests, who are somewhat at loggerheads with one another through the course of the play, to unite. It is not a solution that embraces the couple in evening clothes and the class they represent. Obviously, the canned propaganda messages that are so easily used by government and industry do not serve the majority of people well, whether those slogans have to do with the need for stepped-up militarism, as in the first scene, or the presentation of individualism, as opposed to solidarity, as the real way to be American. Finally, although the different interest groups portrayed in the play may have conflicting agendas, they all, with the exception of the aristocrats, finally recognize that only historical and economical awareness, fueled by constant discussion, is the way to move forward. The conclusion of the play invites the audience into the colloquium:

FARMER: We *need* you.

CHORUS OF FARMERS: We *need* you.

LEADER OF UNEMPLOYED: We need *you*.

CHORUS OF UNEMPLOYED: We need *you*. (FARMERS *and* UNEMPLOYED *jump close together, arms extended. Light on them is intensified. Lights on* WALLACE *and* WOMAN *in evening clothes fade. Tableau of* FARMERS, WOMEN *and* UNEMPLOYED *hold.*) (57)

Ultimately, the spotlight is not on the rich and the powerful—that is, the woman in evening clothes and Secretary Wallace. It is on the masses of people, whose role it will be to work in educated concert. Included in this alliance, of course, will be members of the audience who, through their spectatorship of the play, have been involved in just the type of historical education that *Triple-A* implies will finally lead to a successful formulation of American identity.

The Failures of Dirt

If *Triple-A* is an example of what the Living Newspaper can be at its best, *Dirt* is a Living Newspaper that illustrates some of the pitfalls of the form.[29] It is memorable, not as art but for the ways in which it embodies the decade's tensions over the implications of American identity. Like *Triple-A, Dirt* uses documentary sources to further political understanding and looks to American history to furnish inspiration for the solution of present problems. However, in its nativist hysteria and anxiety about the formation of a national identity, *Dirt* ends up being more frightening than inspiring.

One of the key issues of *Dirt* is the need for Americans to define their own identity and the desire of other nations, specifically England, to formulate what is American. There are several plays (among them, *Flax,* produced in Oregon in 1937) that deal with trade issues between the United States and England. *Dirt,* a script dealing with farmers' problems—and, most specifically, with the Dust Bowl that resulted from topsoil erosion in the thirties—includes the most explicit discussion of the need to define a national identity. The tensions are set up in the beginning of the play, as Swaffle, the British drama critic, enters late and tries to climb over a seated farmer in the audience. Between the farmer's "Hey! Get off my foot, yuh sonova . . ." and Swaffle's "I say, old chap . . . move over . . . blast it"[30] lies a cultural gulf. More serious, however, is Swaffle's misunderstanding of midwestern culture. He explains to the Loudspeaker voice (a loudspeaker was a tool used in most, if not all, Living Newspapers as a guiding dramatic agent) that he is "Looking for your jolly *typical* mid-western town, y'know. Typical. Sinclair Lewis sort of thing. Sour [*sic*] Center. Peoria. Dubuque. Boone. Oskaloosa. Not bad, Oskaloosa. Des Moines . . . insurance companies . . . pretty girls . . . LOOK magazine" (1.1.3).

Just as Studs Lonigan and many of Dos Passos's characters are led astray by relying on mass media images to understand American culture, so it becomes clear that Swaffle, reciting his litany of prefabricated images, cannot understand anything about the way the Midwest works. Swaffle, though British, is reminiscent of Lester Tolman, the journalist in Josephine Herbst's trilogy. Tolman's research tour through the Midwest to investigate farmers' conditions is complicated by his refusal to give up his prefabricated images of rural life and his romantic categories drawn from literature. "When they came to the Dakotas, he wanted to hurry to Montana where he had heard of the big open spaces and longed to get a glimpse of a wildwest town. The first town across the border was dead as a doornail with a local prohibition option that soured Lester on the whole project for twenty-four hours."[31] Like Tolman, Swaffle must learn that his literary notions have little to do with the hard lives of farmers. Moreover, the drama critic's tools are completely inadequate for judging the Living Newspaper that he is watching. He is put in his place, time and time again, by the Loudspeaker voice. It is striking that his mistaken impressions of the Midwest are formed, in part, by his reading of classic American novels. The Loudspeaker voice quickly, and sternly, disabuses him of his notions: "London, huh? And you want to see something typical here in the middlewest? Sit still . . . we'll give you a look! You know how much a ton of dirt is? An acre of dirt? A field of dirt?" (1.1.3).

As "stereopticon slides of above" are shown, the Loudspeaker voice continues his tirade: "Soil conservation payments, if they are to be subsidies at all, subsidize a great national purpose, socially necessary and deplorably long delayed. They are not mere subsidies to fatten the farmer, in the degree that ship subsidies, sugar tariffs and some other things have been subsidies to fatten special interests." An asterisk, at this point, offers the reader a footnoted reference to the source of this information—an editorial in the *Des Moines Register*. Factual, footnoted harangue supportive of a specific change in government policy meets romantic, literary vision, and materialism wins out: Carol Kennicott of Gopher Prairie pales in importance compared to the problem of soil erosion. As Swaffle wonders vaguely just what these farmers want, the Loudspeaker voice poses a question. Why do corporations, rather than farmers, own the dirt of Iowa? This question is framed in terms stressing the alienation of these conglomerates from the earth, in opposition to the close relationship to the soil of the farmers themselves: "Insurance companies in Iowa owned over 50% of Iowa farms a few years ago. More than half of the black soil of Iowa was owned by companies, by corporations, who have installed air-conditioning devices in their offices to keep dust and dirt off their desks and from the air they breathe. Farmers breathe the dirt . . . eat it behind their harrows and plows. AND LIKE IT!" (1.1.4). His subsequent question, "WHY? WHY? WHY?" is echoed not only by the word "WHY," flashing on the front curtain, which is still down, but also by Swaffle and the farmers in the audience. The question can be answered only by providing a historical overview of conditions in Iowa, going back to the development of British-owned land companies in the 1870s. Thus, within the first few pages of *Dirt*, we see elements reminiscent of the historical trilogies. There is the stress on formulating an American identity based less on iconographic images of American life than on the material difficulties faced by farmers.

Dirt is marred by some of the common flaws of its genre: Characters within even "realistic" scenes have a tendency to spout endless statistics, as witness this conversation between a group of second sons of English noblemen, shown relaxing in a tavern in Le Mars, Iowa, in 1879.

> THIRD BOY: Sutherland ought to be interested. He could invest some pounds to good advantage here. The Close brothers cleared over 50% on their investment in crops last year. [A footnote here explains the source of this statistic.] I heard Captain Moreton talking to John last evening. They plan to buy 100,000 more acres soon. They own more than three thousand acres in Crawford county now, bought at $3.50 per acre.
>
> SECOND BOY: They'll have half of England over here at this rate! Too many, I say. The St. Paul papers have been vicious in their editorials against what they call our "British invasion."
>
> THIRD BOY: Let them write. English money has done more in developing this part of Iowa than all of the rest put together. *It's a free country!* (1.2.2)

The occasional calls for more Chianti and joking references to the local gardener's daughter do little to cut the density of the flow of information, and in fact the Loudspeaker cannot allow the young noblemen to carry on their innocent, albeit overly footnoted, conversation for more than a few sentences.

> LOUDSPEAKER: (with force) *A free country?* Is it? IS IT? Let's see. Let's see how free a country is when a corporation can own a half million acres of the finest land obtainable . . . can impose upon country after country a system of almost *feudal* land ownership. LET'S TAKE A LOOK AT THOSE CLOSE BROTHERS! (1.2.3)

It is perhaps above all the bossiness of the Loudspeaker voice, his inability to allow audience members any unsupervised enjoyment, that dooms the play. When Swaffle, hearing one of the Close brothers say that "an Englishman always finds something to complain about, in any part of the world!" is heard to chuckle and say that "He's bloody right, at that!" (1.3.2), the Loudspeaker is quick to silence him: "Quiet! Do you have to dump those cigaret ashes all over your vest? You look like the top of a bridge table! QUIET!" (1.3.2). It is no wonder that a reader of the script, "H." (perhaps for Hallie Flanagan?), was finally compelled to write, in the margins of my copy of the script, that "a lot of this is terrible and under no circumstances could be done until extensively rewritten" (1.6.3). At any rate, it was not produced. The Loudspeaker voice continued its diatribe—against the agricultural policies of President Coolidge, which it explains in detail to the hapless Swaffle—but remained unheard by audiences. The documentary techniques of *Dirt*—the motion picture back-drops depicting closed factories, rioting workers, and unemployment lines, shown while the Loudspeaker voice narrates the progress of the Depression—would remain unseen. And yet here, again, was an attempt, in some ways similar to that of the Communist Party, to link Americanness explicitly with revolutionary tendencies. When Swaffle, for instance, protests that "but in England . . . we have had two generations of the dole . . . fathers and their sons and their son's son's sons" (1.3.3), the Loudspeaker voice retorts "sharply": "I know . . . I know. Your people *accepted* it. Your coal miners starved in Wales. And when your king tried to do something about it. . . . Tradition is strong there in England. The government . . . your government . . . can do no wrong! But here in America . . . we were born in revolution! Freedom of thought and freedom of action are *American traits!* THERE ARE NO CONCENTRA-TION CAMPS IN THIS COUNTRY!" (1.3.4). Freedom of thought and action include the freedom to smash the eggs and pour out the cream of drivers who attempt to deliver these goods in defiance of a farmers' work stoppage. Thus the American identity which the Loudspeaker voice struggles throughout the drama to define turns out to be a radical one, and the Ameri-can farmers, which Swaffle had been anxious to see in terms of *Look* magazine clichés, turn out to be revolutionary followers of Milo Reno.

A family who buys a foreclosed farm, in defiance of a Farmers' Holiday Association plan to stop evictions, is initially portrayed sympathetically. The child complains that "Gosh, Ma, I git pretty tired walkin' to school them two miles. I don't see why they won't let me ride in the bus like th'other kids. They won't tell me why, neither" (1.11.1). The mother quickly becomes deranged, reporting visions of elephants in the chicken coops. This portrayal of insan-ity stands in stark contrast to that included in *Triple-A Plowed Under*. In her final breakdown, while the Loudspeaker whispers its repeated invocations of "DIRT . . . DIRT . . . DIRT" over her insane ramblings, she associates the family with tainted produce: "LIKE OUR POTATOES ROTTING IN TH' GARDEN . . . WE'RE ALL ROTTEN . . . WE STINK!! . . . NO ONE WILL TALK TO US" (1.11.4). When she rushes out of the house carrying a butcher knife, her husband is left to damn farmers and their ideas—but it is unclear where audience sympathies are expected to lie. The Loudspeaker voice, com-ing in on the heels of this family tragedy, does not condemn the farmers for their actions. "The farmers meant business! They were sticking together now. They were using any method to fight with. The law held no aid for them . . .

instead it took their farms away" (1.11.5). The Loudspeaker explicitly links their actions to an older form of American justice, "before law came, before Territorial days in Iowa, when vigilantes were the LAW without a legislature" (1.11.5).

Although the play depicts scenes bound to disturb audiences, such as the one described above or the one in which a judge is nearly lynched for his refusal to stop foreclosure proceedings on a farm, the Loudspeaker does not stop making radical pronouncements about the way in which "capitalistic industry did not hesitate to reduce the supply of manufactured goods to hold prices up—AND THEY DID IT BY CLOSING THEIR FACTORIES AND STARVING MEN AND THEIR FAMILIES" (1.15.1). Given the callousness of industry, the Loudspeaker voice asks: "A man loses his job . . . and he and his wife and children face breadlines and starvation! WHICH WOULD YOUR CHOICE BE AS AN INTELLIGENT THING TO DO?" (1.15.1).

Having posited this fairly radical vision of what being a "good" American entails, the authors of the script, or the Loudspeaker voice, then complicate this notion of patriotism further by depicting a scene from news and fictional accounts of the vigilante nationalism and hysteria prevalent during the Great War. In this scene farmers surround and intimidate an attorney for a bank that is foreclosing on a farmer's mortgage.

FARMER IN FOREGROUND

So you're the guy who sold out John Shaffer? Let's see now . . . what's your name?

MONTZHEIMER

(*smartly dressed man*)

My name is O. H. Montzheimer . . . I'm attorney for the mortgage holder . . .

MAN IN FOREGROUND

Mortgage holder? Sure . . . that's right . . . mortgage holder. *Are you a good American, Mister Montzheimer?*

MONTZHEIMER

(*uncertainly*)

Why . . . I guess so . . . I guess I try to be. What's it to . . .

MAN IN FOREGROUND

Well, we'll show you *how* to be . . .

(*grimly*)

Come on, boys!

(*He seizes MONTZHEIMER . . . the others join in, while DEPUTIES unsuccessfully try to intervene . . . leaders pull MONTZHEIMER over to the wall, force him to his knees near American flag.*) Now . . . if you're a good American . . . you can *kiss this flag!* Or else. (1.15.5)

It is worth recalling that the second volume of Herbst's trilogy, *The Executioner Waits,* opens with a similar flag-kissing scene—but there the heavies are right-wing vigilantes rather than radical farmers. It is a measure of the ideological confusion of *Dirt* that a gesture traditionally used as an acid test of patriotism in times of nationalist fervor should be usurped by radical farmers acting collectively and seeing themselves as engaged in class struggle against big business and banks. These are men who feel that "what this country *needs is more Lincolns an' less Fords*" (1.16.2).

In fact, the play ultimately has an ambivalent relationship to fascism, which is used as both a promise and a threat, as in the penultimate scene of the play, set in 1939, two years after *Dirt* was written. The scene, in which a nightmare version of the Dust Bowl is described, has apocalyptic overtones. We are told by Secretary of Agriculture Wallace that "the very air outside these windows is so filled with the richest DIRT in the world that the top of the Washington Monument is lost to sight! Buses crawl along Fifth Avenue in New York City as they would in a Channel fog in London! . . . our midwestern states are being *depopulated!*" (1.19.3). Not only are conditions dire, but American democracy is incapable of coping with the state of emergency: "We have done what we could . . . what the people of America through their duly elected representatives WOULD PERMIT US TO DO!" (1.19.3). The alternative is not an uprising by the people but action taken from above. "The President has mobilized every force within his power. No longer does America depend upon an unthinking public, a public unattentive to the *public need!*" (1.19.3). Democracy cannot redeem us, the script implies. Should the nightmare scenario of the script's 1939 take place, the Loudspeaker tells us, there will be no redemption,

unless a program of reconstruction is set up in terms of a *national emergency existing NOW!* What would Hitler or Mussolini do against such conditions of soil erosion as exist NOW in the United States? WOULD HITLER OR MUSSOLINI OR STALIN SIT QUIETLY BY AND WATCH THE CONGRESS WASTE YEARS OF TIME WHILE THE SOIL LOSES ITS FERTILITY OR WASHES INTO AN OCEAN? OR WOULD HE FACE THE CONGRESS WITH THE WARNING THAT UNLESS A CONSTRUCTIVE PROGRAM WAS FORTHCOMING IMMEDIATELY, THOSE DULY ELECTED REPRESENTATIVES OF THE PEOPLE WOULD FACE A *FIRING SQUAD* OUTSIDE THE NATIONAL CAPITOL? (1.19.4)

There is little to suggest that assassination of elected officials is not, in fact, the best solution for the problems facing farmers. From this scene, it is hard to derive the notion that the people—romanticized in so many WPA murals and other cultural artifacts of the period—know what's best for them. Instead, they are an "unthinking public" in need of guidance from above. The Loudspeaker voice—hectoring, urgent, unwilling to relinquish control over the action for even a moment, eager to interpret events even as they are unfolding—is praising Stalin, Hitler, and Mussolini. Perhaps, the voice seems to be saying, the Fascists have it right after all; perhaps we are fooling ourselves. The discussion of Americanism that permeates the script, in which to be American means to be revolutionary, to fight the powers that be, has given way to an internationalism embracing the German, Soviet, and Italian solutions to the problems of worldwide depression. That Henry Wallace is seen to endorse this view lends it moral credence.

Thus the play's final scene, in which threats of fascism are washed away by a tide of New Deal optimism, seems finally unconvincing. It portrays a sunnier future, a 1938 in which Roosevelt has signed a crop control bill, and here the Loudspeaker voice comes out in favor of planning. Protesting loudly, as usual, against an unseen and unheard enemy, the Loudspeaker rails against the bill's opponents. "What kind of disgruntled *bosh* is this that would have us believe that sensible plans and systems in effect in industry mean REGIMENTA- TION when applied to the basic industry of our country?" (1.20.1). Retreat- ing from the internationalism of the previous scene, the voice once again invokes the name of an American icon to support his point: "As far back as Alexander Hamilton, careful planning for the farmers was suggested" (1.20.1). Swaffle points out, in response to the Loudspeaker's notion that "the erosion of human character . . . comes from the driving of intelligent and honest farmers to a tenancy system that is making serfs of them" (1.20.3), that "you Americans have always had renters, as we have had in England" (1.20.3). But the Loudspeaker is quick to reframe the question in nationalistic terms. "Renters? Listen, Swaffle . . . and get it through your thick skull . . . renters like you have had in England are long-term tenants" (1.20.3).

After describing the process by which farmers become indebted to the owners of the farms they rent, the Loudspeaker concludes by saying that "The inevitable result is that he NEVER GETS OUT OF DEBT TO THE OWNER OF THE LAND! SERFDOM? SHARECROPPERDOM? Are these things *American?* Have they ever been?" (1.20.3). To preserve the Ameri- can character, the voice more than implies, it will be necessary to do whatever it takes to keep the family farms intact, even if this involves seemingly un- American government intervention. The worst threat here seems to be the anglicization of the United States, and the best promise a sort of populist pride in the redemption of the farming system. As one farmer in a meeting of farmers and businessmen declares, "we *know* that they've given us the auto and some gas to run it . . . but it's up to us to keep it in repair" (1.20.4). As another farmer agrees, "we've got to study the danged thing, understand what makes it run, and learn how to treat it so's it won't get busted again. It's our'n" (1.20.4). It is a businessman who has the last word, though, when he declares that "we don't need collectivism, with the federal government operating the soil as a state function, like in some of the foreign countries. *We ain't goin' fascist yet!* We got brains enough to work together on this ourselves" (1.20.4). The threat of fascism, then, will be turned back by greater public education.

Well, the businessman has almost the last word. It is up to the Loudspeaker, of course, to finish hectoring his hapless English victim, and the audience, in a final advertisement for a new vision of America, and for the form of the Living Newspaper itself. As the word "DIRT" continues to flash on and off the scrim, the Loudspeaker concludes his tirade: "Sit down, Swaffle! I hope you find that typical Iowa farm! And sit down on it the rest of your life in the middle of your quandary" (1.20.5). It is hard to tell here whether the voice is claiming that the only way to understand America, and more specifically the American farm, is to spend a lifetime there—or whether this is simply the Loudspeaker's diffuse hostility at play. However, the final words the voice utters are more ideologically unmuddled:

> Facts! FACTS! F-A-C-T-S-!! THAT'S WHAT YOU HAVE BEEN LIS-TENING TO AND WATCHING FOR THESE PAST TWO HOURS! THINK OF THEM . . . GIVE THEM SOME ATTENTION . . . ALL OF YOU OUT THERE! LET *DIRT* COME TO MEAN AS MUCH TO YOU AS IT MEANS TO THE MEN WHO PLOUGH IT AND PLANT IT!! AFTER ALL . . . THIS IS *YOUR AMERICA!!* (1.20.5)

It is only through education, and more specifically exposure to the kind of documentary presented by the Living Newspaper, that Americans can be drawn together in a sympathetic identification with the farmer and his problems. It is dangerous, according to the Loudspeaker, to accept a prefabricated image of the American farmer—an image based on mass media clichés (one of "insurance companies . . . pretty girls . . . LOOK magazine," as Swaffle impressionistically sums it up). This acceptance can only lead to complacency and, more importantly, to paralysis; an ignorant view of America can only lead to a worsening of its problems. To learn "F-A-C-T-S" is to be a good citizen, to claim one's American birthright. As the farmer in the final scene muses, it will be possible to fix the "danged thing" that is America only by studying it. Watching a Living Newspaper thus can be a way to participate in the democratic process, to reclaim America, and to prevent the creeping tide of fascism, which could encroach on a country populated by "an unthinking public, a public unattentive to the *public need*"—a country in which only "experts" are qualified to make decisions for the American people, who are themselves too lazy to take an interest in their own destiny.

Dirt is not a good play, but a strong case can be made for its importance, both in its obsession with the nature of American identity and the implications of being an American and in its insistence on the political importance of documentary. *Dirt* presents the Living Newspaper as a constituency-building tool, and the viewing of such a play not only as a means of gaining empathy with disenfranchised Americans—in this case, the farmers—but as a blow against fascism. *Dirt* is, above all, an ideologically muddled play, as witness the Loudspeaker's advocating such strong measures as putting congressmen before a firing squad as the next necessary step, should the American public refuse to become educated through such measures as attending the Living Newspapers. Thus the play flirts with what it purports to oppose. In this Living Newspaper, the tools of theatrical criticism are seen as irrelevant to understanding the project: Not only is Swaffle British, and thus less easily able to understand things American, but he is a theater critic, and as such less interested in facts than in impressions. He is incessantly hectored by the Loudspeaker voice, and nothing that he has to say is given credence. At the end of the play, the Loudspeaker doesn't tell him to go away and learn to be a better critic; Swaffle is instead directed to immerse himself in American life. This will be his only chance of understanding the farmers' problems—and, perhaps, the Living Newspaper itself.

Although the Loudspeaker voice of *Dirt* may discourage any considerations of literary or theatrical form, the play is a formal experiment run amok, a case study in the things that can go wrong with a Living Newspaper. With its incessantly flashing signs (like "D-I-R-T" and "F-A-C-T-S"), its shouted imprecations from planted audience members, its iconic film clips, and most of all its domineering Loudspeaker, who seems incapable of giving the audience members space to form their own impressions, *Dirt* is a parody of agit-prop.

Perhaps the difference between the two plays can be best understood by turning to Walter Benjamin's discussion of political art in "Art in the Age of Mechanical Reproduction." Here he writes that "all efforts to render politics aesthetic culminate in one thing: war." It is not just politics but, specifically, the violence of mass movements that he is speaking of. To this end he quotes the futurist Marinetti, who writes that "war is beautiful because it establishes man's dominion over the machinery by means of gas masks, terrifying megaphones, flame throwers and small tanks. . . . War is beautiful because it combines the gunfire, the cannonades, the cease-fire, the scents, and the sense of putrefaction into a symphony."[32] What is *Dirt* if not a loving evocation of attempted lynchings, riots, and subjugation (i.e., the flag-kissing scene)? Much of the drama and excitement of the piece come from the depiction of mass violence. The danger of the Living Newspaper form, ill-used, is that it lends itself to the creation of this kind of spectacle. It is tempting in any theatrical arena to take the quickest route to audience reaction, which is the depiction of violence. In fact, *Dirt* uses the lurid techniques of mass culture in its scenes of violence and cheesily depicted madness. Think of the difference between the mad scene in *Dirt*, in which a farm woman sees circus elephants in her yard, advances on her family with a butcher knife, and then runs screaming outside, to the comparable scene in *Triple-A*, in which a woman shows up at a police station with the infant she has just killed, a scene which is, by contrast, quiet, sad, evocative. If, as Benjamin writes, "The logical result of Fascism is the introduction of aesthetics into political life,"[33] then *Dirt*, with its aestheticization of violence, bears the taint of fascism. This is political art at its most dangerous, art for an audience whose "self-alienation has reached such a degree that it can experience its own destruction as an aesthetic pleasure of the first order."[34] Because violence permeates the play, and because even the dialogue tends to be an exercise in the strong, in the form of the Loudspeaker voice, subjugating the weak, embodied by Swaffle, audiences are given little opportunity for the kind of quiet, detached reflection offered by *Triple-A*.

If, in Benjamin's terms, "this is the situation of politics which Fascism is rendering aesthetic" and "Communism responds by politicizing art,"[35] then *Triple-A* can be seen as political art in its best sense. It is art that demands engagement from the audience rather than the passive enjoyment of the spectator of luridly depicted violence. It is art which concerns itself with the representation not of blood and soil but of the historical forces that shape contemporary political dilemmas. Finally, it is art which insists on the importance of a political activism both within and beyond the theater, on the duties of all citizens to partake in a political process that is often messy, often confusing, and often unsatisfying for many concerned but that is necessary if positive change is to take place. Thus, while the problematic *Dirt* may be a useful vehicle for a discussion of the pitfalls of the Living Newspaper form and the dangers of nativism, it is the more successful *Triple-A Plowed Under* that remains an exemplar of the form.

Liberty Deferred: *When Political Considerations Intervened*

It is easy to see why *Dirt* remained unproduced. However, the blocked pro-duction of another drama, *Liberty Deferred,* is explicable only in the context of the congressional politics that ultimately doomed the Federal Theatre Project to extinction. *Liberty Deferred* was written by two young African American playwrights, Abram Hill and John Silvera. This play, which reexamines south-ern history, opens by explicitly challenging prevailing stage and screen images of blacks: Step'n Fetchit, the Big Apple dancers, "a group of 'cotton pickers'—that is, the musical comedy version of them—in pastel-shaded sateen over-alls. . . . They are all grins and contentment—the popular Hollywood version of the plantation worker singing at his work."[36] Planted black actors in the audience protest these portrayals and demand that the producers "Show us the real Negro. . . . Show us the cause. . . . Show us the unbiased reason for being that way. . . . Tell us about slavery. . . . Tell us about lack of oppor-tunities. . . . Stop that other junk" (254). The portrayal of African American history which is used in response incorporates a range of dramatic techniques and includes not only such documentary evidence as charts detailing the growth of slavery in Virginia but spoken commentary from James Weldon Johnson, Thomas Jefferson, Frederick Douglass, and A. Phillip Randolph. In addition to directly quoted speeches from historical figures, characters include such mythological figures as Jim Crow and Jim Lily White. This blend of fact and fiction is effectively used in what is perhaps the most striking scene, a portrayal of "Lynchotopia"—"the fabled land where all lynch victims go" (291). The keeper of records in this establishment muses aloud: "Well—thirteen new members for the year. Thirteen—exactly one half of last year. I wonder what 1937 will bring. The decline is no sign though. Let's see. What's the total number of members now, 5,107 since 1882. Old Judge Lynch is really doing his stuff. Wouldn't surprise me if they didn't send Walter White down to join us" (290).

He goes much further than speculating on the probable assassination of the head of the NAACP when he begins enrolling lynch victims, questioning them about the ways that they died—"Burned by blow torches, eh? Going modern" (292)—and asking them what, if any, was the state action. The accumulation of facts and figures culminates in a contest, "the customary New Year's review. I'll check over your case and the one that's been through the most brutal lynching gets the prize" (293). We then see the preparations for lynching Claude Neal, the winner of this contest, and although we do not see the crime itself, we do see a mother holding up her child for a better view. The scene may incorporate actual events, but the Living Newspaper goes further in its depiction of the nine lynch victims sitting in on the hearings for the Wagner antilynching bill. We see them "in typical holiday mood—chewing gum, eating popcorn, munching an apple and smoking a cigar; they are ghosts of course and unobserved" (297).

Ironically enough, the only deviation from historical fact up until that point—the announced passage, toward the end of the play, of the antilynching bill—was not only not to be but most likely proved the play's undoing. Although scenes were rehearsed and revisions made, the play ultimately fell victim to congressional suppression. In light of its stand in favor of an anti-lynching bill, the production would most likely have offended the southern senators on the Dies committee—the committee that would ultimately be responsible for the demise of the Federal Theatre Project.[37] Flanagan and the other founders of the FTP had envisioned it as "free, adult, uncensored" theater; although she was committed to a vision of progressive theater, she was well aware of the hostility of anti–New Deal congressmen and had no desire to imperil the livelihood of the 10,000 people who worked under her. And she was sometimes forced to compromise, as in the case of *Liberty Deferred,* for the sake of keeping the FTP alive.

The End of the Federal Theatre Project

In the battle over who was to define Americanism, the conservative senators won. On February 7, 1938, in a front-page article, the *New York Herald Tribune* reported that three U.S. senators, all Democrats—Harry F. Byrd of Virginia, Millard E. Tydings of Maryland, and Charles O. Andrews of Flor-ida—had received reports that their onstage portrayals in the New York pro-duction of the Living Newspaper *One-Third of a Nation* were greeted by hisses and boos. *One-Third of a Nation,* which took its title from Roosevelt's inaugu-ral speech and dealt with the problem of inadequate housing, was, like all Living Newspapers, founded on a solid documentary basis. Using the *Con-gressional Record* as its source, *One-Third of a Nation* included a scene in which "The three Senators, portrayed by relief-paid actors, are shown in a Senate scene as the apparent opposition to Senator Robert F. Wagner, Democrat, of New York, on his low-cost housing bill, now enacted into law." Of course, this was factually true. However, "Friends of Senators Byrd, Tydings and Andrews say they are thus associated with all the social evils and calamities of the slums. They point out that in this role, with the aid of public money voted by the Senate, they may be presented to audiences throughout the country."[38] The senators were particularly disturbed by the success of the FTP, whose au-diences by that date numbered over twenty million nationwide. A sympathetic article in *Motion Picture Herald* that week quoted Andrews as impugning the patriotism of the show's authors: "I don't think Americans are responsible for this kind of presentation," the senator said. "I think some foreign element must be behind this."[39]

Debate raged in the papers over the next few days: Arthur Arent blandly pointed out both the scene's brevity and its factual basis, while mentioning that he had never heard the senators booed onstage. He pointed out that it was necessary to cut down the senators' speeches for the twenty-second scene. He declined to alter the scene.[40] Meanwhile, ticket sales soared.

The commercial and critical success of the Living Newspapers, and of the FTP in general, was not enough to keep the project alive. The first round of budget cuts came in June of 1937, reducing the New York project rolls by nearly 30 percent and halting the publication of the *Federal Theatre Magazine*, which had grown from a mimeographed house organ to a journal that sold out more rapidly than it could be reprinted. This was nothing to what was to come, however: The House Committee on Un-American Activities (or the Dies committee) held hearings in which witnesses claimed that the FTP was dominated by Communists and that one had to belong to the Workers' Alliance to get work on the project, both untruths. (It is true that Flanagan had a policy of never inquiring about the political affiliations of her employees.) J. Parnell Thomas, the Republican congressman from New Jersey, claimed that "every play was clear unadulterated propaganda." Representative Everett M. Dirksen (Republican, Illinois) called the FTP productions "salacious tripe."[41]

When, in November of that year, Flanagan herself went before the Dies Committee, she was peppered with questions from the senators: Hadn't she been to Russia? Was it true that audiences were interested only in Communist plays? Waving an eight-year-old copy of *Theatre Arts Monthly* that contained an article by Flanagan, Representative Joseph Starnes questioned her about her comment that workers' theaters had "a certain Marlowesque madness." "You are quoting from this Marlowe," observed Starnes. "Is he a Communist?"[42] The report the committee filed with the House of Representatives on January 3, 1939, reflected their conviction that "a rather large number of employees on the Federal Theatre Project are either members of the Communist Party or are sympathetic with the Communist Party." Although a large group of New York drama critics, including among others the *New Yorker*'s Wolcott Gibbs, the *New York Times*' Brooks Atkinson, *The Nation*'s Joseph Wood Krutch, *Catholic World*'s Euphemia Van Rensselaer Wyatt, and the *New York Daily News*' Burns Mantle, testified in favor of the FTP before the House Appropriations Committee, and although a number of representatives backed the FTP, the project was doomed. Although Lionel Barrymore characterized any elimination of the arts program as "almost like taking one of the stripes out of the American flag," the project was voted out of existence on June 30, 1939.

It was undoubtedly impossible for the publicly funded relief project known as the Federal Theatre Project to survive for very long when it was forced to rely on an often hostile Congress for funding. Impossible, too, for the Living Newspapers to be produced on the same scale in a commercial venue: The cost of hiring a staff of several hundred for each production, and of reaching millions of people with affordable productions, would be prohibitive. Given the implacable hostility of the Dies Committee, it is amazing that the FTP project lasted as long as it did. Yet during its four years of existence, the FTP produced a series of Living Newspapers that would hold a mirror up to America, would do what so many radical writers of the thirties had only dreamed of accomplishing: address the burning issues of the day with politically and aesthetically sophisticated works that reached millions.

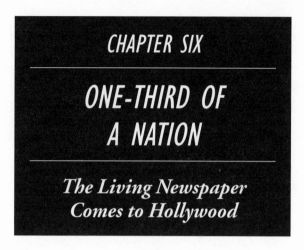

CHAPTER SIX

ONE-THIRD OF A NATION

The Living Newspaper Comes to Hollywood

As successful as the Federal Theatre Project's Living Newspapers were, they reached perhaps thirty million people all told. The size of that audience may have been something that novelists such as Dos Passos, Farrell, and Herbst could only dream of, but at Hollywood's peak it was less than half of the audience for the movies in a single week. Given the popularity of film during the Depression, and given many radical writers' fascination with popular culture (not to mention, of course, the enormous salaries paid to creative personnel in the movies), it is unsurprising that many leftist writers, actors, and directors packed their bags and headed for Hollywood, where studios like Warner Brothers were churning out "social problem" movies about Depression America.

In 1939 Paramount Pictures released a movie called *One-Third of a Nation*, derived from the successful Federal Theatre Project's Living Newspaper of the same name. This was to be the first Hollywood translation of one of the modernist documentary dramas that were the hallmark of the Federal Theatre Project. Written by Arthur Arent and the staff of the Living Newspaper, *One-Third of a Nation* premiered in New York in 1937 and subsequently opened in nine other cities, including Detroit, Cincinnati, Portland (Oregon), Philadelphia, Hartford, and New Orleans. The play ran for two years in San Francisco, its run ending only with the demise of the FTP in 1939.

As Hallie Flanagan noted, "The press considered *One-Third of a Nation* the most important contribution to date." She herself judged it "the most mature living newspaper we had done."[1] Eleanor Roosevelt told Flanagan that the play achieved "something for which we will be grateful for many years to come, something which will mean a tremendous amount in the future, socially, and in the education and growing up of America . . . far more than any amount of speeches which Langdon Post or I—or even the President—might make."[2]

The title of the play was taken, in fact, from Roosevelt's second inaugural address: "I see one-third of a nation ill-housed, ill-clad, ill-nourished." The play's aim was explicitly to effect social change. As Flanagan wrote, "our theatre to be worthy of its creation by the government must at all times concern itself with the aim of our government—a better life for more people."[3] *One-Third of a Nation* achieved remarkable audience and critical popularity. It was seen by 217,458 people in New York City alone. Revised to meet local conditions, it garnered praise from regional newspapers. In New Orleans, the *Times-Picayune* called it "as timely and shrewdly staged theatrical entertainment as has been witnessed in New Orleans for many a season." The *Cincinnati Post* reviewer wrote that the play "is not only the most ambitious production yet presented by the Federal Theatre, but unquestionably the most successful."[4]

From Stage to Screen

With this degree of success, Paramount Pictures had reason to hope for a blockbuster when they purchased the film rights in 1938. The cast for the picture included such luminaries as Sylvia Sydney, Leif Erikson, on loan from the Group Theatre, and a very young Sidney Lumet. Paramount devoted a great deal of attention to the ad campaign, which included a four-page color spread in *Motion Picture Herald* (February 18, 1939) and explicitly linked the movie to the Living Newspaper. "As a play presented by Federal Theatre, [it] won laurels of critics, attracting record crowds and reams of publicity," the ad copy blared. "Life magazine devoted three full pages to '. . . one third of a nation.' Other important national publications right now keeping public interest fanned to fever pitch!" Paramount promised "DRAMA! Real and true, scraped from the shadows . . . teeming with the full-blooded excitement of its seething, turbulent background!" Along with drama would come verisimilitude and "SPECTACLE! Huge tenement fire . . . tenants fighting for lives while flames scorch heavens. Actually filmed on streets of New York!" A headline in the *Hollywood Reporter* (January 11, 1939) read: " '. . . ONE THIRD OF A NATION' STRONG STUFF WITH B.O. PULL."

The opening of the movie in New York was a gala affair, as noted in the

February 10 *Hollywood Reporter* headline, "Paramount Sets Big Bow for 'Nation' Friday." Stars like Franchot Tone, Errol Flynn, Fredric March, and John Barrymore were in attendance, as well as public figures like Senator Robert F. Wagner, Mariner Eccles, the director of the Federal Reserve Bank, borough president Stanley Isaacs, Dr. Rex Tugwell, Victor Ridder, Dorothy Thompson, and Fannie Hurst. The carefully crafted guest list served to present a "serious" image for the film, one of public service as well as entertainment. It was the kind of movie Hollywood could feel good about presenting. As the *Hollywood Reporter* review noted, "this drama of the tenements is a compelling and human document. It should furnish a welcome relief to the jaded film fan, and the hard-pressed exhibitor. It's a combination of prestige and box-office that is a tribute to the value of the screen as a medium of universal entertainment and enlightenment." With the right "exploitation help," noted the reviewer, the picture "should pep up box-offices in all situations."[5] Paramount was certainly willing to offer that help. In the *New Orleans Times-Picayune,* for example, the film's arrival was presaged by publicity stills and by large advertisements which mentioned that "President Roosevelt Wrote the Title" and that the movie had been "Adapted from the Federal Theatre Triumph!"[6]

On the whole, reviews were strong. The *Times-Picayune* in its introductory blurb promised that, "Far from being merely a tract, or a statistical discussion of unhappy conditions of modern life, the film follows the play in being a dramatic and exciting presentation—of problems which are the concern of every American."[7] If this was a film that Hollywood could feel good about making, it was also a picture that audiences could view and feel as though they were doing their civic duty. The reviews quoted in Paramount's four-page spread ranged from the *New York Sun*'s pointing out that this was "One of the rare occasions on which the movies have turned their attention to controversial, contemporary problems affecting the welfare and happiness of a considerable portion of the population" to the *New York Telegraph*'s rave: "A distinct milestone in the progress of the movies. Something to be viewed." The *Brooklyn Eagle* deemed the film "A real screen triumph." The *New York World Telegram* called it "a bitter and two-fisted indictment of an unforgivable situation which exists in this country today." Perhaps the strongest review came from the left: The *New Masses* reviewer asked to be "the first to congratulate Mr. Harold Orlob and Paramount Pictures for the rare feat of making a picture in which the hero is a house." The reviewer went on to praise *One-Third of a Nation* as "a thrilling picture: a hard-hitting, intensely dramatic, and serious picture, a landmark in the American film."[8]

To be sure, some reviews, though positive, highlighted the differences between the Living Newspaper and the movie. The *New York Times* reviewer, for example, noted that "Arthur Arent, who wrote the play, probably would have difficulty in recognizing his brainchild." However, the reviewer concluded, "that matters only to Mr. Arent, his company and the Adelphians who saw the play. We uninstructed of the movie audience will take it for what it's worth, which is considerable, as an interestingly presented editorial for slum clearance."[9] The reviewer for *Variety* went further in his criticisms, maintaining that the movie's indirection "minimizes the sock of the WPA play source." Although praising the acting and direction and predicting that the movie "will do mild business in the dualers as it percolates into release," the review concluded by noting that " 'One Third of a Nation' was the first WPA play production sold for films. The cinematic transition, however, seems to have almost wholly ditched the Federal Housing 'living newspaper' purpose of the stage version, emphasizing the boy-meets-girl premise against the shocking slum background."[10]

It is not that the film is apolitical in its approach; but it is certainly less sanguine about the prospects for widespread change than is the play. Whereas the play consistently emphasizes the role of government in improving civic life, the first representative of the state that we see in the film version is the Irish cop who admonishes an unruly young Sidney Lumet that "It's time you learned to respect private property." Unlike the stage version, the film never questions whether property should remain private and does not outline ways in which the government might help to ameliorate the problem of inadequate housing. However, it does point up the inadequacy of even the most benevolent of capitalists in changing social conditions.

In Hollywood, the Political Becomes Personal

It is true, as the *Variety* and *New York Times* reviewers commented, that the film departs sharply from the Living Newspaper. In its original form, *One-Third of a Nation* is notable for that combination of theatrical innovation and historical reexamination that was a hallmark of the most successful Living Newspapers. Though both play and film open with a contemporary scene of a tenement going up in flames and a character dangling helplessly from a broken fire escape, in the play version it is an anonymous man, whose death is not even seen onstage. A blackout occurs just before he plunges to the ground, and we hear nothing more about him; his demise is important statistically but not sentimentally. In the film version, by contrast, it is the young Joey Rogers, played by Sidney Lumet, whose fall is occasioned by his refusal to give up his hold on his baseball bat and roller skates. When he does fall, his beautiful older sister Mary, played by Sylvia Sydney, is watching from the crowd, as is the handsome young man, Peter Cortland (Leif Erikson), who turns out to be, to her surprise and even his own, the landlord who owns the tenement. He first arrives on the scene, in fact, not because of his own connection with the tragedy but because his sidekick, Donald, played by Hiram Sherman, hears sirens and thinks watching the fire would be a great lark. (He turns triumphantly to Peter as the tenement burns, saying "What'd I tell you—isn't this a lulu?") Thus the specificity of the tragedy is immediately established: The romantic bond is, if not cemented, at least tentatively established shortly thereafter when Peter takes Mary and Joey to the hospital, where they wait for news from the doctor while he agrees with her that the owner of such a building is a murderer. He pays the hospital bill and comforts her when she learns that her brother will survive but is destined to live out his life as a cripple. With Peter's discovery the next day that he himself is the landlord whom he had asserted should be punished with worse than a prison sentence, and his inability to resist the advice of his lawyer, played by Percy Waram, not to express sympathy for the victims, the plot machinery is fully set in motion. With Mary's leftist boyfriend Sam, played by Myron McCormick, to provide occasional ideological pronouncements about the nature of capitalism, the conflict between spineless yet well-meaning heir and fiery young social worker has plenty of room to develop.

In the Living Newspaper, on the other hand, romance and individual tragedy are subordinated to a larger vision of history. Though we see plenty of personal loss—a mother grieving for her baby, newly dead of the cholera caused by tenement overcrowding—there is as much, or more, emphasis on the conditions and laws responsible for that epidemic. Although a few historically important individual slumlords, such as John Jacob Astor and Robert Goelet, are named, the focus is always coolly Brechtian rather than warmly sentimental. When a landlord is introduced, "dressed in a costume that somehow suggests the period from 1775 to 1850,"[11] and the Loudspeaker voice, the trademark of the Living Newspapers, asks him who he is, he replies: "Well, I might be a lot of people. My name might be Rhinelander, Astor, Goelet, Wendell, or—er, Schultz" (28)—the latter being the owner of the tenement that we have seen on fire in the first scene. The scene itself is a graphic representation of the way a landlord can, as he declares upon purchasing his original five-acre plot for $300, "sit here on my land, and make a lot of money" (29). By the end of the scene, his first tenant, who has gotten a twenty-year lease on a "very tiny segment at extreme corner" (31) of the land for fifty dollars a year, is joined by generations of other tenants, whose rents swell to $300 a year for even more minuscule plots. While historical bulletins on such events as the defeat of Cornwallis at Yorktown, the completion of the Erie Canal, and the beginning of the Great Immigration—each announcement accompanied by a note on the exact population of New York during that year—punctuate the scene, we see the worsening of conditions. As the stage directions inform us,

> By this time the TENANTS are sitting in restricted, cramped positions. They can hardly move. Their arms are pressed close to their sides. In these positions they are all engaged in going through some part of their daily routine. For instance, one is shaving; another is reading a newspaper; another is trying to eat; a fourth is washing himself. Still another is attempting to tie his shoe lace. Needless to say, all these activities must be cramped and hemmed in or the point of the scene is lost. (34)

By the time the final tenant, an extremely fat man, has spotted "a few blades of green grass still visible at the end of the carpet" (34), has agreed to pay an exorbitant rent for a plot the landlord assures him is "a little small, but right in the heart of the business section," and has managed to squeeze himself onto his spot with the help of a running start and an exhortation of "Home! Sweet Home!" (35), the audience has received a capsule lesson in urban history, complete with reminiscences by some of the most prominent landlords of the period—men like Astor and Goelet, whose stories are entirely concerned with dollars and cents. The scene, like all scenes in the play, is heavily footnoted.

In the film, we get a more personal account of the ways in which Peter's ancestors, particularly the great-grandfather whose portrait dominates his living room, accrued their wealth—and, more importantly for the sake of the plot, of the ways in which his inherited wealth has made Peter weak, incapable of opposing his father's wishes and fulfilling his childhood dream of becoming a doctor or other professional, incapable, in fact, of making many decisions on his own. In some ways, the movie is as much about Peter's self-actualization as about social change. When Peter tries to individualize the problem of slum housing, making it a matter of rescuing Mary from the terrible conditions that surround her, Mary refuses to let him forget the scope of the problem. This is a microcosm of the film's own ambivalence: Although in the end Peter does come through, tearing down Mary's building and replacing it with modern low-income housing, complete with playgrounds, windows, and other amenities, we cannot forget that there are thousands of other tenements in the city which are not destined to be razed by kindhearted owners.

To be fair, there are some scenes that overlap between movie and play. The second scene of the play, concerning the commissioner's investigation into the conditions responsible for causing the tenement fire, is largely reproduced in the film. In the film, as in the play, we learn of the laws governing tenements—and the exemption from those laws of tenements built before 1901. The statistics on the exact number of such unsafe buildings in New York and the paucity of housing inspectors to enforce even the regulations that apply are quoted in film as in play. In fact, much of the dialogue from this scene is transferred wholesale from play to movie. However, we see once again the difference between the larger social focus of the play and the more personal focus of the movie. In the scene from the play, a man who has lost his wife and two children in the fire asks the responsibility-dodging landlord, "And me? What about me?" The landlord replies:

> Mr. Rosen, believe me, I'm sorry for you. I'll do anything I can to help you. . . . But if you can only afford to pay $24 a month you'll have to live in my house or one just like it—and you cannot blame me. (*A pause—even more slowly.*) You'll have to go back into history and blame whatever it was that made New York City real estate the soundest and most profitable speculation on the face of the earth. (23)

The play refuses to let Mr. Rosen's loss overwhelm the larger social and historical lesson. But in the movie the investigation results in a confrontation between Peter, who volunteers to take the stand against his lawyer's advice, and Mary, and there is an unmistakable undercurrent not only of her leftist boyfriend's jealousy but of her disappointment that her white knight has turned out to be the man responsible for the inferno that has taken her brother's good health and will in the end take his sanity. The callousness of the idle rich is highlighted when Peter announces his intention to testify to his sister Ethel, played by Muriel Hutchinson, and to Donald; they are amused:

ETHEL: Oh, we'll all go—it will be fun.
DONALD: Yes, Peter will give a speech and I'll heckle.
ETHEL: And I'll vamp the district attorney.

In the Living Newspaper, the frivolity of the rich is simply irrelevant. The Living Newspaper has other things to do: It effectively outlines the sources of the problem of overcrowded, crime- and disease-breeding slums and explores tenants' attempts to rectify the situation, including the October 11, 1936, rent strikes in Harlem. Unlike the movie, the play has a multiracial cast. (By contrast, Sam, Mary's boyfriend, talks about how "You turn any city in this country upside down like a rock and you'll find us underneath—the poor, like grubs, all of us, white and sick-looking." All of the poor in the play may be sick-looking, but they are not all white.) Audience members are helpfully assigned a surrogate, the character of the Little Man, who appears onstage, demands to have the light placed on him, tells the Loudspeaker that "I'd like some information" (39), and explains his own difficulties in obtaining low-cost housing. As he tells the Loudspeaker, "I went down to see the Tenement Housing Commissioner. He told me the Living Newspaper was doing a show on housing and I ought to see it . . . so here I am" (40). Eventually, the play explores the inadequacy of most available solutions, including the then-current Wagner–Steagall housing bill, whose funding had been severely slashed from one billion dollars to 526 million dollars. The play ends by pointing out that the budget of the army and the navy for one year would be just about adequate to wipe out slums in New York, and with the Little Man and his wife agreeing that "We're going to holler. And we're going to keep hollering until they admit in Washington that it's just as important to keep a man alive as it is to kill him!" (120). The final image is a reenactment of the fire scene—a reminder that conditions continue to be dire—and the Loud-speaker's announcement: "Ladies and gentlemen, this might be Boston, New York, Chicago, St. Louis, Philadelphia—but just let's call it, 'one-third of a nation!' " (121).

Both the historical analysis of the problem and the exploration of a range of possible political solutions are largely absent from the movie. We see instead Mary's insistence that Peter visit the tenement in which she lives and his appalled reaction to the roaches, the overcrowding, the prostitution that is endemic there. We see the humiliation Mary must experience as she is forced to undress in front of her father, because there is no room for privacy. And we see young Joey slowly losing his mind as he finds himself shunned as a cripple by his former playmates. Indeed, one of the innovative features of the Living Newspaper—the talking tenement—appears here as a hallucination of Joey's. The history he learns—of the cholera epidemic that occurred fifty years pre-viously in his building—is not made available to other characters. And just as the problems are individualized, so is the solution. Peter, at Mary's insistence, cooks up a plan whereby he will be able to offer mortgages to the tenants currently living in his buildings. Although he promises her that he will go through with this plan, he quickly finds it squelched by his lawyer and his sister, who threatens him with a court fight, noting that although she would probably lose, "At least I'd discredit your whole scheme, show up your fine philanthropic gesture for what it is—an irresponsible, undignified, disgusting affair with a cheap little East Side parasite." Although a viewer may disagree with Ethel's choice of adjectives, it is clear that Peter's motivations are a little less than purely ideological. It takes Joey's derangement, induced by his realization that he will never escape the tenement, and his subsequent death in the tenement fire he sets (standing defiantly on the roof, waving his crutch, silhouetted against the night sky) to get Peter to stand up to his sister and lawyer and do what's right.

Although the film ends with a cheerful montage of workmen building a new, modern building, of children playing in the apartment complex playground—and of Joey looking down on the proceedings from above—it is hard for a viewer not to remember the grim statistics recited by the tenement commissioner in the investigation scene. If there are indeed 105,000 tenements in New York City alone, and if getting just one torn down and rebuilt requires not only the presence of the lovely Sylvia Sydney in a young heir's life but the death of a child, it is hard to be optimistic about this particular approach to urban renewal. As Joseph F. Coughlin noted, tongue planted rather firmly in cheek, in the "Showmen's Reviews of Product," a regular column in the *Motion Picture Herald,* "According to the story's solution, it would seem that the best way to meet the slum problem is to have a bevy of young women from the Ghetto meet up with an equal number of plutocratic playboys, who are as socially minded and as generous as 'Cortland' is drawn to be."[12]

Any lingering doubts that a viewer may have about the film's upbeat ending are reinforced by the visual structure of the movie. Perhaps the most powerful presence in the film is the tenement itself, which looms over the action, dwarfing the characters. The movie's director, Dudley Murphy, makes particularly effective use of the building as he shows just how different it looks when seen from within—crumbling, roach-infested, filthy—and when viewed at night, lights twinkling, from Peter Cortland's yacht, anchored in the nearby harbor. As Mary says, "I guess that's what money can do for you—change the angle—make what's ugly and rotten look picturesque." Although the ever-frivolous Peter may reply that, "Young lady, that's entirely too profound an observation on an empty stomach," viewers of the film cannot forget just how ugly the tenement looks up close—or how easy it is for those viewing it from afar to remain in blissful ignorance of its squalor and danger.

All in all, it is hard to disagree with the *Times* reviewer who noted that, "although the personal story is obviously a box office expedient, it has been sensibly and vividly told by a diligent cast and it never moves out of the shadow of the tenement itself." Given this combination of the personal and the political, it would be natural to expect the film to do as well as the successful Warner Brothers social-consciousness movies like *I Am a Fugitive from a Chain Gang* (1932), *Wild Boys of the Road* (1933), *Fury* (1936), *Black Legion* (1936), or *They Won't Forget* (1937). Yet a week after its New York opening, *One-Third of a Nation* was gone, replaced by *You Can't Cheat an*

Honest Man. The movie did equally badly across the country. In the *Motion Picture Herald* column "What the Picture Did for Me," disgruntled exhibitors reported audience reactions that ranged from tepid to downright hostile. From the Paramount Theatre in Dewey, Oklahoma, E. M. Freiburger described the movie as a "fair action picture which failed to draw. No kicks; no compliments. Played March 19"—a single day, that is. From Paynesville, Minnesota, at the Rialto Theatre (small town and rural patronage), the report was still more discouraging: "Am very sorry I played this. It has an interesting story but it leaves a very bad taste in the mouths of the few who will come out for a picture of this type. Not for small situations like this." The indictment from the owner of the Palace Theatre in Eufala, Oklahoma, was harshest of all: "Just a lot of wasted film. No one liked it. You will be better off if you leave it in the exchange."[13] In the end, the movie sank like a stone. Today, it is forgotten: The theoretically encyclopedic volume *1939: The Year in Movies* does not even list it. Why did *One-Third of a Nation* disappear into oblivion while a number of the social-consciousness films produced by Warner Brothers did at least moderate box-office business and are now enshrined in memory?

It is difficult to pinpoint a single cause to explain the movie's failure. Rather, a constellation of factors contributed to its premature death at the box office and in public consciousness. Generic expectations, conservative exhibitors, and a shift in public consciousness (and in Hollywood's consciousness) away from domestic problems and toward the threat of fascism all diluted the film's impact. The death of the Federal Theatre Project the same year of the film's release, thanks to the House Committee on Un-American Activities, can't have helped. And, ironically enough, the movie's very shift away from the message of the Living Newspaper from which it was derived—federal intervention as an effective method of solving social problems—may well have worked against its success. As Purdy and Roffman define the genre, social problem films were "indictment[s] of personal villainy which the films' social agencies do away with in the final reel."[14] In *One-Third of a Nation* the villain turns out to be a nice, weak-willed guy, who in the end becomes the agent of change. This, then, is more along the lines of a conversion experience than anything else and serves to muddy the film ideologically.

The Social Problem Film

Hollywood approaches to social problems tended to be weakened by studio ambivalence and, after its establishment in 1934, the sometimes heavy hand of the Production Code Administration headed by Joseph Breen. It was Breen who decreed that antilynching films like *Fury* and *Black Legion* should not deal with racial prejudice or criticize southern mores. In addition, studio owners often had fixed notions of what should or should not be represented on the screen. William Wyler tells the story of Sam Goldwyn's visit to the set of *Dead End.* Goldwyn was upset by the garbage littering the slum streets. When Wyler pointed out that, in fact, tenements tended to be dirty, Goldwyn snapped, "Not in my movies they don't," and ordered the trash picked up.

Exhibitors often maintained an implacable hostility toward anything they construed as on-screen propaganda. As Hollywood began to respond to the threat of fascism, the producer Walter Wanger issued a series of statements urging his colleagues to use the film medium to take a political stand. The response from the industry was swift. In *Motion Picture Herald,* the editor and publisher Martin Quigley inveighed against "the efforts of those who would invade the entertainment screen with political propaganda." Couching his argument in the language of Americanism, he declared that "the political propagandists would enslave the screen, just as they have done in all of the totalitarian states. My efforts are for the preservation of the freedom of the screen."

> It is my belief, which you seem more intent on suppressing than disproving, that motion pictures of a political, controversial character, embracing support of any one of the three institutions—Nazism, Fascism and Communism—would be commercially and strategically disastrous to the welfare of the industry.[15]

Of course, Wanger, a staunch Democrat, was not advocating the production of pro-Fascist, pro-Nazi, or pro-Communist films. The social problem films that Hollywood produced during the thirties were, on the whole, hardly radical. Compared to the expressions of support he received from exhibitors, however, Quigley's reaction to Wanger's proposals was positively mild. The publication of Quigley's broadside drew letters from what the *Motion Picture Herald* editor, stressing the economic clout of the respondents, described as "a cross section of the industry representing both distribution and exhibition, especially exhibition. There are expressions of the buying power, the authority of the consumers." In the excerpts published in the March 4, 1939, issue, exhibitors came out strenuously against anything other than apolitical entertainment. The president of the Allied-Independent Theatre Owners of Iowa-Nebraska wrote that "We believe the American motion picture industry, as an industry, should carefully refrain from becoming involved in any political, religious or racial controversy, either national or international." Thus, not only were Communist or Nazi movies objectionable, but any movies that touched on any political events were dangerous. The owner of the Hastings

Strand Theatre in Hastings, Michigan, seemed concerned about what show-ing controversial pictures might say about him: "Perhaps the producer loses sight of the fact that little or no attention is paid to who wrote the article or produced the picture, but when an exhibitor plays the picture, his public assume[s] that he sanctions its showing, and he more or less is on the spot." This exhibitor seemed nervous about being identified with controversial ideas—ideas he, in a small-town context, might be challenged on or asked to answer for. Some took up Quigley's refrain, equating the "propaganda" that Wanger endorsed with Communist ideas: "Not so long ago Communism, for instance, was tagged as a crazy cult of whiskered devotees in Russia, far removed from the daily round of life in the Middle West," wrote an exhibitor from Mason, Michigan. "But when the seed of Communism burgeoned in the sit-down strikes which paralyzed Michigan industry two years ago . . . Communism became at once a very real danger." Finally, many stressed eco-nomic arguments: As an exhibitor from Atlanta, Georgia, noted, "when the motion picture becomes propaganda it drives from the theatre those people who do not agree with the theories advanced in pictures." "I have always found," agreed an exhibitor in Griswold, Iowa, "that any kind of propaganda picture is poison at the box office." Interestingly enough, though, most ex-hibitors mentioned their personal status in the community as a reason for keeping politics out of movies. As one exhibitor from Custer, South Dakota, wrote, "We not only suffer from diminishing returns on pictures of this type, but get considerable criticism also, and that is bad for a business that caters to the general public. 'Blockade' did no business and it also caused some very, very adverse comment in my small town."

What was the "propaganda" that so many of these people were objecting to? Was it the hard-hitting radical message of *Black Fury* (1935), a film in which happy, comfortably housed, well-fed coal miners are duped into going on strike by a crook who works for an agency that stirs up labor unrest in order to hire out scabs and guards to management? (The workers end up much worse off as the result of their impulsive strike.) Or was the radical message con-tained in movies like *Black Legion* (1936) or *Fury* (1936), which, although their subject is lynching, make no allusion to racial relations for fear of offending southern audiences?

It is true that earlier films like *I Am a Fugitive from a Chain Gang* (1932) and *Heroes for Sale* (1933) offer a somewhat bleaker, less sanitized vision of the social problems of the Depression. In the former film, based on a popular autobiography of the period, a war veteran slides gradually into a life as a penniless hobo, is framed for a crime he has not committed, and eventually is sentenced to hard labor. His escape from the chain gang, his surrender on the condition that he will have a short sentence, his betrayal by authorities, and his final escape from the hell to which he has been indefinitely consigned leave him bitter, alone, living by his wits as a petty criminal. No benevolent federal authority intervenes on his behalf; there is no hope at movie's end, no promise of redemption through romance or hard work. Although it is not finally so bleak, *Heroes for Sale* treats the problems of a veteran, played by Richard Barthelmess, whose wife dies in a labor melee caused by callous management; he is thrown into prison for inciting the riot and is later branded a dangerous radical for starting a soup kitchen to help the unfortunate. Although Barthelmess does end the film with an optimistic declaration of faith in Roosevelt's programs, he ends it in a state of homelessness and destitution, a fugitive from justice.

To understand the difference between 1932's *I Am a Fugitive from a Chain Gang* and 1935's *Black Fury,* it is necessary to understand what a difference the Production Code of 1934 made. The Code solidified into Hollywood law what until that point had been only an intermittently obeyed Hollywood instinct. Enforced by Joseph Breen, the head of the Hays Office, the Production Code mandated filmic representations that would not offend important constituencies like southern audiences or the Catholic Legion for Decency. It called for producers to create the kind of "correct entertainment" that "tends to improve the race, or at least to re-create or rebuild human beings exhausted with the realities of life."[16] It was Joseph Breen who insisted that *Fury* not deal with racial prejudice. When Louis B. Mayer invited a representative of the Nazi regime to view an advance screening of the 1938 anti-Fascist drama *Three Comrades,* Breen, in order to mollify the Nazis, suggested that the film be changed to focus on the rise of communism rather than of nazism.[17] The gangster films viewed so avidly by Studs Lonigan, who completely identifies with the gangster protagonists of such (imaginary) films as *Doomed Victory,* are pre-Code and thus provide him with ample opportunity to imagine the on-screen criminals, and by extension himself, as heroes. As he watches the gangster work his way up in the criminal hierarchy, "Joey Studs Lonigan Gallagher laughing loudly," the blurring of identities is complete: "Joey Gallagher again fading, in the mind of Studs Lonigan, into Studs Lonigan. Studs Lonigan, the world is yours. Take it. Oh, Christ, why hadn't he had an exciting life like Joey Gallagher? It happened to some people. Look at Al Capone."[18] The tough gangster dying in a blaze of glory in 1932 would by 1938 become James Cagney in *Angels with Dirty Faces,* acceding to a priest's request that he deglamorize his profession by deliberately acting cowardly on the way to the electric chair in order to dissuade neighborhood kids from embarking upon a life of crime.

Yet the Code, while bleaching certain forms of sexual and criminal be-havior from the screen and enforcing conservative, family-oriented plots, was not necessarily running roughshod over the desires of producers. The fact of the matter is that the very forms of the classic Hollywood cinema made the production of radical texts difficult. While fiction writers and playwrights, such as those working on the Living Newspapers, were using modernist tech-nique and documentary to create a complex vision of American history and the current dilemmas facing Americans, Hollywood directors were creating a series of products recognizable and predictable enough that Depression au-diences could view them several times a week without undue discomfort. Studs Lonigan, the prototypical consumer of mass culture, when troubled by thoughts of his own mortality, "couldn't stand this, and [he] quickened his steps to get home and read the newspaper, listen to the radio, do anything to get those thoughts out of his head" (*JD,* 172). Studs also watches movies as a way of numbing the pain and anxiety caused by his Depression woes. Studs may be a product of the Marxist Farrell's worst fears about how the working class experiences culture, how formula comforts audiences who would be better off considering their predicament analytically rather than escaping into the comforts of predictability: "Studs yawned without reading the credit list or cast of characters, and slumped in his seat ready to let the picture afford him an interesting good time" (61). Whether or not most audience members resembled him in their desire for mindless formula, that was what Hollywood generally offered. While writers and playwrights of the period ranged freely through a storehouse of modernist and documentary techniques in search of a new approach—one that would entertain audiences while presenting them with a perspective new enough to make the familiar unrecognizable, or at least disquietingly different enough to merit fresh study—filmmakers adhered to the formula that seemed to guarantee box-office success.

Hollywood during the thirties may have been full of radical writers like Samuel Ornitz, author of the immigrant classic *Haunch, Paunch, and Jowl,* a caustic reworking of Abraham Cahan's *Rise of David Levinsky,* and a member of the first writers' delegation to Harlan County. (He later became one of the Hollywood Ten.) Yet, despite the presence of enough leftists in Hollywood to induce V. J. Jerome, the Communist Party's cultural commissar, to make a trip to California to set up a movie-industry branch of the Party, it was clear to all concerned that the influence of these members on the culture industry would be limited, at best. Party head William Z. Foster told those in attendance at a secret meeting at Dalton Trumbo's house, "We can't expect to put any propa-ganda in the films, but we can try to keep anti-Soviet propaganda out."[19] Indeed, years later, when the House Committee on Un-American Activities tried its hardest to unearth evidence of Communist influence in the movies, about the best that committee members could come up with was Lionel Stander whistling the "Internationale" while waiting for an elevator. By the midthirties, selling out to Hollywood had already become a cliché: Radical writers like Clifford Odets of the Group Theatre who left New York and headed west knew that, if they were not quite selling their souls, they were at least unlikely to create the kind of transgressive art that was possible onstage or between the covers of books. *Waiting for Lefty* could never be translated onto celluloid. In fact, the playwright had resisted the blandishments of movie producers for quite a while before finally capitulating. Odets had deliberately sabotaged his first Hollywood offers to film *Awake and Sing* by insisting on a contractual commitment not to change the political dialogue. When he finally decided to sign a studio contract, it was, as Wendy Smith writes, "all for a good cause. He would cut a quick deal, make a couple of fast bucks, send money home to the Group, and be home in a few weeks."[20] Odets, like his radical colleagues, may have spent a good deal of his time in Hollywood raising money for the Scottsboro Boys, but his politics and his work life remained fairly separate.

Sullivan's Travels:
The Road in Search of America, Hollywood-Style

Despite an adherence to formula, despite a reluctance to delve fully into the political problems of the era, filmmakers were often quite aware of the tension between their own inability to move beyond the constraints of formula and their sometime desire to grapple with the same issues as artists working in other genres. Perhaps the best exemplar of the journey Hollywood made throughout the thirties is *Sullivan's Travels,* Preston Sturges's 1941 comedy. A discussion of this movie is perhaps a fitting note to end on, since the protagonist of the movie, the highly successful movie director John L. Sullivan, embarks upon the journey with which so many artists began the thirties. Like Edmund Wilson, John Dos Passos, Waldo Frank, Sherwood Anderson, and others, Sullivan will traverse the American landscape in an effort not only to understand the nature of the political problems besetting the nation but to address the question of how to make radical art. Yet not only will the solution Sullivan devises for the problem of making art for the masses in a time of despair be markedly different from that of American writers and artists, but the journey upon which he embarks can stand as a metaphor for the distance Hollywood travels from the beginning to the end of the Depression in its representation of social problems.

The film-within-a-film with which *Sullivan's Travels* opens provides us with our first clue that there may be little hope for this pop director with a conscience. Although the sequence of two men engaged in a struggle to the death atop a moving train may be emblematic of capital and labor destroying one another, as Sullivan tells the studio executives screening the film, and although, as he excitedly continues, "it teaches a lesson, a moral lesson and it has social significance," it sure looks like formula to us, albeit formula overlaid with literary pretension. And that, it turns out, is the trouble: Sullivan, director of such blockbuster hits as *Ants in Your Pants* and *Hey, Hey in the Hayloft* wants to make real, gritty movies about the dilemma of the American worker. Though the studio bosses may be able to convince him of his inexperience and inadequacy by regaling him with (invented) tales of their Horatio Alger–like backgrounds, which stand in stark contrast to his life of privilege, they ultimately cannot dissuade him from embarking upon his trip across America. What we get, then, is the documentary record of this early thirties trope: Like Wilson and others, Sullivan will talk to the homeless, will question the small businessman, will get to the heart of the American malaise. Yet all we see is his failure to get anywhere close. A handsomely outfitted tour bus, courtesy of the studio, follows him wherever he goes, ready to cater to his every whim; his bum's outfit is furnished by wardrobe; and his hitchhiking efforts land him back in Hollywood.

There is a sour tone beneath the comedy, one that grows stronger as the picture draws to a close and Sullivan finds himself for the first time in serious trouble: suffering from amnesia, presumed dead by the studio, his bum's wardrobe all too convincing, sentenced to six years of hard labor on a chain gang for slugging a cop who has insulted him. Yet while a pre-Code, early thirties film like *I Am a Fugitive from a Chain Gang* could draw audiences into the claustrophobic prison environment of its protagonist and refuse to offer the escape hatch of a happy ending, *Sullivan's Travels* insists on its own unreality. When Sullivan finally remembers who he is, it is as though he has reawakened into the plot of his own life: "Hollywood directors don't end up on chain gangs," he tells the warden, and from there it is a matter of minutes until he attains his release. Although he has been sentenced for a crime he did indeed commit, and although his sentence is not out of line with those of the convicts whose fortunes he shares (who never, however, become more than shadowy background presences to us), the social order, as in any true comedy, has been restored. Rather than making *I Am a Fugitive from a Chain Gang of 1941*, in order to expose audiences to the conditions still suffered by his former cell mates, Sullivan's next movie will be *Ants in Their Pants of 1939*, as has been suggested by the studio executives. This prototypical director, convinced that the best he can do is to provide audiences with the predictable, amusing fare that will let them forget their troubles, will relinquish any attempt at accurate representation.

Sturges was no fool: *Sullivan's Travels,* like the best comic films of the period, hovers barely within its formulaic constraints, playfully self-conscious, yet ultimately never fully transgressive. Though Farrell may have dangled the possibilities afforded by mass culture before the noses of his readerless radical colleagues, he, and they, knew that the best they could hope for was to borrow some of the more lurid preoccupations and techniques of Hollywood and rework them within less corporate genres.

An American Comedy

Having begun with a late-thirties Paramount picture that provided at least a botched version of a Soviet-derived, documentary, modernist drama, it may be fitting to close with a Paramount picture of the early thirties that never got made: one which would have involved a collaboration between a great Soviet experimenter and a grandfather of the American radical novel. When Sergei Eisenstein arrived in Hollywood in the spring of 1930 with a $3,000-a-week contract from Paramount, the studio suggested that he film Dreiser's *An American Tragedy,* a notion that appealed to both Eisenstein and Dreiser tremendously. It would have been a pairing that perfectly expressed the possibilities for radical art in the thirties. At a time when writers and other artists were combining what they had learned from the naturalists and journalists of the teens and from the modernist experiments of the twenties, this collaboration could have perfectly inaugurated the new decade. As Edmund Wilson writes in *The American Jitters,*

> This interested Eisenstein very much: he understood it as Dreiser meant it to be understood, as a tragedy of American bourgeois ideals. He made a scenario in which Clyde Griffiths' early environment was given its full value—in which after his glimpses as a bellboy of the luxurious life in the hotel, he is brought back home to the dreary mission again; and in which the murder trial was made an indictment of the society which was condemning him and whose standards he had been doing his best to live up to.[21]

Eisenstein saw the real tragedy of the novel as "the tragic course pursued by Clyde, whom the social structure drives to murder."[22] This vision was rather different from that of the studio, one of whose writers described the novel as "the story about the guy who got hot nuts, screwed a girl and drowned her."[23]

Moreover, Eisenstein wanted to further violate the conventions of Hollywood by casting nonprofessional actors for the major parts in the film, as he had been accustomed to doing in the Soviet Union. He proposed finding Clyde Griffiths in a filling station or a hotel, and Roberta Alden among the shop girls of Hollywood. Not only did he want the "realism" of this casting, but, having recently discussed *Ulysses* with Joyce in Paris, he had invented a technique that was the cinematic equivalent of Joyce's stream of consciousness, one which he called the "interior monologue." In the end, Paramount didn't allow him to make *An American Tragedy,* or any other film for that matter. Hiring Eisenstein presented political problems: A Los Angeles professional patriot, Major Frank Pease, was telegraphing senators and congressmen to complain about the Russian's presence, and Hamilton Fish was beginning his investigations into Communist influence in Hollywood. The day his contract ran out, the studio bought Eisenstein a ticket back to Russia, and the film was made instead by Joseph von Sternberg, in a version that so angered Dreiser that he not only made a public protest but sued the studio for having misrepresented his whole meaning and therefore having violated his contract. In his statement, Wilson writes,

> Dreiser had called on American writers to stand up for their work in the films. He reminded them that the imagination of the Americans got most of its food from the movies; and that at a time when the country had reached a crisis which peculiarly demanded realistic understanding the movies were still bemusing them systematically with sentimental lies about their own lives and lies about life in general.[24]

Unsurprisingly, Dreiser lost his suit, although he did get the studio to agree to make some minor changes in the film. The experiments of the decade would continue but not in Hollywood, or at least not in such a stylistically and politically radical fashion. And by the end of the decade Paramount would be no closer to being willing or able to embrace fully the possibilities afforded them than they had been when they invited Eisenstein into their studio.

THE
SEARCH ABANDONED

The 1930s were marked by concern across the political spectrum with defining an American identity, whether it be the Communist Party's slogan "Communism Is Twentieth Century Americanism" or Ezra Pound's book *Jefferson and/or Mussolini?* It was the last time in our country's history that the left focused to such a degree on reclaiming the nation's past and present, when it was possible to be both radical and patriotic. It was also the last time that the federal government not only tolerated widespread debate over the nature of Americanism but actually funded such debate. For although political debate certainly took place in conventional contexts such as presidential campaigns and on the editorial pages of newspapers, the decade of the thirties was a time when arguments about the nature of American identity, and revisionary views of American history, were presented in the form of song, dance, literature, theater, and film.

Much of this work was produced with government funding under the auspices of the Federal Arts Projects. The Living Newspapers of the Federal Theatre Project reached an audience that ultimately numbered thirty million. The Federal Writers Project produced approximately a thousand publications, among them the state guidebooks. Perhaps the best-remembered projects of the Federal Arts Project were 2,500 murals painted by a range of distinguished and soon-to-be-distinguished artists, including Thomas Hart Benton, Grant Wood, Willem de Kooning, Reginald Marsh, Jackson Pollock, Rockwell Kent, Philip Guston, and Stuart Davis. Working for the Federal Dance Project, Helen Tamiris produced a dance interpretation of Walt Whitman's *Salut au Monde* as well as the more contemporary *How Long Brethren* (1937), a dramatization of black protest songs.[1]

The WPA's Joint Committee on Folk Arts sponsored the fieldwork of John A. Lomax and his son Alan for the swiftly growing Archive of American Folk Music in the Library of Congress. Beginning with their tour of southern prison camps in the early thirties, the Lomaxes made further recordings in the South, New England, and the Midwest. By 1940 the archives contained over 4,000 folk-music discs. Federal Music Project staffers went to Oklahoma to record and notate Native American music, to New Mexico for Spanish folk songs, to Mississippi for African American work songs.

The Farm Security Administration's Photography Unit, directed by Roy Stryker, was engaged in building a "picture record of rural America," and to this end photographers Ben Shahn, Dorothea Lange, Walker Evans, Russell Lee, Carl Mydans, Marion Post, and Arthur Rothstein compiled tens of thousands of images of Americans whose lives had hitherto gone unrecorded: sharecroppers, migrant workers, laborers.

For the government to consider the cultural productions of the dispossessed—convicts, sharecroppers, and the homeless—as serious art, worth not only recording but preserving as an integral contribution to the American identity, seems more than progressive; it seems, on the face of the matter, downright radical. Yet, though many of the decade's leftist artists and writers were on the government payroll, either through the Federal Arts Projects or under the auspices of the Farm Security Administration (FSA), it would be a mistake to characterize most government-sponsored art, or even most Americanist art and thought of the decade, as being radical. It is easy to conflate two distinct strands of thought during this period, a class conflict model and what we would today call a multiculturalist approach, and indeed, there is an overlap. It is, however, important to preserve some distinctions between the two camps. For while Dos Passos, Farrell, Herbst, and other class-conscious, politically oriented artists and thinkers were producing their work, many of their less radical colleagues were focusing on similar subject matter and using, often, the same documentary methods to achieve a very different result. This group included people like Margaret Mead and Constance Rourke, whose work is generally viewed as part of the American Studies movement; visual artists such as Ben Shahn and Thomas Hart Benton; and composers ranging from George Gershwin, whose 1935 opera *Porgy and Bess* was hailed for its Americanist themes, to Virgil Thomson, who scored the FSA-funded documentaries by Pare Lorentz, *The Plough That Broke the Plains* (1936) and *The River* (1938), which dealt with, respectively, the problems caused by the Dust

Bowl and the construction of the TVA dams. It included, as well, choreographers: in ballet, Lincoln Kirstein, who produced such Americanist works as *Filling Station* (1938), scored by Virgil Thomson, and *Billy the Kid* (1939), scored by Aaron Copland; in modern dance, Martha Graham, whose works during the thirties included *American Document* (1938), a ballet that reviewed the country's past, incorporating such documents as the preamble to the Declaration of Independence, as well as *American Provincials* (1934) and *American Lyric* (1938).

This group was spearheaded by those who stressed culture over class, who often used new materials, like folk songs and stories, prints and paintings, and oral histories, to forge a vision of America that was more inclusive than traditional histories. Like many of their radical counterparts, these artists and scholars often focused their attention on those who had hitherto been excluded from traditional histories—groups such as the industrial workers painted by Thomas Hart Benton and the sharecroppers photographed by Margaret Bourke-White. However, rather than using a model of class conflict, those in the American Studies movement used a more ethnographic model.

Constance Rourke, whose work involved collecting and publishing (and thus ratifying the importance of) American folk culture, remains one of the best exemplars of the ethnographic approach. Rourke, who became the director of the Federal Art Project's Index of American Design and who was perhaps the most famous of Depression-era American ethnographers, tended toward a generally celebratory view of American history. As Marcus Klein points out about her most famous book, *American Humor: A Study of the National Character,* "Given the perspective, Rourke could award honor to, for instance, the probable inventor of blackface minstrelsy, the white theatrical producer Jim Crow Rice—now forgotten except as an epithet but in his time, by Rourke's measure, an authentic and imaginative maker of tradition."[2]

Though writers like Rourke as well as documentarians like Dorothea Lange did embark on projects that recorded the lives of forgotten Americans, their aim was not necessarily to offer a Marxist perspective on the trouble they saw. For instance, Thomas Hart Benton's 1936 Missouri State Capitol mural did present aspects of state history and legend that many citizens would rather not acknowledge. Mark Twain's Huck Finn and Jim, Frankie and Johnny, the doomed lovers celebrated in American folk song, and the outlaw Jesse James gazed down at visitors and aroused protests. However, Benton preceded his move back to Missouri by circulating a farewell letter to New York in which he condemned the city as being overrun by Communists and homosexuals. Faulkner could offer his vision of the lives of dispossessed southerners and even provide his audiences with a history of their decline and fall, without necessarily speculating on the larger political reasons for the events in question. Some writers are harder to place in one camp or another: Agee, for instance, used documentary in *Let Us Now Praise Famous Men* but sidestepped attempts to place himself, or this work, in a radical camp.

What complicates the issue further is that the American Studies group and the radicals not only worked together on many government projects but were often able to use the same work for both ethnographic and explicitly political purposes. The convict songs collected by the Lomaxes were used to build an archive of American music, in much the same spirit as Rourke collected thousands of traditional images, from cigar-store Indians to farmers' weather vanes, for the Federal Art Project's Index of American Design. However, Lawrence Gellert used the Lomaxes' work as the basis for his collection, *Negro Songs of Protest* (1936), published under the auspices of the Communist-sponsored American Music League. The open political climate of not only the Depression cultural scene in general but the Federal Art Projects in particular facilitated intellectual and artistic exchanges between those who wanted to celebrate the richness of American heritage and those who had more radical political uses for that heritage.

History viewed through a cultural lens was indisputably less threatening to the troubled American regime of the thirties than history framed in terms of class struggle. When many perceived the country as falling apart, it was certainly in the government's interest to promulgate an image of America as a culturally diverse place that could include everybody. In many ways the Federal Arts Projects embody the tension between these two models: The thirties was probably the last time that radicals entered government jobs in the hope of being able to offer their vision of America to a large public. Their struggles to do so help illuminate the fate of radical culture since the Depression era.

Although the Federal Arts Projects were federally funded and centrally administered from Washington, battles over the representation of American life and history often took place at a strictly local level. The debate raged particularly fiercely, not only within a state but within a community, over the meaning of local history as depicted in the murals of the Federal Art Project, which were painted in post offices, state capitols, and other public buildings throughout the country. While heroic workers and smiling children certainly occupied their share of space in the murals, so did the poor, the homeless, and a range of historical figures, such as Abraham Lincoln and Frederick Douglass. Many murals were controversial: Industrialists in Kellogg, Idaho, condemned Fletcher Martin's design, "Mine Rescue," while officials of the Mine Workers and Smelt Workers Union praised it. The industrialists prevailed, and Martin substituted a design depicting the arrival of a local prospector for whom the town was named. In Watango, Oklahoma, Cheyenne Indians pitched a teepee on the post office lawn until Edith Mahier changed the Indian ponies on her mural, which Chief Red Bird complained looked like "oversized swans." However, on the whole the murals received, and continue to receive, their share of acclaim on social and aesthetic grounds, both from critics and from grateful citizens, including the postmaster of Pleasant Hill, Missouri, who wrote: "In behalf of many smaller cities, wholly without objects of art, as ours was, may I beseech you and the Treasury to give them some art, more of it, whenever you find it possible to do so. How can a finished citizen be made in an artless town?"[3]

Arguments over mural content often took place at an extremely local level; the state guidebooks of the Federal Writers Project, on the other hand, illuminate the debate that went on within different branches of the government, as well as within the Federal Arts Projects themselves, over how best to promote a vision of America that was not only inclusive but acknowledged past injustices. The guidebooks were collectively written reexaminations of the history of a particular state. The historical approach taken by the guidebook writers often stressed the class conflict and racial tension that had shaped the prevailing power structure of the area. Thus the official, government-produced history of a southern state included accounts of lynching, the Massachusetts guide included a sympathetic account of Sacco and Vanzetti's trial, and the Colorado guide focused on the Ludlow mining massacre. The guides were as comprehensively researched as the FTP Living Newspapers. As a result, project workers sometimes came across hitherto forgotten episodes which, in the words of one reviewer, supplied "a terrible and yet engaging corrective to the success stories that dominate our literature."[4]

The state guidebooks were products of a struggle that pitted local interests against federal administrators, reds against red-baiters, revisionists against reactionaries. Roosevelt and Harry Hopkins were both committed to the principle that the WPA would neither discriminate because of political beliefs nor inquire of its employees the nature of their politics. As a result, the political views shaping the project were heterogeneous—the first Federal Emergency Relief Agency plans for writers' projects reflected the influence of both the Communist-backed Writers' Union and the Authors' League, a group that represented most of the country's more established writers on issues of copyright and contract and that tended to be somewhat conservative. The Federal Writers Project (FWP) tended to stand behind authors who included guidebook pieces on Sacco and Vanzetti and on Tom Mooney, even when it meant bucking substantial pressure from state authorities. The Writers Project published autobiographical works by Richard Wright such as "The

Ethics of Jim Crow" and an essay by Charles S. Johnson on "Negroes in Tennessee," which served to break down traditional stereotypes.

However, although they did cut lines from the Mississippi guide like "the passing of public hanging was, in the eyes of the Negro, a sad mistake," the central administrators allowed sections offering stereotyped views of plantation culture to slip through. Given the exigencies of politics and the difficulties of maintaining a delicate balance of power between local and federal administrators of the project, it is remarkable that the Writers Project managed to produce as much radical material as it did. Moreover, the very structure of the project was one which broke down the hierarchies between the more successful and powerful writers and their struggling, hitherto largely unheard colleagues: Writers, both established and unknown, worked collectively, mostly within their own communities, to produce a comprehensive, thoroughly researched history of a state, a history that placed more emphasis, in general, on the stories of ordinary working Americans than on "great men." Black writers like Richard Wright and Zora Neale Hurston were actually paid by the government to write about the experience of being poor and black in the segregated South, and their stories, instead of being read by the hundred readers of a tiny radical magazine, were widely reviewed and disseminated to tens of thousands of readers.

When the Massachusetts guide came out with forty-one lines on the Sacco and Vanzetti case, Senators Henry Cabot Lodge, Jr., and David I. Walsh demanded an investigation, former governor Joseph B. Ely recommended that the volume be burned on the Boston Common, and Governor Hurley suggested that the writers of the guidebook go back where they came from. However, the federal government stood by the guide, and Harry Hopkins refused to hold up current printings of the book, although subsequent editions did incorporate slight changes, such as an essay that paid a little more attention to current industrial conditions and a little less to Sacco and Vanzetti.

In some ways it is difficult to see the Federal Writers Project as having a clear direction. Project administrator Henry Alsberg, though impassioned about the notion of producing the guidebooks, was so disorganized that he did not even keep carbons and thus had less than total control of the overall project. There were great ideological variations between the guidebooks from state to state, particularly on racial issues.

By contrast, the plan that Hallie Flanagan presented to Harry Hopkins for the FTP stated that its primary aim was "To set up theatres which have possibilities of growing into social institutions in the communities in which they are located and thus to provide possible future employment for at least some of those who now present an immediate and acute problem for the government."[5] The idea of theater as a tool of community empowerment was in itself fairly radical in a Broadway, big-money theater culture. More radical was the notion that theater could be used, as in the Living Newspapers, to increase the political awareness of audiences. Like the Writers Project, the Theatre Project stressed collective work and eschewed a star system in which "name" writers and actors would be given the greatest share of glory at the expense of unknowns.

However, the FTP ran into some of the same problems with recalcitrant state administrators as had the Writers Project. As Flanagan acknowledged, for example, "Texas was a tough nut to crack and we failed to crack it." Although she pushed hard to encourage the state director to produce plays like *Triple-A Plowed Under,* he was apprehensive and anxious to avoid controversy, preferring stock shows. "The Texas WPA feared what it referred to as 'any new type of show,' "[6] recalled Flanagan, and because of her stated emphasis on community choice and community empowerment, the Texas project consisted mainly of tent shows and stock shows.

All in all, the Theatre Project would have to be placed solidly on the radical side of the ledger, in that the Living Newspapers it produced were political dramas intended, among other things, to educate their audiences to understand current events using the tools of political—often class-based—analysis. In *1935* the U.S. justice system was indicted with a well-researched scene on the collusion between racketeers and courts in the Dutch Schulz case, and in *Power* the development of electrical monopolies and their detrimental impact on the workers of this country were discussed.

A verdict on the Writers Project would have to be mixed. There seemed to be more at stake for states in their representation of their own history, whereas the Living Newspapers, which frequently dealt with national rather than local issues, were by and large free from interference before they actually hit the stage. Governors and state senators, as well as powerful business interests, were more than likely to want a somewhat sugar-coated version of the history of their state, to present it as a place that welcomed all of its citizens, rather than as a site of class conflict and racial strife. And because the state guidebooks were in a form that was somewhat familiar to readers, they were easier targets for political criticism. More people knew how to read a history essay for political content than knew how to analyze a theatrical production that was a strange melange of film clips, newspaper quotations, and skits. The Living Newspapers had a chance to garner critical acclaim and attract large audiences before coming under attack from red-baiters, whereas the guidebooks originated in the states themselves and thus were subject to scrutiny by local government leaders before they ever hit print. Although the Writers Project leaders did their best to keep a somewhat prolabor, revisionist tone to the histories they produced, officials in each state tended to fight them hard over inclusion of data that would make their state seem less appealing as a destination for visitors.

The Federal Writers Project lasted longer than the Federal Theatre Project, but in somewhat altered form. In 1939, as a result of the Dies hearings, Congress voted not only to defund the FTP but to severely limit funding for the FWP. During the Dies committee hearings, Alsberg was questioned about such matters as a letter he had written to the editor of *The Nation,* ten years previously, protesting the inhumane treatment of prisoners and calling for the unionization of convicts. Although the letter was a decade old, had been written in a spirit of irony, and by no means reflected FWP policy, Alsberg was fired as director of the Writers Project and replaced with the more conservative John Dimmick Newsom. Allegations of Communist infiltration of the Federal Arts Projects led to the 1940 Relief Act, which required all WPA workers to sign affidavits that they were not Communists, Bund members, or aliens. At the same time, the country's entrance into World War II brought much of the FWP's work, like W. E. B. Du Bois's proposed encyclopedia of the Negro, to a screeching halt. Days after the invasion of Poland, Newsom circulated a memo among project staff suggesting that the efforts of the FWP be closely linked to the national emergency. In an additional memo, Newsom argued that "the Writers' Program alone could supply 'cultural content' to patriotism by providing the realistic awareness of 'a unified tradition—the most powerful stimulus to integrated action.' "[7] The state guides, the Living Newspapers, the dances, the murals, the Archive of American Folk Music had portrayed a highly heterogeneous nation, one populated by citizens of often competing interests, one often fraught with contradictions. Now the government was interested in presenting a united front to the outside world. The Writers Program, as it was now called, shifted its focus to war themes.

By the time America entered the war, the debate on Americanism was beginning to narrow. The left was in disarray, following the signing of the Soviet–Nazi pact in 1939. The government's focus shifted, from tolerating and even encouraging a wider cultural debate on national identity to maintaining the war effort. The uneasy wartime alliances of left and right, of the Soviet Union and the United States, were not stable enough to permit the kinds of questions that were possible during the thirties. Charges of disloyalty carried greater weight during wartime than they had in the thirties. In 1942 Josephine Herbst was abruptly dismissed from her job at the Office of the Coordinator of Information in Washington, where she worked at the German desk writing anti-Nazi propaganda for broadcast overseas, a position she had volunteered for after the bombing of Pearl Harbor. Just before her dismissal she was visited by investigators who asked her why she had gone to the Soviet Union in 1930 and told her that it was reported that in Madrid, in 1937, she had broadcast on behalf of the Spanish Loyalists and that, in 1932, she had signed a petition protesting the violation of civil rights in Detroit.[8] In later years these activities would have specific, familiar names, like premature antifascism; at this point they were still enough to get Herbst fired. The national focus had shifted: Americans were no longer gazing inward and had largely stopped searching for a usable past. Instead, they were looking overseas. And when the war was over, the cultural landscape of the thirties would be radically altered.

With the end of the Second World War, and the beginning of the Cold War, the acceptable options for Americanism narrowed further. Just as there were fewer ways to be American, so there were many more ways to be considered un-American. The House Committee on Un-American Activities, which began hearings shortly after the war, called writers, directors, and actors to the stand to defend their unpatriotic activities during the thirties. Loyalty oaths became commonplace in business and government; by the fifties, it seemed almost inconceivable that, less than twenty years previously, an American president had strenuously insisted that government relief projects should hire workers regardless of their political affiliations.

Introduction. From Uncle Tom's Cabin *to* Gone with the Wind

1. Matthew Josephson, *Portrait of the Artist as American* (1930; rpt., New York: Farrar, Straus & Giroux, 1979), p. xv.

2. Quoted in Alan Trachtenberg, *Reading American Photographs* (New York: Hill & Wang, 1989), p. 231.

3. See G. Kurt Piehler, *Remembering War the American Way* (Washington, D.C.: Smithsonian Institution Press, 1995), p. 73.

4. Edmund Wilson, *Patriotic Gore* (New York: Oxford University Press, 1962), p. 3.

5. Emerson to James Eliot Cabot, August 4, 1861, *The Letters of Ralph Waldo Emerson,* ed. Ralph L. Rusk (New York, 1939), 5: 253. Quoted in George Frederickson, *The Inner Civil War: Northern Intellectuals and the Crisis of the Union* (New York: Harper & Row, 1965), p. 176.

6. Michael Denning, *Mechanic Accents* (London: Verso Books, 1987), p. 26.

7. Ibid., p. 34.

8. Lawrence W. Levine, *Highbrow/Lowbrow* (Cambridge: Harvard University Press, 1988), p. 146; Sinclair Lewis quoted on p. 144.

9. Quoted in Roland Marchand, *Advertising the American Dream: Making Way for Modernity, 1920–1940* (Berkeley: University of California Press, 1985), p. 52.

10. Quoted in Denning, *Mechanic Accents,* pp. 30–38.

11. Robert S. Lynd and Helen Merrell Lynd, *Middletown* (New York: Harcourt Brace & World, 1929), p. 233.

12. Although the Lynds, when they came back to Middletown in 1935, found that the onset of the Depression had caused a new surge in reading and that reading rates

had actually gone up with the new, involuntary leisure afforded the unemployed, they also noted that as the Depression wore on reading rates began to sink again. It is possible that Depression writers, had they read *Middletown in Transition,* could have taken hope from the Lynds' statistics on readership rates. However, they might also have lost hope from statements such as the one from a local businessman, whom the Lynds quote to explain why an abrupt slacking-off in 1933 followed the dramatic rise in nonfiction reading of 1932: "We small businessmen began to see that we had to save our own necks. And so we stopped trying to understand the big issues and kind of lost touch with them. They're too big for us anyway." Robert S. Lynd and Helen Merrell Lynd, *Middletown in Transition* (New York: Harcourt Brace, 1937), p. 256.

13. Robert S. McElvaine, *The Great Depression* (New York: Times Books, 1984), p. 208.

14. In fact, *Gone with the Wind* was only one of many Civil War novels that appeared in the thirties; among the most notable were Joseph Hergesheimer's *The Limestone Tree* (1931), T. S. Stribling's *The Forge* (1931), Du Bose Heyward's *Peter Ashley* (1932), Roark Bradford's *Kingdom Coming* (1933), MacKinlay Kantor's *Long Remember* (1934), Stark Young's *So Red the Rose* (1934), Andrew Lytle's *The Long Night* (1936), Clifford Dowdey's *Bugles Blow No More* (1937), Caroline Gordon's *None Shall Look Back* (1937), Edgar Lee Masters's *The Tide of Time* (1937), Hervey Allen's *Action at Aquila* (1938), William Faulkner's *The Unvanquished* (1938), Allen Tate's *The Fathers* (1938), Francis Griswold's *A Sea Island Lady* (1939). See Richard Harwell, "Gone with Miss Ravenel's Courage; or, Bugles Blow So Red: A Note on the Civil War Novel," in Richard Harwell, ed., *"Gone with the Wind" as Book and Film* (Columbia: University of South Carolina Press, 1983), p. 8.

15. See Jack Temple Kirby, *Media-Made Dixie: The South in the American Imagination* (Baton Rouge: Louisiana State University Press, 1978), pp. 69–73, and Jim Cullen, *The Civil War in Popular Culture: A Reusable Past* (Washington, D.C.: Smithsonian Institution Press, 1995), pp. 40–44.

16. Theodor Adorno, "Perennial Fashion—Jazz," in *Prisms,* trans. Samuel and Sherry Weber (London: Neville Spearman, 1967), p. 121; Adorno, "On the Fetish-Character in Music and the Regression of Listening," in *The Essential Frankfurt School Reader* (New York: Urizen Books, 1978), pp. 278, 287; Adorno and Max Horkheimer, "The Culture Industry: Enlightenment as Mass Deception," in *Dialectic of Enlightenment,* trans. John Cumming (New York: Seabury Press, 1972), pp. 120, 126, 278; Martin Jay, *The Dialectical Imagination* (Boston: Little, Brown, 1973), p. 190.

17. Arnold Rampersand, *The Life of Langston Hughes* (New York: Oxford University Press, 1986), 1:359.

18. Adorno and Horkheimer, "Culture Industry," p. 120; Adorno, "On the Fetish Character in Music," p. 287. Odets quoted in Margaret Brenman-Gibson, *Clifford Odets, American Playwright: The Years from 1906 to 1940* (New York: Atheneum, 1982), p. 393.

19. Malcolm Bradbury and James McFarlane, eds., *Modernism* (1976; rpt., New York: Penguin Books, 1991), p. 27.

20. James Agee and Walker Evans, *Let Us Now Praise Famous Men* (1941; rpt., Boston: Houghton Mifflin, 1980), p. 197.

21. Bradbury and McFarlane, *Modernism*, p. 27.

22. Quoted in Malcolm Cowley, *The Dream of the Golden Mountains: Remembering the 1930s* (1964; rpt., New York: Viking-Penguin, 1981), p. 271.

1. The Road

1. Sherwood Anderson, *Puzzled America* (New York: Charles Scribner's Sons, 1935), p. ix.

2. Sherwood Anderson, *A Story Teller's Story* (1922; rpt., New York: Viking Press, 1927), p. 78.

3. Indeed, it seems fitting that it would be Edmund Wilson, whose *American Jitters* is one of the great entries into the genre of thirties travel writing, who would produce what remains one of the best studies of Civil War literature, *Patriotic Gore.*

4. Studs Terkel, *Hard Times: An Oral History of the Great Depression* (New York: Pantheon Books, 1970), pp. 85, 93, 207, 30, 107.

5. For general accounts of the Depression, see William Leuchtenberg, *Franklin D. Roosevelt and the New Deal, 1932–1940* (New York: Harper & Row, 1963), Robert S. McElvaine, *The Great Depression* (New York: Times Books, 1984). For a contemporary treatment of events, look to Frederick Lewis Allen, *Since Yesterday: The Nineteen-Thirties in America* (New York: Harper & Brothers, 1939). For a detailed account of the Bonus March, see Malcolm Cowley's *Dream of the Golden Mountains: Remembering the 1930s* (1964; rpt. New York: Viking-Penguin, 1981).

6. For the best account of this tragedy, see Donald Worster, *Dust Bowl* (New York: Oxford University Press, 1979). For a great account of traveling through the dust belt, see Nathan Asch, *The Road: In Search of America* (New York: W. W. Norton, 1937), pp. 99–104.

7. Ruth McKenney, *Industrial Valley* (New York: Harcourt Brace & World, 1939), pp. 9, 12, 34, 49, 54, 64, 78.

8. McElvaine, *Great Depression*, p. 142.

9. Roosevelt quoted in ibid., p. 117.

10. Cowley, *Dream*, p. 11.

11. Ibid., p. 16.

12. James Rorty, *Where Life Is Better: An Unsentimental American Journey* (New York: Reynal & Hitchcock, 1936), p. 11.

13. Louis Adamic, *My America* (New York: Harper & Brothers, 1938), p. xi.

14. Ibid., p. 48.

15. James Agee and Walker Evans, *Let Us Now Praise Famous Men* (1941; rpt., Boston: Houghton Mifflin, 1980), p. xv.

16. Asch, *The Road*, pp. 23, 59, 58, 268.

17. Ibid., p. 269.

18. Richard H. Pells, *Radical Visions & American Dreams: Culture and Social*

Thought in the Depression Years (Middletown, Conn.: Wesleyan University Press, 1973), p. 196.

19. Rorty, *Where Life Is Better,* p. 30. Nathan Asch, *Pay Day* (New York: Brewer & Warren, Payson & Clarke, 1930), pp. 254–55.

20. Anderson, *Puzzled America,* p. x.

21. Rorty, *Where Life Is Better,* pp. 49–50.

22. Henry Hart, ed., *American Writers Congress* (New York: International Publishers, 1935), p. 9.

23. In 1935 the Seventh World Congress of the Communist Party International issued a call for a Popular Front to fight the rise of fascism throughout the world. This began a period during which Communists and other leftists formed alliances with liberals and began supporting many aspects of the New Deal. Earl Browder, the general secretary of the Communist Party, ran for president in 1936 only because the Party did not want to hurt Roosevelt's chances for reelection by openly supporting him.

24. Fred J. Ringel, ed., *America: As Americans See It* (New York: Harcourt Brace, 1932). As Ringel explained in his foreword, the book began as an attempt "to present to Europeans a real commentary on America. [Though] [i]ntended and edited for publication in European countries, the book when assembled promised to be equally interesting at least, to American readers. So, strangely enough, it is being published first in this country" (vii)—where it became a best seller.

25. Joan Shelley Rubin, *Constance Rourke and American Culture* (Chapel Hill: University of North Carolina Press, 1980), p. 53.

26. Joseph Freeman, *An American Testament* (New York: Farrar, Straus & Giroux, 1973), p. 34.

27. It was also marked by its extreme thoroughness. As S. S. McClure, the editor of *McClure's Magazine,* recalled, the preparation of the five articles Ida Tarbell produced on Standard Oil took her fifteen years to write. The form of journalism pioneered in his magazine, McClure wrote, was predicated on a dramatic change in the pace and economics of journalism: "I decided . . . to pay my writers for their study rather than for the amount of copy they turned out—to put the writer on such a salary as would relieve him of all financial worry and let him master a subject to such a degree that he could write upon it, if not with the authority of the specialist, at least with such accuracy as could inform the public and meet with the corroboration of experts." S. S. McClure, *My Autobiography* (New York: Frederick A. Stokes, 1914), p. 245.

28. Freeman, *American Testament,* pp. 56, 173. Cowley, *Dream,* pp. 28, 31.

29. Freeman, *American Testament,* p. 114; Williams quoted on p. 112.

30. In his introduction to the 1984 reissue of Stearns's *The Street I Know,* under the title *Confessions of a Harvard Man* (1935; Santa Barbara: Paget Press, 1984), Hugh Ford disputes Cowley's account of Stearns as the "Moses who led young Americans out of the contaminated New World into the cultural folds of the Old" (xiii), pointing out that Stearns's departure was motivated not just by intellectual and ideological reasons but also by the loss of his wife in childbirth and the adoption of his infant son by his

parents-in-law. Stearns's life, in fact, had its tragic aspects; he interrupted a promising American career to end up as a racecourse tout (albeit a very successful one) and alcoholic moocher in Paris. He returned to this country only in 1932, when the last of his options had run out.

31. Freeman, *American Testament,* pp. 183, 232. William Wiser, *The Crazy Years: Paris in the Twenties* (New York: Atheneum, 1983), p. 25.

32. Freeman, *American Testament,* p. 221.

33. Matthew Josephson, *Infidel in the Temple* (New York: Alfred A. Knopf, 1967), p. 5.

34. Malcolm Cowley, *Exile's Return* (1934; rpt., New York: Penguin Books, 1969), pp. 170, 174.

35. Matthew Josephson, *Life among the Surrealists* (New York: Holt, Rinehart & Winston, 1962), p. 274.

36. Virgil Thomson, *Virgil Thomson* (New York: Alfred A. Knopf, 1966), pp. 116–17.

37. Freeman, *American Testament,* p. 250.

38. Claude McKay, *A Long Way from Home* (1937; rpt., New York: Harcourt Brace & World, 1970), p. 103.

39. Freeman, *American Testament,* p. 375.

40. Frances Perkins, secretary of labor under Roosevelt, traced the reforms of the 1930s to the report of the factory commission responsible for investigating the Triangle Shirtwaist fire, a commission on which she served: "The stirring up of the public conscience and the act of the people in penitence brought about not only these laws which make New York State to this day the best state in relation to factory laws; it was also that stirring of conscience which brought about in 1932 the introduction of a new element into the life of the whole United States. We had in the election of Franklin Roosevelt the beginning of what has come to be called a New Deal for the United States. But it was based really upon the experiences we had had in New York State and upon the sacrifices of those who . . . died in that terrible fire on March 25, 1911." From a speech by Perkins on March 25, 1961, quoted in Leon Stein, *The Triangle Fire* (Philadelphia: J. B. Lippincott, 1962), p. 211.

41. Editors of *Direction* included Thomas Cochran, John Hyde Preston, Harriet Bissell, and M. Tjader Harris. Bissell was replaced by H. L. River after the first three issues. Preston was the author of the 1938 proletarian novel *The Liberators.*

42. *Direction* 1.3 (April 1938): 30.

43. The project of redefining Americanism would occupy radicals of various stripes throughout the thirties. A typical example of this rhetoric may be found in the prologue to Granville Hicks's 1938 travelogue, *I Like America,* in which he contrasts the Americanism of red-baiters with his own revolutionary form of patriotism: "My kind of patriotism, unlike yours, is, as I have said, the patriotism that believes in change. And I think it is more clearly akin than yours to the patriotism of the men who fought in the American Revolution, of the abolitionists, of the westward-moving pioneers. We have made some drastic changes in our history as a nation, and it seems

to me truly America needs to be ready to make another great change if the need exists" (New York: Modern Age Books, 1938), p. 5.

44. See Michael Gold, "A Love Letter for France," anthologized in *Mike Gold: A Literary Anthology,* ed. Mike Folsom (New York: International Publishers, 1972), p. 236.

45. *Books,* July 24, 1938, p. 2.

46. *Commonweal* 28 (July 15, 1938): 332.

47. Ruth McKenney, *My Sister Eileen* (New York: Harcourt Brace & World, 1938), p. vii; hereafter, page numbers are cited parenthetically in text.

48. *New Republic* 98 (February 22, 1939): 77.

49. Quoted on the back cover of the paperback edition of *Industrial Valley.*

50. McKenney, *Industrial Valley,* pp. 16–17, 61, 52.

51. A great deal of recent scholarship has focused on the reinterpretation of proletarian fiction of the thirties. See, for instance, Barbara Foley's comprehensive *Radical Representations: Politics and Form in U.S. Proletarian Fiction, 1929–1941* (Durham: Duke University Press, 1993). Foley, as she states in her introduction, eschews detailed readings of individual texts in favor of "omnibus analyses generalizing about the relation of generic to doctrinal politics in a broad range of novels" (xi); as this statement and her subtitle suggest, her analysis is focused more closely on the role of the proletarian novel within radical movements than on the function of radical fiction within the culture at large, and on the ways that the "culture wars" were enacted within specific texts. For recent work on radical literature of the Depression, see also James D. Bloom, *Left Letters: The Culture Wars of Mike Gold and Joseph Freeman* (New York: Columbia University Press, 1992), which focuses attention on the debates of radical writers in the thirties—over such issues as attaining readership, as well as over the use of experimental forms—through the work of Gold and Freeman. I agree with Foley, however, that Bloom's work is overreliant on hegemonic notions of a "party line" which (presumably) dominated writers' thought during the Depression. The bogey of Stalinism still haunts most discussions of radical literature of the period; obviously, nobody wants to be put in the position of seeming to stand up for Stalinism. What I would like to propose is an alternative model for looking at radical literature, a more assimilationist view, as it were. While the work that has been done on the Trotskyist-Stalinist "culture wars" of the period is important, it is equally important, I think, to keep in mind the mutability of ideology during the period—which is why I'm more interested in situating radical thought within the context of Depression debates over the nature and function of Americanism. James Murphy, *The Proletarian Moment: The Controversy over Leftism in Literature* (Urbana and Chicago: University of Illinois Press, 1991), challenges the notion of an ideologically hegemonic Communist Party battling the *Partisan Review*'s more open, literarily sophisticated crowd, espoused most recently in Alan Wald, *The New York Intellectuals: The Rise and Fall of the Anti-Stalinist Left from the 1930s to the 1980s* (Chapel Hill: University of North Carolina Press, 1986), which posits a richer revolutionary tradition of Trotsky-

ist thought against a more stultifying Stalinist left. Much recent scholarship has focused on the reasons for the critical neglect of or contempt for the proletarian literature of the thirties. Most notably, Cary Nelson discusses Cold War suppression of radical Depression texts in *Repression and Recovery: Modern American Poetry and the Politics of Cultural Memory* (Madison: University of Wisconsin Press, 1989). Nelson's work stands against Daniel Aaron's notion that the Communist Party was a uniformly suffocating influence on American writers of the period. See Aaron's *Writers on the Left: Odysseys in American Literary Communism* (New York: Harcourt Brace & World, 1961). Paula Rabinowitz uses feminist and psychoanalytic theory to discuss proletarian novels written by women in *Labor and Desire: Women's Revolutionary Fiction in Depression America* (Chapel Hill: University of North Carolina Press, 1991). Walter Rideout's *The Radical Novel in the United States, 1900–1954* (Cambridge: Harvard University Press, 1956) remains a wonderfully clear overview of a great number of texts and movements.

2. Dos Passos Issues a Challenge

1. Donald Pizer, *Dos Passos' U.S.A.* (Charlottesville: University Press of Virginia, 1988), p. 29.

2. Melvin Landsberg, *Dos Passos' Path to U.S.A.* (Boulder: Colorado Associated University Press, 1972), p. 1.

3. Pizer, *Dos Passos' U.S.A.,* p. 30.

4. In this article, which appeared in the *New Republic* in October 1916, Dos Passos complained that "No ghosts hover about our fields; there are no nymphs in our fountains; there is no tradition of countless generations tilling and tending to give us reverence for those rocks and rills and templed hills so glibly mentioned in the national anthem" (*New Republic* 8 [October 14, 1916]: 269–71)—an echo of Henry James's 1887 lament about America's insufficiencies for writers: "one might enumerate the items of high civilization, as it exists in other countries, which are absent from the textures of American life, until it should become a wonder to know what was left . . . no country gentlemen, no palaces, no castles, nor manors, nor old country-houses, nor parsonages, nor thatched cottages nor ivied ruins" (Henry James, *Hawthorne* [1887; rpt., New York: AMS Press, 1968], p. 43). Where Dos Passos parts company from James is in his somewhat unsettling talk of soul and soil, in his nostalgia for "primitive savageries" and his distaste for American "floundering, without rudder or compass, in the sea of modern life." American literature, wrote Dos Passos, reflected all too well "that genial, ineffectual, blandly energetic affair," the American soul, in itself insufficient for the production of great literature. "As a result of this constant need to draw on foreign sources our literature has become a hybrid which, like the mule, is barren and must be produced afresh each time by the crossing of other strains." This decidedly antimodern tone would, of course, be gone by the time Dos Passos wrote *U.S.A.;* what clearly carried over into the trilogy, however, was Dos

Passos's concern about the gentility, which he associated with the feminization, of American literature: "It is significant," he wrote, "that, quite unconsciously, I chose the works of two women to typify American novels."

5. Among other American writers who were ambulance drivers in 1917 were e. e. cummings, Dashiell Hammett, Robert Hillyer, Louis Bromfield, Sidney Howard, John Howard Lawson, Ernest Hemingway, Harry Crosby, William Seabrook, Slater Brown, and Julian Green.

6. Nathan Asch, *Pay Day* (New York: Brewer & Warren, Payson & Clarke, 1930), pp. 254–55.

7. John Dos Passos, *Facing the Chair: Sacco and Vanzetti: The Story of Two Foreign Born Workmen* (Boston: Sacco and Vanzetti Defense Committee, 1927), p. 25.

8. Landsberg, *Dos Passos' Path*, p. 143.

9. *Americana* 1.1 (1932): 10–20. This doggedly nonsectarian humor magazine, edited in its final incarnation by Alexander King, Gilbert Seldes, Nathanael West, and George Grosz was devoted in large part to documenting the ironic distance between official and unofficial realities. As the editors declared in their opening manifesto, "We are Americans who believe that our civilization exudes a miasmic stench and that we had better prepare to give it a decent but rapid burial. . . . We are the laughing morticians of the present" (1.1 [1932]: 1).

10. John Dos Passos, *The Big Money* (1936; rpt., New York: New American Library, 1969), p. 519; hereafter cited parenthetically in text as *BM.*

11. Ruth McKenney studs the text of *Industrial Valley* with actual examples of such unfounded optimism as, in 1932, the "*Beacon Journal,* Akron's leading newspaper, published an editorial which read, in part: 'It is manifest that this pinch cannot abide forever and that in the long run it is going to be a good thing for the country.'" In 1933, McKenney notes, Henry Ford, interviewed by the same journal, was quoted as saying that "This nation is on the threshold of an inconceivably bright future." *Industrial Valley* (New York: Harcourt Brace & World, 1939), pp. 19, 61.

12. Gilbert Seldes, *The Years of the Locust* (Boston: Little, Brown, 1933), p. 56. Among Seldes's illustrations are a facsimile of a *Boston Herald* front page for 1930. The headline reads: "Confidence Is Keynote of New Year." Smaller headlines trumpet: "Leader of Investment Bankers Has No Fears for Normal Prosperity" and "Secretary Lamont Says General Business Is on Sound and Stable Basis" (55).

13. See, for instance, William Stott, *Documentary Expression and Thirties America* (Chicago: University of Chicago Press, 1973), pp. 67–73.

14. Ibid., p. 69.

15. Robert S. McElvaine, *The Great Depression* (New York: Times Books, 1984), p. 53.

16. The "Newsreels" of *U.S.A.* stand in sharp contrast to the autobiographic, "truer" "Camera Eye" sections. Actual newsreels, as Raymond Fielding points out, "were compromised from the beginning by fakery, re-creation, manipulation and staging. None of these practices is necessarily inappropriate in certain types of docu-

NOTES TO PAGES 44–63   191

mentary films, but all are certainly suspect in a medium that tries to pass as reportorial journalism." Raymond Fielding, *The March of Time, 1935–1951* (New York: Oxford University Press, 1981), p. 5.

17. As Walter Rideout points out, at the end of Robert Cantwell's strike novel *The Land of Plenty* two husky journalists assist policemen in beating up a striker, whereas an entire chapter in Clara Weatherwax's prizewinning *Marching! Marching!* is devoted to two parallel columns offering divergent accounts of a strike: one from a local newspaper and another from the union's own paper (Walter Rideout, *The Radical Novel in the United States* [Cambridge: Harvard University Press, 1956], p. 200).

18. See, for instance, Peter Ellis's critical article on a "March of Time" feature on sharecroppers, "King Cotton's Slaves," which appeared in *New Masses*, August 18, 1936.

19. "Time Marches On!" *New Theatre*, August 1936. In its very next issue the magazine editorialized against newsreel manufacturers who signed a contract with Hitler, agreeing to his terms on how they should document the 1936 Olympic games. "Newsreel Muzzle," *New Theatre*, September 1936.

20. Thomas Sugrue, "The Newsreels," *Scribner's Magazine* 101.4 (April 1937): 9–18.

21. Dos Passos, *The Big Money*, p. 444.

22. John Dos Passos, *The 42nd Parallel* (1930; rpt., New York: New American Library, 1969), p. 42; hereafter cited parenthetically in text as *FP*.

23. John Dos Passos, *Nineteen Nineteen* (1932; rpt., New York: New American Library, 1969), p. 98; hereafter cited parenthetically in text as *NN*.

24. Roland Marchand, *Advertising the American Dream: Making Way for Modernity, 1920–1940* (Berkeley: University of California Press, 1985), p. 6.

25. See Landsberg, *Dos Passos' Path*, p. 213.

26. In the autobiographical Camera Eye (25), Dos Passos offers readers a far more oppressive version of a Harvard education: "haven't got the nerve to break out of the bellglass four years under the etherdome breathe deep gently now that's the way be a good boy one two three four five six get A's in some courses but don't be a grin be interested in literature but remain a gentleman don't be seen with Jews or Socialists" (*FP*, 311).

27. Frederick Lewis Allen, *Only Yesterday: An Informal History of the 1920's* (1931; rpt., New York: Harper & Row, 1964), p. 149.

28. James Harvey Young, "Patent Medicines and the Self-Help Syndrome," in *Medicine without Doctors*, ed. Guenter B. Risse (New York: Science History Publications, 1977), p. 98.

29. Barbara Foley, "The Treatment of Time in *The Big Money*: An Examination of Ideology and Literary Form," *Modern Fiction Studies* 26.3 (Autumn 1980): 457–58.

30. James Harvey Young, *The Toadstool Millionaires* (Princeton: Princeton University Press, 1961), p. 239.

31. David Vanderwerken, *Dos Passos and the "Old Words"* (Ann Arbor: University Microfilms, 1973), p. 88.

3. Boys Will Be Boys

1. Louis Adamic, "What the Proletariat Reads," *Saturday Review of Literature* 11 (December 1, 1934): 321–22. As Barbara Foley points out, Adamic's article fueled a growing controversy over the readership of proletarian novels. Defenders of the proletarian novel attacked Adamic's methodology and pointed out that, relative to their incomes, many workers actually spent a great deal of money on books, whereas critics of proletarian literature suggested that the real proletarian literature consisted of the romances and westerns which the working class consumed at a great rate (Foley, "The Treatment of Time in *The Big Money*," *Modern Fiction Studies* 26 [Autumn 1980]: 102–9). Low sales figures were a matter of concern for even the staunchest defenders of the proletarian novel, however.

2. Henry Hart, ed., *American Writers Congress* (New York: International Publishers, 1935), p. 161.

3. James T. Farrell, *Studs Lonigan* (New York: Modern Library, 1938), p. xv.

4. Although Richard Wright would present an equally problematic hero in *Native Son*, Bigger Thomas is a character easier to view as a case study, as a type, than as a person. His position throughout the novel, from the point of view of characters ranging from Mr. Dalton to Max, his Communist lawyer, to, of course, his prosecutors is that of an example—whether of a black youth to be uplifted by charity, of a victim of racism and capitalism, or of a dangerous beast. Bigger never has the angst of Studs—he has no real consciousness, in fact. Farrell's achievement lies in portraying a working-class character who is neither idealized nor bestial.

5. James T. Farrell, *The Young Manhood of Studs Lonigan* (New York: Vanguard Press, 1934), pp. 99–100; hereafter cited parenthetically in text as *YMSL*.

6. James T. Farrell, *Young Lonigan: A Boyhood in Chicago Streets* (New York: Vanguard Press, 1932), p. 13; hereafter cited parenthetically in text as *YL*.

7. Paula Rabinowitz, *Labor and Desire: Women's Revolutionary Fiction in Depression America* (Chapel Hill: University of North Carolina Press, 1991), p. 8.

8. Michael Gold, "Wilder: Prophet of the Genteel Christ," *New Republic*, October 22, 1930, pp. 266–67. Gold's article provoked a violent debate in the letters pages of the magazine, which a disdainful Edmund Wilson would characterize in his 1932 essay, "The Literary Class War," as "Strange cries from the depths . . . illiterate and hardly articulate" (*The Shores of Light* [New York: Farrar, Straus & Giroux, 1952], p. 535).

9. Quoted in Daniel Aaron, *Writers on the Left* (New York: Harcourt Brace & World, 1961), p. 240.

10. Michael Gold, "Go Left, Young Writers!" *New Masses* 4 (January 1929): 3–4.

11. Jack Conroy, "Authors' Field Day: A Symposium on Marxist Criticism," *New Masses*, July 3, 1934, p. 28.

12. Walter Rideout, *The Radical Novel in the United States, 1900–1954* (Cambridge: Harvard University Press, 1956), p. 190; Rabinowitz, *Labor and Desire*, p. 89.

13. Frank Norris, *McTeague* (1899; rpt., New York: New American Library, 1964), p. 151.

14. Ibid.

15. Theodore Dreiser, *Sister Carrie* (1900; rpt., New York: New American Library, 1961), pp. 42, 46, 54.

16. Roland Marchand, *Advertising the American Dream: Making Way for Modernity, 1920–1940* (Berkeley: University of California Press, 1985), pp. xvii, 66, 138, 131. It is not difficult to draw a connection between Gold's insistence on brawny fiction and the aversion he and critics such as D. S. Mirsky shared for the "stylishness" of modernist literature.

17. James T. Farrell, *Judgment Day* (New York: Vanguard Press, 1935), p. 81; hereafter cited parenthetically in text as *JD*.

18. Dennis Flynn and Jack Salzman, "An Interview with Farrell," *Twentieth Century Literature* 22.1 (February 1976).

19. Joan Shelley Rubin, *The Making of Middlebrow Culture* (Chapel Hill: University of North Carolina Press, 1992), p. 100.

20. Donald Pizer, *Twentieth-Century American Literary Naturalism: An Interpretation* (Carbondale: Southern Illinois University Press, 1982), pp. 24–25.

21. Eve Sedgwick, *Epistemology of the Closet* (Berkeley: University of California Press, 1990), p. 15.

22. Kate Millett, *Sexual Politics* (London: Sphere Books, 1971), p. 303.

23. Ann Douglas, "*Studs Lonigan* and the Failure of History in Mass Society: A Study in Claustrophobia," *American Quarterly* 29.5 (Winter, 1977), p. 502.

24. Irving Howe and Lewis Coser, *The American Communist Party* (Boston: Beacon Press, 1957), p. 339.

25. Minor quoted in ibid., p. 340.

4. Herbst's Trexler Trilogy

1. Elinor Langer, afterword to Josephine Herbst, *Rope of Gold* (1939; rpt., Old Westbury, NY: Feminist Press, 1984); hereafter cited parenthetically in text as *RG*.

2. Edwin Berry Burgum, "Josephine Herbst's *Rope of Gold*," *New Masses*, March 21, 1939.

3. Elinor Langer, *Josephine Herbst* (Boston: Atlantic/Little, Brown, 1984). Although Langer's biography has helped somewhat to recover the reputation of Josephine Herbst, scholarship even since that biography's publication in 1983 has been scanty at best.

4. Tess Slesinger, *The Unpossessed* (New York: Simon & Schuster, 1934), p. 13.

5. Ibid., pp. 17, 10, 41.

6. C. C. Regier, *The Era of the Muckrakers* (1932; rpt., Gloucester, Mass.: Peter Smith, 1957), p. 214.

7. See Louis Filler, *The Muckrakers* (University Park: Pennsylvania State University

Press, 1976); Alfred Kazin, *On Native Grounds* (New York: Reynal & Hitchcock, 1942), as well as Walter Rideout, *The Radical Novel in the United States, 1900–1954,* rev. ed. (New York: Columbia University Press, 1992).

8. Anthologized in Harvey Swados, *Years of Conscience: The Muckrakers* (Cleveland: Meridian Books, 1962).

9. See Madelon Golden Schilpp and Sharon M. Murphy, *Great Women of the Press* (Carbondale: Southern Illinois University Press, 1983), p. 162.

10. Harriet Woodbridge Gilfillan [Lauren Gilfillan], *I Went to Pit College* (New York: Literary Guild, 1934), p. 10.

11. It is unclear which Trexler girl is the narrator, which suggests that Herbst was employing, at least briefly, the technique of the collective novel—one used by Clara Weatherwax in *Marching! Marching!,* a once acclaimed, now forgotten, 1935 proletarian novel.

12. Josephine Herbst, *Pity Is Not Enough* (1933; rpt., New York: Warner Books, 1985), p. 1; hereafter cited parenthetically in text as *PINE.*

13. Josephine Herbst, *The Executioner Waits* (New York: Harcourt Brace, 1934), p. 125; hereafter cited parenthetically in text as *EW.*

14. See Langer, *Josephine Herbst,* pp. 143–46.

5. Finding a Collective Solution

1. Other alumni of English 47 included Eugene O'Neill, Philip Barry, Sidney Howard, George Sklar, S. N. Behrman, George Abbott, and Albert Maltz.

2. Quotation from Joanne Bentley, *Hallie Flanagan: A Life in the American Theatre* (New York: Alfred A. Knopf, 1988), p. 121.

3. Stuart Cosgrove, "The Living Newspaper: History, Production, Form" (Ph.D. diss., University of Hull, 1982), p. 9.

4. John Bonn, who supervised the German-speaking unit for the FTP, had previously headed the Proletbuehne. Several members of the Workers' Laboratory Theatre and of Theatre Collective also joined the FTP, including Stephen Karnot, who had studied under Vsevolod Meyerhold in Russia and who headed the Suitcase Theatre. See John O'Connor, "The Federal Theatre Project's Search for an Audience," in *Theatre for Working Class Audiences in the United States, 1830–1980* (Westport, Conn.: Greenwood Press, 1985), pp. 171–82.

5. Hallie Flanagan, *Arena* (1940; rpt., New York: Limelight Editions, 1985), p. 72.

6. Generally speaking, studies of the Living Newspapers have largely been confined to production histories and memoirs. See, for instance, Willson Whitman's *Bread and Circuses: A Study of Federal Theatre* (New York: Oxford University Press, 1937) or Lorraine Brown and John O'Connor's edited collection, *Free, Adult, Uncensored: The Living History of the Federal Theatre Project* (Washington, D.C.: New Republic Books, 1978). For an excellent study focusing on the political struggles surrounding productions, see Jane De Hart-Mathews, *The Federal Theatre, 1935–1939: Plays, Relief, and Politics* (Princeton: Princeton University Press, 1967). Recently, Barbara Melosh has

examined the gender politics embodied in New Deal public art and theater, including the Living Newspapers, in *Engendering Culture: Manhood and Womanhood in New Deal Public Art and Theater* (Washington, D.C.: Smithsonian Institution Press, 1991); and Stuart Cosgrove, in "Living Newspaper," has provided a thorough history of the form, from its Soviet origins to its use in Peruvian literacy campaigns of the 1970s.

7. Federal Theatre Project, "Writing the Living Newspaper," pp. 2–3, Library of Congress, Federal Theatre Collection.

8. Morris Watson, "The Living Newspaper," *Scholastic*, October 31, 1936, pp. 4–7.

9. FTP, "Writing," pp. 9–10.

10. Ibid., p. 9.

11. Brown and O'Connor, *Free, Adult, Uncensored*, p. 195.

12. FTP, "Writing," p. 10.

13. Arthur Arent, "The Technique of the Living Newspaper," *Theatre Arts*, November 1938.

14. Flanagan, *Arena*, p. 70. Morris Watson, who headed the Living Newspaper unit of the FTP, explained in a *New Theatre* article that "Inevitably, the Living Newspaper's technique is compared to the March of Time movie and radio programs. The difference between the two is essentially the point of view. March of Time is put out by a rich magazine and a rich advertiser. The Living Newspaper is written, edited, staged and acted by people who struggle for their living. It is bound to catch the flavor of that struggle" (*New Theatre*, June 1936, p. 7).

15. Georg Lukács, *The Historical Novel* (Lincoln: University of Nebraska Press, 1983), p. 335.

16. In fact, labor groups and workers' theaters recognized the potential of the Living Newspapers to effect political change. In 1937 the New Theatre League (formerly the League of Workers' Theatre), a Communist Party–backed organization, circulated copies of a Living Newspaper entitled *What Can the Union Do for Me?*, a piece based on the policies of the Steel Workers' Organizing Committee. Each script included a booklet instructing members how to write and perform their own Living Newspapers. That same year, the Brookwood Labor College staged a Living Newspaper entitled *Sit-Down*. The Living Newspaper was truly an art form that could be used by workers to forward a radical agenda.

17. Cosgrove, "Living Newspaper," p. 80.

18. Jerre Mangione, *An Ethnic at Large* (1978; rpt., Philadelphia: University of Pennsylvania Press, 1983), pp. 231–33.

19. The Living Newspapers were often rewritten during the production run to reflect political change; for instance, the *New York Herald Tribune* of February 10, 1938, reported that the last act of *Power*, a show about the electric light and power industry, would not be completed until just before curtain time, pending the outcome of an expected Supreme Court decision. The play's author, Arthur Arent—who had originally ended the play with the question "What will the Supreme Court do?"—had prepared three endings: one for a positive decision, one for a negative, and one for no decision (*New York Herald Tribune*, February 10, 1938, p. 12).

20. Flanagan, *Arena,* p. 70.

21. Ibid., p. 72.

22. John Mullen, "A Worker Looks at Broadway," *New Theatre,* May 1936, pp. 25–27.

23. Garet Garrett, "Federal Theatre for the Masses," *Saturday Evening Post* 207 (June 20, 1936): 8–9. Garrett was concerned, however, about the communist influence on this project.

24. Robert Benchley, in *New Yorker,* March 28, 1936, p. 34.

25. "The Living Newspaper Finally Gets Under Way with 'Triple-A Plowed Under,'" *New York Times,* March 16, 1936, p. 21.

26. "Triple A Plowed Under," *Variety,* March 18, 1936, p. 62.

27. Living Newspaper Staff, *Triple-A Plowed Under,* in *Federal Theatre Plays* (New York: Random House, 1938), pp. 9–10; hereafter, page numbers are cited parenthetically in text.

28. Bentley, *Flanagan,* p. 220.

29. See John O'Connor, "The Drama of Farming: The Federal Theatre Living Newspapers on Agriculture," *Prospects* 15 (1990): 325–58.

30. Don Farran and Ruth Stewart, *Dirt* (unpublished script, 1937), act 1, scene 1, p. 2; hereafter cited parenthetically in text.

31. Josephine Herbst, *Rope of Gold* (Old Westbury, N.Y.: Feminist Press, 1984), p. 244.

32. Walter Benjamin, *Illuminations,* trans. Harry Zohn (New York: Harcourt Brace & World, 1968), p. 241.

33. Ibid.

34. Ibid., p. 242.

35. Ibid.

36. Abram Hill and John Silvera, *Liberty Deferred,* in Lorraine Brown, ed., and Tamara Liller and Barbara Jones Smith, co-eds., *"Liberty Deferred" and Other Living Newspapers of the 1930s* (Fairfax, Va.: George Mason University Press, 1989), p. 253; hereafter cited parenthetically in text.

37. The play was rejected by Emmet Lavery, director of the National Service Bureau, which was responsible for play selection. This rejection was cited specifically as an example of discrimination in a brief prepared by the Negro Arts Council. In fact, Abram Hill recalled that "we got a tremendous amount of encouragement out of Mrs. Flanagan, and one or two others in the higher echelons." Flanagan was known to fight for the production of such potentially controversial dramas as Theodore Ward's *Big White Fog,* in which some characters advocated a merger of black and white labor for the common good. See E. Quita Craig, *Black Drama of the Federal Theatre Era* (Amherst: University of Massachusetts Press, 1980), pp. 61, 64. *Liberty Deferred* was not the only black-authored drama that remained unproduced. Zora Neale Hurston wrote a version of *Lysistrata,* remembers John Houseman, head of New York's Negro Theatre, "updated and located in a Florida fishing community, where the men's wives refused them intercourse until they won their fight with the canning company for a

living wage. It scandalized both Left and Right by its saltiness, which was considered injurious to the serious Negro image they both, in their different ways, desired to create. So I had to give that one up." See John Houseman, *Run-Through* (New York: Simon & Schuster, 1972), p. 204.

38. "3 Senators Say W.P.A. Theater Holds Them Up to Public's Boos," *New York Herald Tribune,* February 7, 1938, p. 1.

39. "WPA Play Juggles Their Words to Draw 'Boos,' Senators Charge," *Motion Picture Herald,* February 12, 1938, p. 21. The journal was generally critical of the "hell-raising militant interlopers of the WPA theatre." See Terry Ramsaye, "Curtain," *Motion Picture Herald,* July 8, 1939, pp. 7–8.

40. " '3rd of a Nation' Will Remain as Arent Wrote It," *New York Herald Tribune,* February 10, 1938, p. 13.

41. Flanagan, *Arena,* p. 337. For the most thorough account of the political battle to keep the FTP alive in the face of congressional opposition, see also De Hart-Mathews, *Federal Theatre.*

42. De Hart-Mathews, *Federal Theatre,* p. 342.

6. One-Third of a Nation

1. Hallie Flanagan, *Arena* (1940; rpt., New York: Limelight Editions, 1985), p. 217.

2. Ibid., p. 222.

3. Ibid., p. 211.

4. Newspapers quoted in ibid., pp. 87, 171.

5. *Hollywood Reporter,* January 11, 1939.

6. *Times-Picayune,* March 31, 1939.

7. Ibid.

8. "Housing Goes to Town," *New Masses,* February 14, 1939, p. 28.

9. *New York Times,* February 13, 1939.

10. *Variety,* February 15, 1939.

11. Arthur Arent, *One-Third of a Nation,* in *Federal Theatre Plays* (New York: Random House, 1938), p. 28; hereafter, page numbers are cited parenthetically in text.

12. *Motion Picture Herald,* February 18, 1939.

13. Ibid., April 8, April 29, March 25, 1939.

14. Jim Purdy and Peter Roffman, *The Hollywood Social Problem Film* (Bloomington: University of Indiana Press, 1981), p. 138.

15. *Motion Picture Herald,* January 21, 1939.

16. Gregory D. Black, "Hollywood Censored: The Production Code Administration and the Hollywood Film Industry, 1930–1940," *Film History* 3.3 (1989): 185–87.

17. Purdy and Roffman, *Social Problem Film,* p. 210.

18. Farrell, *Judgment Day* (*JD*), p. 68.

19. Victor Navasky, *Naming Names* (New York: Viking Press, 1980), p. 78.

20. Wendy Smith, *Real Life Drama: The Group Theatre and America, 1931–1940* (New York: Alfred A. Knopf, 1990), p. 250.

21. Edmund Wilson, *The American Jitters* (New York: Charles Scribner's Sons, 1932), p. 245.

22. Sergei Eisenstein, *Film Form and the Film Sense* (New York: Meridian Books, 1957), p. 96.

23. Richard Lingeman, *Theodore Dreiser: An American Journey, 1908–1945* (New York: G. P. Putnam's Sons, 1990), p. 341.

24. Wilson, *American Jitters,* p. 248.

Conclusion. The Search Abandoned

1. Tamiris also choreographed the Living Newspaper *One-Third of a Nation* for the FTP.

2. Marcus Klein, *Foreigners: The Making of American Literature, 1900–1940* (Chicago: University of Chicago Press, 1981), p. 176.

3. Richard D. McKinzie, *The New Deal for Artists* (Princeton: Princeton University Press, 1973), p. 72.

4. Monty Penkower, *The Federal Writers Project* (Urbana: University of Illinois Press, 1977), p. 114.

5. Hallie Flanagan, *Arena* (1940; rpt., New York: Limelight Editions, 1985), p. 23.

6. Ibid., p. 93.

7. Penkower, *Federal Writers Project,* p. 230.

8. Josephine Herbst, *The Starched Blue Sky of Spain and Other Memoirs* (New York: HarperCollins, 1991), pp. 101, 107.

WORKS CONSULTED

The scripts of many Living Newspapers, including those cited in this book, as well as the article "Writing the Living Newspaper," referred to in chapter 4, can be found at the Federal Theatre Collection, located at the Library of Congress.

Aaron, Daniel. *Writers on the Left: Odysseys in American Literary Communism.* New York: Harcourt Brace & World, 1961.

Adamic, Louis. *My America.* New York: Harper & Brothers, 1938.

——. "What the Proletariat Reads." *Saturday Review of Literature* 11 (December 1, 1934): 321–22.

Adorno, Theodor. "On the Fetish-Character in Music and the Regression of Listening." In *The Essential Frankfurt School Reader.* New York: Urizen Books, 1978.

——. "Perennial Fashion—Jazz." In *Prisms,* translated by Samuel and Shierry Weber. London: Neville Spearman, 1967.

Adorno, Theodor, and Max Horkheimer. "The Culture Industry: Enlightenment as Mass Deception." In *Dialectic of Enlightenment,* translated by John Cumming. New York: Seabury Press, 1972.

Agee, James, and Walker Evans. *Let Us Now Praise Famous Men.* 1941. Reprint. Boston: Houghton Mifflin, 1980.

Alexander, Charles C. *Here the Country Lies.* Bloomington: Indiana University Press, 1980.

Allen, Frederick Lewis. *Only Yesterday: An Informal History of the 1920's.* 1931. Reprint. New York: Harper & Row, 1964.

——. *Since Yesterday: The Nineteen-Thirties in America.* New York: Harper & Brothers, 1939.

Anderson, Sherwood. *Puzzled America*. New York: Charles Scribner's Sons, 1935.

———. *A Story Teller's Story*. 1922. Reprint. New York: Viking Press, 1927.

Arent, Arthur. "The Technique of the Living Newspaper." *Theatre Arts*, November 1938.

———, ed. *One-Third of a Nation*. In *Federal Theatre Plays*, vol. 1. New York: Random House, 1938.

Asch, Nathan. *Pay Day*. New York: Brewer & Warren, Payson & Clarke, 1930.

———. *The Road: In Search of America*. New York: W. W. Norton, 1937.

Benjamin, Walter. *Illuminations*. Translated by Harry Zohn. New York: Harcourt Brace & World, 1968.

Bentley, Joanne. *Hallie Flanagan: A Life in the American Theatre*. New York: Alfred A. Knopf, 1988.

Bessie, Alvah. *Inquisition in Eden*. New York: Macmillan, 1965.

Bloom, James D. *Left Letters: The Culture Wars of Mike Gold and Joseph Freeman*. New York: Columbia University Press, 1992.

Bordwell, David; Janet Staiger; and Kristin Thompson. *The Classic Hollywood Cinema: Film Style and Mode of Production to 1960*. New York: Columbia University Press, 1985.

Bradbury, Malcolm, and James McFarlane, eds. *Modernism*. 1976. Reprint. New York: Penguin Books, 1991.

Brenman-Gibson, Margaret. *Clifford Odets, American Playwright: The Years from 1906 to 1940*. New York: Atheneum, 1982.

Brooks, Cleanth, and Robert Penn Warren. *Understanding Fiction*. Englewood Cliffs, N.J.: Prentice-Hall, 1959.

Brooks, Cleanth; R. W. B. Lewis; and Robert Penn Warren. *American Literature: The Makers and the Making*. New York: St. Martin's Press, 1973.

Brown, Elaine. *A Taste of Power*. New York: Pantheon, 1992.

Brown, Lorraine, and John O'Connor. *Free, Adult, Uncensored: The Living History of the Federal Theatre Project*. Washington, D.C.: New Republic Books, 1978.

Brown, Lorraine, ed., and Tamara Liller and Barbara Jones Smith, co-eds. *"Liberty Deferred" and Other Living Newspapers of the 1930s*. Fairfax, Va.: George Mason University Press, 1989.

Burgum, Edwin Berry. "Josephine Herbst's *Rope of Gold*." *New Masses*, March 21, 1939.

Burrow, James G. *AMA: Voice of American Medicine*. Baltimore: Johns Hopkins University Press, 1963.

Cantwell, Robert. *The Land of Plenty*. New York: Farrar & Rinehart, 1934.

Conder, John J. *Naturalism in American Fiction*. Lexington: University Press of Kentucky, 1984.

Conroy, Jack. "Authors' Field Day: A Symposium on Marxist Criticism." *New Masses*, July 3, 1934, 27–32.

———. *The Disinherited*. New York: Covici, Friede, 1933.

Cosgrove, Stuart. "The Living Newspaper: History, Production, Form." Ph.D. dissertation, University of Hull, 1982.

Cowley, Malcolm. *The Dream of the Golden Mountains: Remembering the 1930s.* New York: Viking Press, 1964.

——. *Exile's Return.* 1934. Reprint. New York: Penguin Books, 1969.

Craig, E. Quita. *Black Drama of the Federal Theatre Era.* Amherst: University of Massachusetts Press, 1980.

Cullen, Jim. *The Civil War in Popular Culture: A Reusable Past.* Washington, D.C.: Smithsonian Institution Press, 1995.

Dahlberg, Edward. *Bottom Dogs.* New York: Simon & Schuster, 1930.

De Hart-Mathews, Jane. *The Federal Theatre, 1935–1939: Plays, Relief, and Politics.* Princeton: Princeton University Press, 1967.

Denning, Michael. *Mechanic Accents.* London: Verso Books, 1987.

Doctorow, E. L. *Ragtime.* New York: Bantam Books, 1976.

Dos Passos, John. *Facing the Chair: Sacco and Vanzetti: The Story of Two Foreign Born Workmen.* Boston: Sacco and Vanzetti Defense Committee, 1927.

——. *The 42nd Parallel.* 1930. Reprint. New York: New American Library, 1969.

——. *Nineteen Nineteen.* 1932. Reprint. New York: New American Library, 1969.

——. *The Big Money.* 1933. Reprint. New York: New American Library, 1969.

——. "Working under the Gun." Reprinted in Jack Salzman, *Years of Protest.* Indianapolis: Bobbs-Merrill Educational Publishing, 1967.

Douglas, Ann. "*Studs Lonigan* and the Failure of History in Mass Society: A Study in Claustrophobia." *American Quarterly* 29.5 (Winter 1977), pp. 487–505.

Dreiser, Theodore. *An American Tragedy.* 1925. Reprint. New York: New American Library, 1981.

——. *Sister Carrie.* 1900. Reprint. New York: New American Library, 1961.

Dubofsky, Melvyn, ed. *American Labor since the New Deal.* Chicago: Quadrangle Books, 1971.

Eisenstein, Sergei. *Film Form and the Film Sense.* New York: Meridian Books, 1957.

Farrell, James T. *Young Lonigan: A Boyhood in Chicago Streets.* New York: Vanguard Press, 1932.

——. *The Young Manhood of Studs Lonigan.* New York: Vanguard Press, 1934.

——. *Judgment Day.* New York: Vanguard Press, 1935.

——. *A Note on Literary Criticism.* New York: Vanguard Press, 1936.

Fielding, Raymond. *The March of Time, 1935–1951.* New York: Oxford University Press, 1981.

Filler, Louis. *The Muckrakers.* University Park: Pennsylvania State University Press, 1976.

Flanagan, Hallie. *Arena.* 1940. Reprint. New York: Limelight Editions, 1985.

Flynn, Dennis, and Jack Salzman. "An Interview with Farrell." *Twentieth Century Literature* 22.1 (February 1976): 1–10.

Foley, Barbara. *Radical Representations: Politics and Form in U.S. Proletarian Fiction, 1929–1941.* Durham: Duke University Press, 1993.

——. "The Treatment of Time in *The Big Money:* An Examination of Ideology and Literary Form." *Modern Fiction Studies* 26.3 (Autumn 1980), pp. 447–67.

Folsom, Michael, ed. *Mike Gold: A Literary Anthology.* New York: International Publishers, 1972.

Frederickson, George. *The Inner Civil War: Northern Intellectuals and the Crisis of the Union.* New York: Harper & Row, 1965.

Freeman, Joseph. *An American Testament.* New York: Farrar, Straus & Giroux, 1973.

Galeano, Eduardo. *Century of the Wind.* Translated by Cedric Balfrage. New York: Pantheon, 1986.

——. *Faces and Masks.* Translated by Cedric Balfrage. New York: Pantheon, 1984.

——. *Genesis.* Translated by Cedric Balfrage. New York: Pantheon, 1982.

Geoghegan, Thomas. *Which Side Are You On? Trying to Be for Labor When It's Flat on Its Back.* New York: Farrar, Straus & Giroux, 1991.

Gilfillan, Harriet Woodbridge [Lauren Gilfillan]. *I Went to Pit College.* New York: Literary Guild, 1934.

Gold, Michael. "A Love Letter for France." Anthologized in *Mike Gold: A Literary Anthology,* ed. Mike Folsom. New York: International Publishers, 1972.

——. "Go Left, Young Writers!" *New Masses* 4 (January 1929): 3–4.

——. "Letters Column." *New Masses,* August 1930, p. 22.

——. "Wilder: Prophet of the Genteel Christ." *New Republic,* October 22, 1930, pp. 266–67.

Graff, Gerald. *Professing Literature.* Chicago: University of Chicago Press, 1987.

Gruber, Carol S. *Mars and Minerva: World War I and the Uses of Higher Learning in America.* Baton Rouge: Louisiana State University Press, 1975.

Hart, Henry, ed. *American Writers Congress.* New York: International Publishers, 1935.

Harwell, Richard, ed. *"Gone with the Wind" as Book and Film.* Columbia: University of South Carolina Press, 1983.

Herbst, Josephine. *Pity Is Not Enough.* 1933. Reprint. New York: Warner Books, 1985.

——. *The Executioner Waits.* New York: Harcourt Brace, 1934.

——. *Rope of Gold.* 1939. Reprint. Old Westbury, N.Y.: Feminist Press, 1984.

——. *The Starched Blue Sky of Spain and Other Memoirs.* New York: HarperCollins, 1991.

Hicks, Granville. *I Like America.* New York: Modern Age Books, 1938.

Houseman, John. *Run-Through.* New York: Simon & Schuster, 1972.

Howe, Irving, and Lewis Coser. *The American Communist Party.* Boston: Beacon Press, 1957.

Jaffe, Philip J. *The Rise and Fall of American Communism.* New York: Horizon Press, 1975.

James, Henry. *Hawthorne.* 1887. Reprint. New York: AMS Press, 1968.

Jay, Martin. *The Dialectical Imagination.* Boston: Little, Brown, 1973.

Josephson, Matthew. *Infidel in the Temple.* New York: Alfred A. Knopf, 1967.

——. *Life among the Surrealists.* New York: Holt, Rinehart & Winston, 1962.

——. *Portrait of the Artist as American.* 1930. Reprint. New York: Farrar, Straus & Giroux, 1979.

Kazin, Alfred. *On Native Grounds.* New York: Reynal & Hitchcock, 1942.

Kirby, Jack Temple. *Media-Made Dixie: The South in the American Imagination*. Baton Rouge: Louisiana State University Press, 1978.

Klein, Marcus. *Foreigners: The Making of American Literature, 1900–1940*. Chicago: University of Chicago Press, 1981.

Kramer, Hilton. "Who Was Josephine Herbst?" *New Criterion* 3.1 (September 1984): pp. 1–14.

Kriegel, Leonard. "Homage to Mr. Farrell." *Nation,* October 16, 1976, pp. 373–76.

Landsberg, Melvin. *Dos Passos' Path to U.S.A.* Boulder: Colorado Associated University Press, 1972.

Langer, Elinor. *Josephine Herbst*. Boston: Atlantic/Little, Brown, 1984.

Leffland, Ella. *Rumors of Peace*. New York: Harper & Row, 1979.

Leitch, Vincent B. *American Literary Criticism from the Thirties to the Eighties*. New York: Columbia University Press, 1988.

Leuchtenberg, William. *Franklin D. Roosevelt and the New Deal, 1932–1940*. New York: Harper & Row, 1963.

Levine, Ira A. *Left-Wing Dramatic Theory in the American Theatre*. Ann Arbor: University of Michigan Press, 1985.

Levine, Lawrence W. *Highbrow/Lowbrow*. Cambridge: Harvard University Press, 1988.

Lingeman, Richard. *Theodore Dreiser: An American Journey, 1908–1945*. New York: G. P. Putnam's Sons, 1990.

Living Newspaper Staff. *Triple-A Plowed Under*. In *Federal Theatre Plays,* vol. 2. New York: Random House, 1938.

Ludington, Townsend. *John Dos Passos: A Twentieth Century Odyssey*. New York: E. P. Dutton, 1980.

Lukács, Georg. *The Historical Novel*. Lincoln: University of Nebraska Press, 1983.

Lynd, Robert S., and Helen Merrell Lynd. *Middletown*. New York: Harcourt Brace & World, 1929.

——. *Middletown in Transition*. New York: Harcourt Brace, 1937.

McAdam, Doug. *Freedom Summer*. New York: Oxford University Press, 1988.

McClure, S. S. *My Autobiography*. New York: Frederick A. Stokes, 1914.

McElvaine, Robert S. *The Great Depression*. New York: Times Books, 1984.

McKay, Claude. *A Long Way from Home*. 1937. Reprint. New York: Harcourt Brace & World, 1970.

McKenney, Ruth. *Industrial Valley*. New York: Harcourt Brace & World, 1939.

——. *My Sister Eileen*. New York: Harcourt Brace & World, 1938.

Mangione, Jerre. *An Ethnic at Large*. 1978. Reprint. Philadelphia: University of Pennsylvania Press, 1983.

Marchand, Roland. *Advertising the American Dream: Making Way for Modernity, 1920–1940*. Berkeley: University of California Press, 1985.

Melosh, Barbara. *Engendering Culture: Manhood and Womanhood in New Deal Public Art and Theatre*. Washington, D.C.: Smithsonian Institution Press, 1991.

Millett, Kate. *Sexual Politics*. London: Sphere Books, 1971.

Mirsky, D. S. "Joyce and Irish Literature." *New Masses,* April 3, 1934, p. 85.

Murphy, James. *The Proletarian Moment: The Controversy over Leftism in Literature.* Urbana and Chicago: University of Illinois Press, 1991.

Navasky, Victor. *Naming Names.* New York: Viking Press, 1980.

Nelson, Cary. *Repression and Recovery: Modern American Poetry and the Politics of Cultural Memory.* Madison: University of Wisconsin Press, 1989.

Neve, Brian. *Film and Politics in America: A Social Tradition.* London: Routledge, 1992.

Ninkovich, Frank. "The New Criticism and Cold War America." *Southern Quarterly: A Journal of the Arts in the South* 20.1 (Fall 1981): 1–24.

Norris, Frank. *McTeague.* 1899. Reprint. New York: New American Library, 1964.

Odets, Clifford. *Waiting for Lefty.* In *Six Plays.* New York: Random House, 1939.

Parrington, Vernon Louis. *Main Currents in American Thought.* New York: Harcourt Brace, 1930.

Pease, Donald E. *Visionary Compacts.* Madison: University of Wisconsin Press, 1987.

Pells, Richard H. *Radical Visions & American Dreams: Culture and Social Thought in the Depression Years.* Middletown, Conn.: Wesleyan University Press, 1973.

Penkower, Monty Noam. *The Federal Writers Project.* Urbana: University of Illinois Press, 1977.

Piehler, G. Kurt. *Remembering War the American Way.* Washington, D.C.: Smithsonian Institution Press, 1995.

Pizer, Donald. *Dos Passos' U.S.A.* Charlottesville: University Press of Virginia, 1988.

——. *Twentieth-Century American Literary Naturalism: An Interpretation.* Carbondale: Southern Illinois University Press, 1982.

Purdy, Jim, and Peter Roffman. *The Hollywood Social Problem Film.* Bloomington: University of Indiana Press, 1981.

Rabinowitz, Paula. *Labor and Desire: Women's Revolutionary Fiction in Depression America.* Chapel Hill: University of North Carolina Press, 1991.

Rampersand, Arnold. *The Life of Langston Hughes.* Vol. 1. New York: Oxford University Press, 1986.

Ransom, John Crowe. "Criticism, Inc." In *The World's Body.* New York: Charles Scribner's Sons, 1938.

Ravn, Ole. *Litteraturhistorisk Oversigt.* Herning: Forlaget Systeme, 1984.

Regier, C. C. *The Era of the Muckrakers.* 1932. Reprint. Gloucester, Mass.: Peter Smith, 1957.

Rideout, Walter. *The Radical Novel in the United States, 1900–1954.* Cambridge: Harvard University Press, 1956.

Ringel, Fred J., ed. *America: As Americans See It.* New York: Harcourt Brace, 1932.

Rorty, James. *Where Life Is Better: An Unsentimental American Journey.* New York: Reynal & Hitchcock, 1936.

Rubin, Joan Shelley. *Constance Rourke and American Culture.* Chapel Hill: University of North Carolina Press, 1980.

——. *The Making of Middlebrow Culture.* Chapel Hill: University of North Carolina Press, 1992.

Schilpp, Madelon Golden, and Sharon M. Murphy. *Great Women of the Press*. Carbondale: Southern Illinois University Press, 1983.

Schrecker, Ellen W. *No Ivory Tower: McCarthyism and the Universities*. New York: Oxford University Press, 1986.

Sedgwick, Eve. *Epistemology of the Closet*. Berkeley: University of California Press, 1990.

Seldes, Gilbert. *The Years of the Locust*. Boston: Little, Brown, 1933.

Sinclair, Upton. *Money Writes!* London: T. Werner Lauries, 1931.

Slesinger, Tess. *The Unpossessed*. New York: Simon & Schuster, 1934.

Smedley, Agnes. *Daughter of Earth*. 1923. Reprint. New York: Feminist Press, 1987.

Smith, Wendy. *Real Life Drama: The Group Theatre and America, 1931–1940*. New York: Alfred A. Knopf, 1990.

Stearns, Harold. *The Street I Know*. 1935. Reissued as *Confessions of a Harvard Man*. Santa Barbara: Paget Press, 1984.

Stein, Leon. *The Triangle Fire*. Philadelphia: J. B. Lippincott, 1962.

Steinbeck, John. *The Grapes of Wrath*. New York: Viking Press, 1939.

Stott, William. *Documentary Expression and Thirties America*. Chicago: University of Chicago Press, 1973.

Sugrue, Thomas. "The Newsreels." *Scribner's Magazine* 101.4 (April 1937): 9–18.

Swados, Harvey. *Years of Conscience: The Muckrakers*. Cleveland: Meridian Books, 1962.

Terkel, Studs. *Hard Times: An Oral History of the Great Depression*. New York: Pantheon Books, 1970.

Thomson, Virgil. *Virgil Thomson*. New York: Alfred A. Knopf, 1966.

Trachtenberg, Alan. *Reading American Photographs*. New York: Hill & Wang, 1989.

Vanderwerken, David. *Dos Passos and the "Old Words."* Ann Arbor: University Microfilms, 1973.

Wald, Alan. *The New York Intellectuals: The Rise and Fall of the Anti-Stalinist Left from the 1930s to the 1980s*. Chapel Hill: University of North Carolina Press, 1986.

Weatherwax, Clara. *Marching! Marching!* New York: John Day, 1935.

Whitman, Willson. *Bread and Circuses: A Study of Federal Theatre*. New York: Oxford University Press, 1937.

Wilson, Edmund. *The American Jitters*. New York: Charles Scribner's Sons, 1932.

——. *Patriotic Gore*. New York: Oxford University Press, 1962.

——. *The Shores of Light*. New York: Farrar, Straus & Giroux, 1952.

Worster, Donald. *Dust Bowl*. New York: Oxford University Press, 1979.

Wright, Richard. *Native Son*. New York: Harper & Row, 1940.

Young, James Harvey. "Patent Medicines and the Self-Help Syndrome." In *Medicine without Doctors,* ed. Guenter B. Risse. New York: Science History Publications, 1977.

——. *The Toadstool Millionaires*. Princeton: Princeton University Press, 1961.

Young, Thomas Daniel. *Gentleman in a Dustcoat: A Biography of John Crowe Ransom*. Baton Rouge: Louisiana State University Press, 1976.

INDEX